The Management of the Tourism Sector

Roger Doswell

about the author

Roger Doswell originally studied hotel management at Battersea Polytechnic. After completing national service as a Pilot Officer in the Royal Air Force Catering Branch in the 1950s, he spent four years working in France and Spain before leaving for the United States. Working for Hotel Corporation of America (later to become Sonesta Hotels), he joined the Management Services Department at the central office in Boston, Mass. After a further period at the Royal Orleans Hotel, in New Orleans, he returned to the company's Carlton Tower Hotel, in London.

Granted leave of absence, he was appointed Kobler Research Fellow at the University of Surrey where he undertook a study of hotel planning. He continued as a lecturer, helping to develop the University's first degree course in hotel and catering management. Returning to Hotel Corporation of America he was made Director of Operational Planning for the company's European expansion programme. He entered the field of international consultancy in 1971, when he was appointed Tourism Development Adviser to the Caribbean Development Bank. He followed this with assignments in the Caribbean and Latin America for Canadian Pacific Hotels, and then went to Syria as team leader of a human resources task group for the International Labour Organisation (ILO) and United Nations Development Programme (UNDP).

After further missions to Pakistan, Iraq and Bulgaria, he was appointed Chief Technical Adviser for the ILO/UNDP project – the Centre for Tourism Studies – in Havana, Cuba. He then moved to the ILO/UNDP tourism project in Puerto Plata, Dominican Republic. Among assignments for the World Tourism Organisation (WTO), he undertook missions to Ethiopia and Equatorial Guinea before moving to Kuala Lumpur as adviser on human resource development to Malaysia's Tourist Development Corporation. In 1987, he helped WTO on its technical cooperation programme, at its headquarters in Madrid, before leaving for the South Pacific on the WTO/UNDP regional tourism project. He was then appointed Chief Technical Adviser on the ILO/UNDP project in Bali, later becoming Senior Tourism Development Adviser to Indonesia's Ministry of Tourism. In recent years he has undertaken further missions to Africa; to Zimbabwe, Zanzibar, Kenya, Nigeria, Ghana and Eritrea. Also to Jordan, Saudi Arabia and Iran as well as the countries of South Asia. His career has spanned the twentieth century's tourism explosion, and he has confronted at close hand many of the successes as well as the failures.

by the same author

1967   (with Philip Nailon), *Case Studies in Hotel Management*, Barrie & Jenkins.

1970   *Towards an Integrated Approach to Hotel Planning*, New University Education.

   (with John Beavis, Graham Campbell Smith, Peter Copp, Louis Erdi and Fred Lawson), *Principles of Hotel Design*, Architectural Press.

1972   Tourism – A Phenomenon of our Time *in The Role of Tourism in Caribbean Development*, Christian Action for Development in the Eastern Caribbean – CADEC.

1977   (with Philip Nailon), *Further Case Studies in Hotel Management*, Barrie & Jenkins.

1978   *Case Studies in Tourism*, Barrie & Jenkins.

1979   *Further Case Studies in Tourism*, Barrie & Jenkins.

1979   (with Guy Blanchard and Paul Gamble), *Anatomia de un Hotel*, Centro de Estudios Turísticos, Havana.

1980   (with Paul Gamble), *Marketing and Planning Hotels and Tourism Projects*, Hutchinson.

1982   *Administración de Hoteles – Estudio de Casos*, Puerta del Sol/Textos, Madrid.

1990   New Destinations for Developed Countries in the *Horwath Book of Tourism*, The MacMillan Press.

1997   *Tourism – How Effective Management Makes the Difference*, Butterworth Heinemann.

2000   African Tourism Training and Education – Hits and Misses in *The Political Economy of Tourism in Africa*, Cognizant Communication Corporation.

Published by Columbus Publishing Limited on behalf of the Institute of Commercial Management.

Columbus Travel Guides, Columbus House,
28 Charles Square, London N1 6HT, United Kingdom.
Tel: +44 (0)20 7608 6666
Fax: +44 (0)20 7608 6569
E-mail: booksales@columbus-group.co.uk

First published 2000

Designed & produced by
Space Design and Production Services Limited, London N1
Printed & bound by
Thanet Press Limited, Margate

ISBN: 1 902221 45 1

contents

preface

This book is complementary to a previous book *Tourism – How Effective Management Makes the Difference* published by Butterworth Heinemann in 1997, with a special edition prepared for the Institute of Commercial Management in 1998. Both books take a planning and management perspective but in a different way. The first book focuses on planning. It provides an understanding of the sector, the identification of its needs and the preparation of plans. It examines the characteristics of the tourism sector, and the organisation and responsibilities of a government tourism administration (GTA). It goes on to review the influences on tourism's public administration and its economic, environmental and cultural impacts. It then puts planning into an overall management context, and structures the planning function accordingly.

This book places more emphasis on tourism's ongoing management. It helps translate the plans, policies and strategies into the "what do I do next" step – and the "how do I continue to manage tourism". The book is divided into two parts. The first part develops the framework for tourism management. It does this by tracing the development of places into tourist destinations, explaining the needs of visitors, cyclical trends, the influence of transport, and the importance of market research. It focuses on the formulation of the mix of marketing mixes (products, images, prices, promotion and sales), and indicates how they interact to position the destination.

The second part deals with implementation; the overall marketing mix, the GTA's coordination, sales, the essential management tools, the regeneration, re-engineering and expansion of tourism, and the importance of quality. It dedicates chapters to some of the key tools; legislation, physical planning, classification and grading, and human resources. It finishes with a checklist designed to pull the various strands of tourism management together. It helps the reader to do this. The book shows how the sector can coordinate all of its diverse interests, ensuring the widest possible involvement and participation of owners, managers, employees and the community at large.

Tourism's economic, social and environmental impacts were treated, in the first book, as chapters apart. In real life they are not apart but among tourism management's everyday ingredients. For this reason, in this book, they are made part of the overall management process and subsumed accordingly within the various chapters. In the first book I spoke about the danger of one-off tourism development plans, which often emphasise physical planning and deal only cursorily with other aspects of tourism management. Such plans are usually prepared within a short time frame by hastily organised teams of consultants, in a manner external to the permanent government tourism administration and remote from the sector itself. Yet intergovernmental bodies and international agencies continue to waste resources on this approach, without providing sufficient assistance in the development of managerial capacities. This is true even in the UK where local authorities continue to focus on physical planning aspects, ignoring many other important management needs.

The key to tourism development lies in the management of the sector. Planning is an integral part of management. And management is an ongoing incremental process, it doesn't begin or end, once in place it continues.

It is sometimes argued that government involvement in sectoral management is interventionist. This need not be true. A government agency, like a GTA, can prevent unnecessary intervention. It is also mistaken to argue that the management of the sector as such is unnecessary. "One can leave it to the private sector", people say. However, the prospect of different sub-sectors and innumerable businesses working in the dark, in isolation, without agreed directions or objectives, without coordination, without agreed plans or programmes, cannot be argued sensibly. This is often what one has now. Tourism as a sector involves many enterprises and sections of society. It needs a common approach, and agreed objectives and activities. It needs management, not by the government but by the sector itself. The book proposes that the sector use the GTA as a key resource and that, in turn, the GTA provide all the help it can give.

We live in a world of time-space compression, not only does physical distance shrink but the distance between ideas and disciplines. Everything is pulled together – part of the high tech informatization and the global media and trade explosion. However, we also see things move the other way, a contradictory spinning off to the periphery. Governments increasingly centralise their policies, guidelines and standards while they also decentralise, pushing down many decisions to the local level. There is totality but there is subsidiarity. Globalisation produces a sameness yet sharpens many differences.

Centralisation lives with decentralisation and globalisation with differentiation. These all appear as beginning-of-the-century contradictions, yet they are important to any contemporary concept of sectoral management.

Against this background, a GTA joins with the sector at three levels:

- coordinating overall plans, policies and strategies and using them to steer and guide the sector's development and operation.
- taking action and providing support in areas such as planning, marketing, training, and public awareness.
- establishing a minimum legislative and regulatory framework.

One government embraces all three levels, another tackles only the last and possibly the second. A role undertaken by one government may be judged as interference by another. This book does not address issues of political ideology neither does it argue for or against government. It argues for a "with" government approach, in favour of a catalytic public sector role. Of course a government should not act dictatorially. It should be open and communicate, consult, collaborate and join with the whole sector. Government itself, and the people who elected it, should watch that management is appropriate and effective. That the sector gets the management it needs.

The book makes reference here and there to the unfinished product, the unfinished image and the unfinished marketing mix. Nothing can ever be called completely finished. There are too many changing characteristics and influences. One can't avoid change. Hence the ongoing process of tourism management. One never finishes. Re-engineering, regeneration and expansion offer a constant challenge.

The book presents a framework to allow everybody to look at tourism in the same way. Each sector may be different but the framework is always the same. The framework provides a sensible sequence and method to follow, ensuring that nothing is forgotten and letting one see the interdependence and interrelationships between the various parts. The framework shows us not only what is happening but what isn't happening. It gives us a consistent way – a model or vehicle – by which to proceed. And it gives us an approach, a method, which allows us to compare our results.

George Steiner pointed out that all discourse approximates. Human behaviour is enormously complex while our power of expression is limited. In the management of the tourism sector there are thousands of variables. Since one cannot include them all on the same page or even in the same chapter, every argument tends to be partial and incomplete. Yet to bring them together, to refer constantly backwards and forwards, can risk duplication and repetition. Even a morass of confusion. I have tried to avoid this, to be straightforward and consistent, to make ideas self evident and easy to grasp. And I have also tried to interconnect the variables, and fit all the bits together. First one has to hear the melody – then make it recurrent – then make it instantly recognisable.

What is put forward as the state-of-the-art and the existing body of knowledge may sometimes comprise a conventional set of viewpoints rather than proven principles. Intellectual conformity, which is an oxymoron, becomes the rule of the day. People are coerced into "receiving and accepting" certain codes and beliefs. There is such a thing as the dogma of the classroom, distorted and imposed on students as absolute. And sometimes teachers are just told to stick unquestioningly to the curriculum or syllabus. Yet we tell students to question, question, question. It is better, Karl Popper said, to try and prove every hypothesis wrong. Fresh thinking always challenges some conventional wisdom. That's why it's fresh. Even so, people need courage to abandon the values which they may have misguidedly cherished.

In the text, I have frequently used contractions, e.g. don't – haven't – can't. Convention maintains that this is wrong. Many writers confine the use of contractions to dialogue, and consider them inappropriate for serious writing. However, conventions change and I find that they add to the book's readability.

Alan de Botton says there is a culture of quotation. Quotations and references are often heaped into a text to give a false impression of rigorous scholarship. Many falsely claim to represent the "commonly recognised" or "already established" but are only included to support the writer's arguments. Others are included as padding, irrelevant and hardly verifiable. I did not want to clutter the book in this way, and have kept references to a minimum. I may have included some general ideas from the public domain, but the book as a whole is structured and written according to my own interpretation and analysis. However, where appropriate I have given the sources of certain ideas or data. I have also included a list of recommended further reading.

We have reached a stage in tourism when we are seldom given a clean canvas on which to paint. In many locations there are now few pristine sites waiting to be developed for tourism. Sites are already full of hotels and the current question is – What do we do now? Much of the present and future task is to correct what has gone before. I have attempted to address this point.

The book is written as 24 modules (chapters) – mostly between 2,800 and 3,300 words. They are written in a concise way and each could be read in about 30 minutes. The book could therefore be read in 12 hours. In this time anybody can get a comprehensive understanding about the tourism sector and its management. The book can also be used and studied in greater depth, and serve as a continuing reference.

Management books tend to couch their theories in parables in an almost biblical way. For example, there is a man who lives in ignorance and does the wrong things – then there is a man who is enlightened and does the right things. One has the righteous (progressive and dynamic) and the unrighteous (static and out-of-touch). This device, also used by preachers, is common. "Be one of us – think like us," says the management teacher, "or stay unenlightened and become obsolescent". I certainly hope that I haven't preached but I do believe that the management of the tourism sector will take on more and more importance. It should improve and become more effective. There is no other way to avoid the mistakes and abuses tourism has suffered, and the many continuing dangers it faces as it expands and grows.

Good luck.

section one
the framework

chapter one
The Place

This chapter starts by defining places and their importance. It goes on to describe what makes a place: population growth, the natural characteristics, the built environment, the people, the economic situation, political systems and traditions, patterns of life, historic and artistic characteristics, the media, entertainment and recreation, and the place's international links. The chapter then examines change and urbanisation, and concludes by discussing the unfinished nature of places.

Inhabited Places

Places are of great importance to us. Where we live or have lived, the places we visit, the places we love, the new places we discover, the places we dream of visiting. In tourism they are our starting and ending points. This sense of place is aptly captured by Lawrence Durrell when he wrote about Venice, "Cloud and water mixed into each other, dripping with colours, merging, overlapping, liquefying, with steeples and balconies and roofs floating in space, like the fragments of history touched with the colours of wine, tar, ochre, blood, fire-opal, and ripening grain" (Durrell, 1957).

Inhabited places are normally town or country; the urban or the rural environment. They are portions of space where people live as a community – either large or small – village, town or city.

An inhabited place reflects the culture of the people who live and work there. This determines how a place looks, functions and feels, given the other influences of natural features such as climate, landscape and resources. A place also reflects the nature and strength of its economy, and the local political will and capacity to provide acceptable and sustainable levels of environmental quality.

If a place is uninhabited it generally has its status legally defined. Uninhabited places may be reserves, protected areas, national parks or common land. They may comprise areas set aside indefinitely for the protection of wildlife and, or, the recreation and enjoyment of the population. Or they may be uninhabited because of their inhospitable bleakness; e.g. the expanses of desert sand or arctic tundra.

What Makes a Place?

The factors which make up or influence an inhabited place include population growth, natural characteristics, the people themselves, the built environment, the economic situation, the political systems and traditions, the international links, historic and artistic characteristics, and the local media, entertainment and recreational activities. This is illustrated in Figure 1.1. Different places are also subject to varying degrees of change. Some enter periods of dynamic redevelopment and expansion, others suffer periods of stagnation, decline and depopulation.

These considerations interact with different environmental factors: adequate infrastructure, physical planning regulations and controls, pollution control, conservation and protection, orderly expansion, renovation and redevelopment, and respect for the spirit of the place.

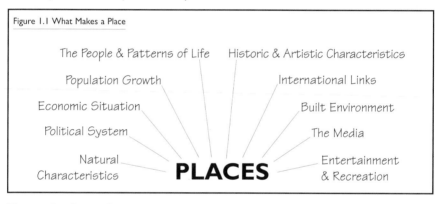

Figure 1.1 What Makes a Place

The People & Patterns of Life · Historic & Artistic Characteristics · Population Growth · International Links · Economic Situation · Built Environment · Political System · The Media · Natural Characteristics · **PLACES** · Entertainment & Recreation

Population Growth

As population grows, places have to accommodate more people. Growth puts pressure on the world's environment and resources, and poses a challenge to sustainable development perspectives. Population growth remains high but recent trends are encouraging. The United Nations Population Fund (UNFPA, 1997) reports a fall in fertility rates although global population continues to grow by 81 million people a year. The world population in mid-1997 was 5.85 billion. Fertility declined to an average of 2.96 children per woman in 1997; the 1.48 per cent annual growth rate for 1990-1995 was lower than the rate projected.

The world in 2050 is expected to have between 7.7 billion and 11.1 billion people. Where the 2050 population finally falls depends on the world's capacity to limit fertility rates. UNFPA considers the most likely projection to be 9.4 billion, half a billion less than the 1994 estimate. Such growth is bound to change significantly the size and character of many places.

Natural Characteristics

Climate plays a major part in giving a place its fundamental feel and character; what part the seasons play, how hot or cold it gets, how much rain or snow there is. Climate influences the local flora and fauna and this contributes to the look of a place. The climate determines how much of a life can be spent outdoors. It affects the way people dress and introduces different rhythms to life, deeply affecting people's attitudes and lifestyles.

Landscape is recognised as an important influence on the culture and outlook of people. High mountains, rich agricultural plains, vast deltas of great rivers, rocky and bleak coastlines, snowy and empty expanses, or palm fringed atolls influence the local population in different ways.

The Built Environment

A place's physical infrastructure is the basis of its built environment. Are the roads and transportation networks, water and power supplies, sewerage, drainage and waste disposal well planned and adequate? Are they keeping pace with the place's growth and development?

Planning regulations control what is built where, on what scale, of what height, style and density, while zoning designates particular areas for certain uses. Other regulations control minimum building standards. Planning also dictates the retention of green space, the variety of views preserved or opened up, and the protection of certain areas and historic buildings against development.

Forms of public transport influence the appearance and feeling of a place – for example, places where the horse and carriage are preserved, or the bicycle rickshaw, or the motorised three wheeler. Double decker buses form a part of the image of some places such as London. Urban subway systems are often famous; for example, in Paris, Moscow, London and New York.

Historic downtown areas should be protected, and the architectural style, scale and character of buildings maintained. Some areas or streets can be pedestrianised. Incentives can be provided for the restoration of buildings, while ways can be found to beautify the local surroundings.

The People and the Patterns of Life

Culture describes everything people are; how they dress and behave, what they believe, what they do. A place and the culture of the people who live there are inseparable.

Migration is an important factor in the development of many countries. For example in the Americas, the concentration of a particular nationality such as Germans in Milwaukee, or Poles in Buffalo, or the Irish, Jews and Italians in New York, or the Italians in Argentina and Venezuela, has tended to give these places a special character. In the case of Australia and Canada there are cities with a distinctive English atmosphere. Some places in South East Asia have a Chinese character. Migration has continued to have an influence on many places. In the United Kingdom, for example, there are now large South Asian Muslim and Hindu communities, as well as a West Indian community. France has a large North African minority. Migrants bring their culture with them, making a lasting impact on the host country.

The status or women, their appearance, degree of equality, and general participation in society, also influence the atmosphere of a place. Societies where women are emancipated contrast with more restrictive societies.

The patterns and pace of life affect the place's ambience: the way people live, work and relax; their working hours, when they finish and whether they go straight home; the times the streets are full and the shops and markets busy; the ways people dress; the popular items of food and drink, and the habits of eating and drinking out; and the hour when traffic thins and the place closes down.

How well health, education and other services are developed, also contributes significantly to a place. Is everything available and does it work well?

Religion can also influence daily life, requiring particular patterns of behaviour and prayer. At times places of worship can become crowded with followers, while major religious festivals are among the highlights of the year.

Crime too changes the atmosphere of a place. Local crime rates by type of offence are an important consideration. Is it safe to walk around and is there good security? Organised crime, even random street crime, may create fear in a society. This tends to communicate itself immediately.

The way people spend their leisure time contributes to the ambience; whether people stay at home or venture out; and where they go and what they do.

The Economic Situation

The economic situation of a place determines its relative prosperity. In turn this influences the quality of the local infrastructure and the appearance of the place. John Gimlette called Stonetown in Zanzibar "ravaged by neglect" (The Daily Telegraph, 11 July, 1998). However, neglect means to disregard through indifference or carelessness. Stonetown suffers not from neglect but because there is insufficient money to fix it.

The local patterns of employment, and the level of technology are important. What kinds of industry and other economic activities exist? What are the local standards of living – not only in per capita income – but also in access to housing, health and education? Is there unemployment? What is the overall economic and social structure?

High economic growth is usually visible – there is plenty going on with new construction and infrastructural projects in evidence. There is an atmosphere of hustle and bustle; growth communicates itself. By contrast low growth economies cast an air of stagnation and poverty.

Political Standards and Systems

Open political systems are where governments are elected for a given term, there is an effective opposition, democratic institutions hold sway, there is freedom of expression and a sound record of human rights. One can sense a place's political climate together with the observance of basic human freedoms.

Totalitarian regimes are usually restrictive and often oppressive. They may eliminate street crime but tend to generate an atmosphere of anxiety. Kapuscinski quotes an Iranian living under the Shah, "...everyone will be afraid, innocent and guilty, everyone will feel the intimidation, no one will feel safe." (Kapuscinski, 1986).

Open and pluralistic political systems tend to generate feelings of stability and continuity. People don't live in fear of the State. They tend to feel secure and free to get on with their lives.

Historic and Artistic Characteristics

The historic and artistic comprise a place's cultural attractions. This means all those physical or formal expressions of the local culture which can be visited, exhibited or performed. They can be described as either hard or soft:

- *Hard* includes historical sites, museums, architecture in general, monuments, religious buildings (mosques, temples, cathedrals), and cultural centres, archaeological sites, and centres of contemporary community life.

- *Soft* includes music, drama, poetry, literature, painting, sculpture, engraving, folklore and handicrafts.

The hard and soft are often imaginatively combined. Such attractions often give a sense of timelessness to a place; they symbolise its identity, provide continuity in the face of change, and help to maintain a constant image (Doswell, 1997).

Media, Entertainment & Recreation

The media reflect the tempo of society. For example through the size, richness and variety of newspapers; the scope of social and cultural comment, the range of advertisements, the awareness of the world at large, and the reporting of economic and business activity.

All the rest of the media give similar indications, including the number and variety of television and radio stations. They all contribute towards the rhythm and feeling of a place.

The range of available entertainment facilities includes theatres, cinemas, nightclubs, discotheques and concert halls, and gives an indication of the vibrancy of contemporary culture. As noted, strong links may exist with the place's cultural attractions.

Similarly the participation of the society in sports or leisure centres, or just jogging or exercising in local parks or other recreational areas, contributes to the atmosphere of a place. Spectator sports, featuring major games such as football, baseball or cricket, capture the imagination and generate wide support. Particularly big events create a special atmosphere, and tend to take over places on given days or during given periods. Referring to football's World Cup held in France in 1998, which France won, Time Magazine commented, "…if the stadium in Paris was the epicentre, the waves of national euphoria spread right across the country" (Time, 20 July, 1998).

International Links

Ports and border towns or areas may have a number of well established international links. These contribute to the character of a place, bringing various foreign influences. Many of these are of a trading and commercial nature, built up over a long period of time. Others are through tourism and create an international feeling in particular districts or areas. Foreign language signs abound, as well as restaurants and shops catering to the national tastes of visitors. All of these influences affect the character of a place.

Pace of Change

The pace of change is related principally to population and economic growth or decline (see Figure 1.2). Just the look and upkeep of buildings and the environment are a sign. As already noted, the intensity of economic activity tends to communicate itself. For example, new construction, outdoor advertising and the variety of retail outlets. The media reveals cultural change, social reform and new community initiatives. The whole appearance and feel of a place tend to convey its relative state of well being.

Places do not tend to have life cycles in the same way as businesses. Chapter 7 explains cycles and their effect. Changes in markets and technology may end some of a place's principal economic activities, but usually this does not put an end to the place itself. Places usually adjust, diversify and revitalise

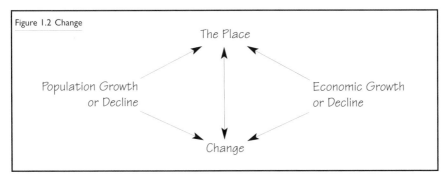

Figure 1.2 Change

The Place

Population Growth
or Decline

Economic Growth
or Decline

Change

themselves. However, there are places which have been known to die. For example, a few nineteenth century towns which were formerly based on mining or industry.

Tourism puts places under increasing pressure. International visitor arrivals could increase from the 650 million arrivals expected in the year 2000 to between 2.5 billion and 3.0 billion by 2050. This will create major new needs in terms of transport and accommodation alone, while exerting enormous additional pressures on the places visited.

Urbanisation

As countries modernise and industrialise, cities become concentrations of economic activity. People drift from the country to the urban areas. Cities start to have problems to assimilate the increasing numbers of incoming people and to provide enough jobs and places to live. Slum areas and high rates of unemployment develop. Urban crime increases. Vehicular traffic grows at an alarming rate and starts to choke the streets. City services cannot cope and pollution increases. New building escapes any planning and zoning regulations. Inner city areas decline and decay, and some areas remain without basic services. The mass transit system is inadequate. As the quality of the urban environment deteriorates, the character of the place changes.

According to the United Nations Population Fund, half the people in the world will be living in cities by the year 2006. It also points out that in 1950 some 83 cities or city systems had populations of more than 1 million, 34 of them in developing countries. In 1996 there were 280 with this number expected to double by the year 2015. All the new million-cities and 11 of the world's biggest cities were in developing countries (UNFPA, 1996).

In the more developed world, between 1990 and 2015, North America, Australia and New Zealand will record little change in population distribution by city. Europe too should not change much, in either the number of cities or population distribution by city size. About two thirds of the population continue to live in cities of under 500,000 inhabitants.

Any place, and particularly city centres, pose the challenge of carrying capacity. This is the capacity in the number of users at any one time. It can only be exceeded with damaging results. For example: deterioration in the quality of the place itself, its attractions and environment; and overcrowding which causes intolerable queues and bottlenecks – spoiling people's enjoyment. People joke, "Did you hear? They closed London last week, it was full!" It takes skilful management to avert such a possibility.

Impacts and reactions must be studied and evaluated; for example, what pollution? what damage? how many people? where? when? at what times? with what reactions? What changes need to be made? What actions taken? Carrying capacity is not just a concept, it is a tool.

Places are Unfinished

Places have an ethos – everything that makes them up contributes to a particular atmosphere and character. Something about a place may remain constant; other things change and keep on changing. Quite apart from the pressures of growing urbanisation, places change.

As one travels to places worldwide, particularly cities, one usually finds them in a state of repair and disrepair, renovation and deterioration, expansion and contraction, improvement and decline. Districts rise and fall. Transportation patterns change. Industries become obsolete. Businesses come and go. "The place is going to be great when it's finished", people say. Places go on changing, they never remain the same.

Places were either not planned or only partially planned. They have grown up over the years, a reflection of the desires and actions of each succeeding generation. It is seldom that one can plan a place from the start. Plans once prepared are quickly superseded as places continue to grow, responding to changing technology, demographics and lifestyles.

In 1856, Harper's commented on a rapidly changing New York, "A man born in New York forty years ago finds nothing, absolutely nothing, of the New York he knew. If he chances to stumble on a few old houses not yet levelled he is fortunate. But the landmarks, the objects which marked the city to him, as a city, are gone." (Cole, 1992).

The image of a place, the way people perceive and think about it, is formed by different ideas many of which are impalpable. Image is explained fully in Chapter 9.

Lord Alfred Tennyson's "land where all things always seemed the same" hardly exists. When people return to a place once visited it is never quite the same. It will have changed for the better or worse. However, there may exist enough of the old appeal for it to continue to please.

References

Cole, William. (1992). *Quotable New York – A Literary Companion*, Penguin Books.

Durrell, Lawrence. (1959). *Bitter Lemons of Cyprus*, Faber and Faber.

Gimlette, John. (1998). *Zanzibar; Home of an African Queen*, The Daily Telegraph, 11 July, 1998,

Kapuscinski, Ryszard (1986). *Shah of Shahs*, Picador.

Bravo La France. (1998). Time Magazine, 20 July.

United Nations Population Fund. (1996). *The State of World Population 1996, Changing Places, Population, Development and the Urban Future*, UNFPA.

United Nations Population Fund. (1997). *The State of World Population, 1997, The Right to Choose: Reproductive Rights and Reproductive Health*, UNFPA.

chapter two
Tourist Destinations

This chapter carries on from the concept of places described in Chapter 1 and asks – What makes a destination? It defines the terms destination and visitors, and also describes the value of domestic market foundations. It then describes different types of destination and their characteristics. It also explains the categories of visitor. The chapter then goes on to describe the destination characteristics according to market; for general interest and special interest holidays, for business traffic, visiting friends and family travel, and for health, religious and other purposes. It then discusses the three stages of travel to a destination; choice, journey and stay. The chapter concludes pointing out the need for a complete tourism product and describing the marketing mix.

A Destination

A tourist destination is any place which attracts visitors (either tourists who overnight or same-day visitors).

Everywhere normally provides facilities for visitors and some type of overnight accommodation. Any place can be a destination. Everywhere has a tourism sector, large or small.

Domestic Market Foundations

Exports are often built on the basis of satisfactory domestic production and marketing. Tourism is similar. Products and the balance of marketing mixes establish themselves serving a domestic demand, and then move on to serve international markets. This remains true even in many developing countries. Those who launch directly into international markets may miss the learning curve and continuity afforded by domestic customers.

Over reliance on international markets may also make destinations more vulnerable to the ups-and-downs of external events and influences. However, island countries such as the Bahamas or Mauritius have offered little opportunity to develop domestic tourism.

Visitors

The World Tourism Organisation (WTO, 1993) defines travellers as visitors or other travellers. Other travellers are not counted as visitors or included in tourism statistics. They are border workers, transit passengers, immigrants, nomads, refugees, members of the armed forces and diplomats.

Visitors (either domestic or international) are persons who travel to a place other than where they are normally resident for a period not exceeding 12 months. However, they should not have travelled for the purpose of an activity remunerated within the place visited.

WTO then divides visitors into tourists and same day visitors. Same-day visitors do not spend the night. Tourists stay at least one night.

The visitor's experience changes according to the particular mix of happenings, people and places. As Hemingway comments on Paris, "There is never any ending to Paris and the memory of each person who has lived in it differs from that of any other" (Hemingway, 1964).

Types Of Destination

Main, secondary and multiple destinations

Trips are of three types (see Figure 2.1): to a main destination only; to a main destination but with some secondary destinations; or to a number of different destinations (multiple destinations) without there being a main destination.

These can be further described and illustrated as follows:

- *Main destination only.* People travel directly to and from a main destination without stopping en route. For example, they go directly to Bali on holiday or Paris on business.

- *Main destination/secondary destinations.* Some secondary destinations may be transit destinations – places visited while en route to a main

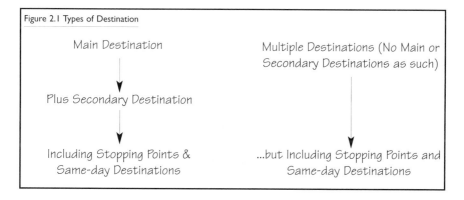

Figure 2.1 Types of Destination

Main Destination

↓

Plus Secondary Destination

↓

Including Stopping Points & Same-day Destinations

Multiple Destinations (No Main or Secondary Destinations as such)

↓

...but Including Stopping Points and Same-day Destinations

destination. Once at their main destination people may also choose to make same-day visits to a number of secondary destinations in the same vicinity. Or they may decide to add a secondary destination to the trip, and spend a few days there. This is generally known as an "add on". People may "add on" Lombok to a holiday in Bali, or Cambodia to a holiday in Thailand.

- Multiple destinations. People may visit a number of different countries or places on the same trip or holiday. There are no main and secondary destinations. Each destination ranks equally.

Stopping points

The stopping points on a journey mentioned above, can be also be called staging points or stopovers.

There are two concepts:

- stopping points on a journey are the places where travellers choose to overnight or spend a few days, while en route to or from a main destination (on the way there or on the way home). Bali or Singapore may be used as stopovers by air travellers from Europe to Australia. The stopping point becomes a secondary destination.

- stopping points (for a stay of one or more nights) on an overland tour, air tour or cruise fit the definition of a multiple destination trip or holiday. An air tour normally covers different countries and cities; an overland tour different places and possibly different countries; a cruise normally different countries. There are no main or secondary destinations.

Same-day destinations

A same-day destination may be covered by an organised excursion. You take a coach tour from London to Canterbury, or from Paris to Versailles. Or you may choose to visit a same-day destination on your own initiative. For example, you take the train from Delhi to visit the Taj Mahal or the train from Colombo to visit Kandy. You may take a ferry from England to spend a day in Boulogne, or in Fiji you may fly from Suva for a visit to Levuka. Or in whatever country you can choose to drive somewhere in your own car.

Destination areas

Normally a destination is best identified as the specific place rather than an area. For example – "I'm going to London" not "I'm going to the South-East of England".

However, the concept of a "tourist destination area" is also used. This does identify the destination as an area rather than a single place. This is quite clear in the case of the Lake District in England or the Loire Valley in France.

When a destination is identified as an area, all the places in it are normally within one-day road access of each other.

However, same day road access depends on driving conditions and these can change according to the weather and time of year. This creates a degree of imprecision.

It is also conceptually confusing to think in terms of same day air access since this can add places some hundreds of kilometres away. For example St Lucia is a same day excursion from Barbados. Lombok, East Java and South Sulawesi are all same day excursions from Bali. Edinburgh, Paris or Brussels could be same day trips from London.

In most cases, it is better to identify destinations as the specific places visited. For touring holidays, however, the region of the country or countries visited (these are multiple destination trips) provide a more comprehensive description.

Tourism destination area should not be confused with a tourism development area. Tourism development area is a term used in national tourism planning and management. This requires the division of the country into a sensible system of tourism development areas. These should be related to the organisation of the government's administrative units; e.g. region, state, county, province, borough, municipality and township.

Purposes Of Travel

The WTO lists the purposes of travel as:

> Leisure, recreation and holidays
> Visiting friends and relatives (VFR)
> Business and professional
> Health treatment
> Religion/pilgrimages
> Other

These various purposes are straightforward although there does exist some ambiguity. For example somebody on holiday may be visiting friends and relatives.

These purposes mean that people travel either by obligation (business, health, religion etc) or for pleasure (leisure, recreation and holidays).

Generally people travel on a trip (when travelling for obligatory reasons), or on holiday (travelling for pleasure).

Pleasure travel divides between general interest tourism (the mainstream) and special interest tourism (the narrower or niche markets).

General Interest Tourism

General interest tourism has the purpose of holidays, rest and recreation. Its destinations have the following main characteristics:

- the destination is a resort where people spend most of their time enjoying the beach or mountains, other recreational attractions, and the overall holiday atmosphere. Resorts are likely to have integrated facilities and services, with shops and entertainment within the immediate environment. Tourists may venture away from the resort to take only one or two local tours. Some examples of major resorts are the Playa Ingles resort in Gran Canaria, or the Costa Dorada in the Dominican Republic, or the Nusa Dua in Bali.

- the destination is used as a base for a general interest overland touring holiday (local). People arrive at a destination by personal car or hire a car on arrival. They tour on a daily basis (most days) making same-day visits to places found within the surrounding area, returning to their hotel or other accommodation each night. For example, people may choose Tours as a base to visit the Loire Valley.

- multiple destinations are chosen as the framework for a general interest overland touring holiday (long distance). People travel by personal car or tour bus from place to place covering as many as seven, eight or more destinations in the one holiday.

- a number of different ports are visited as part of a cruise ship holiday. People are given the opportunity to disembark at each port spending some time shopping, eating out, visiting attractions, and taking local tours. Since people sleep on board the ship, they are not treated for statistical purposes as tourists but as same-day visitors.

- a number of different destinations may also be visited as part of a cruising holiday in chartered and crewed yachts. People who are experienced sailors may crew the yachts themselves, undertaking what are known as bareboat charters.

- a multiple destination holiday may include air travel linked to overland tours and/or cruises or may be further combined with a stay at a resort. Air tours may include a number of countries in a particular region of the world. For example, a tour in South East Asia which includes Bangkok (Thailand), Hong Kong, Bali (Indonesia), Singapore and Penang (Malaysia).

Visits to major historic cities may be included in some types of both general and special interest tourism.

Special Interest Tourism

Special interest tourism describes holidays aimed at a particular, clearly defined range of interests, comprising the purpose or motivation.

This definition covers an immense number of possibilities. Principal among these are the following:

Sports

- Spectator – travelling to watch football matches, tennis competitions, motor racing or any other sports event.
- Participative – for example tennis, golf, yachting, or fishing holidays.

Ecotourism/nature

The destination is a place somewhere in the countryside amidst a variety of attractive natural resources. It may also include the more specialised types of study such as botany, bird watching and entomology.

Way-of-life tourism

This covers a stay at a destination linked to various visits, all aimed at the study of a different culture and way-of-life.

Cultural tourism

Cultural tourism may be aimed at the hardware of a cultural heritage; e.g. particular cultural sites such as cathedrals, castles, chateaux, and archaeological sites. Or it is aimed more at the cultural software of the performing and visual arts; e.g. painting, sculpture, music, dance, opera, theatre and literature. Or it may combine elements of cultural hardware and software together.

Festivals

These may include general cultural festivals or film, song, music and dance festivals.

Arts and handicrafts

- Study visits – an itinerary which includes visits to various collections, the observation of differences in styles and techniques, and stops at various workshops to watch the artists at work.
- Courses and workshops – may include a workshop where people learn and practice the particular skills and techniques.

Photography

This normally involves an itinerary aimed at creating opportunities for outstanding photographs often of a specialised nature. For example, a trip to the Swiss Alps or on safari in East Africa

Other hobbies/pastimes

This may cover many other hobbies or pastimes. For example, stamp collecting, model aeroplanes, dog and bird fancying, and writing.

Adventure

- Soft adventure – this includes an adventure holiday which is not particularly strenuous or tough. It might include horse back riding through particular countryside, safaris, trekking, hiking, game fishing and cycling.

- Hard adventure – these are holidays in often tough and demanding conditions and include mountaineering, white water rafting, canoeing, and deep sea diving.

Special Interest Focus And Purpose

A number of these special interest holidays may be either narrowly or broadly focused. They will be narrow and for those people who are dedicated. For example pottery experts, going to a participative workshop, may wish to learn certain advanced and refined techniques.

Other holidays may be more general with several areas clustered together to meet the needs of the market in question. For example, ecotourism, way-of-life, cultural attractions, and arts and handicrafts may be packaged together to form one programme. These same components could form the basis for a photographer's tour. Various hard and soft adventure experiences may be packaged together. Sports enthusiasts may have the chance to play a number of different games.

With a number of special interest markets the purpose of the holiday is more important than the destination. For example, one may look for excellent deep sea diving regardless of where it is found.

Asked about their trip people put the purpose before the destination – "I'm going skiing", or "We're off to play golf" or "We're going fishing". However, people do tend to mention the place if it is a leader in a particular special interest market. For example, "I'm skiing at Gstaad", or "We're golfing at St Andrews next week", or "We're trekking in the Himalayas", or "We'll be diving in the Cayman Islands".

While the purpose of the trip is the primary consideration, the destination itself still counts. The final choice will be influenced by the product, image, price, promotion and the sales organisation. Together these comprise a destination's marketing mix.

The types of holiday cover all the special interests imaginable. For example, there are many holidays which feature the first world war battlefields in Belgium and Northern France. For example, these may focus on the works of the first world war poets.

Business and Professional Travel

A high proportion of business travel is to a single destination. However, business persons may also travel to a number of places within the same region of the country (e.g. South-East England), or the world (e.g. South-East Asia).

Travel therefore falls into the same three categories described; main destination only, main destination plus secondary destinations, and multiple destinations.

Also related to this category is the MICE market (meetings, incentive travel, conventions and exhibitions). This is an important market segment.

VFR, Health, Religious and Other Travel

Visiting friends and relatives (VFR) is usually to a main destination, sometimes including secondary destinations.

Health, religious and other travel usually has a clear main destination, but can also include secondary destinations. Multiple destination trips may be organised for religious purposes.

Health travel may be particularly related to spas and health resorts. Religious travel is often represented by pilgrimages e.g. the Hadj.

The Destination and its Three Stages

The concept of a destination turns a place into a choice (a decision to travel, to go there and come back, to opt for a means of transport, to undertake the journey). It means to displace oneself temporarily, to embark on an experience, and to live out a period away from one's home setting. One can divide this into three stages (see Figure 2.2):

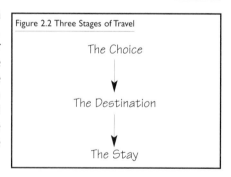

Figure 2.2 Three Stages of Travel

The Choice

The Destination

The Stay

The choice of the destination

What happens before leaving home; studying the publicity, choosing where to go and making the purchase. People choose a destination if it is thought to meet the purposes of their trip or holiday and other needs and motivations, at a price which they can afford and which seems to offer value for money. The success of the promotional message, the appeal of the destination's image, the ease of purchase, and the credibility of the tour operator (if used), all influence the final choice.

The journey to the destination

When one chooses a destination, one also buys travel distance and the means of transport. Generally the farther away the more it costs and the longer it takes. The journey has its own appeal – the relative comfort, the romance of travel, the stopping points and the anticipation of arrival.

The stay at the destination

What happens at the destination forms the basis of memories, satisfactions and dissatisfactions.

The Destination as a Marketing Mix

Figure 2.3 The Marketing Mix
✓ Product
✓ Image
✓ Price
✓ Promotion
✓ Sales

As noted, a destination should be seen as a tourism product together with the other components of the marketing mix (image, price, promotion and sales network – see Figure 2.3). The image is a powerful influence in tourism and is treated as a separate component (Doswell, 1997).

Places are destinations. What kind of destination will depend on the marketing mix and the various potential markets. However, it is not enough to have cultural, scenic or other attractions or to offer just a room or somewhere to sleep. Tourism, to provide benefits for the place itself and satisfactions for its visitors, requires a complete product. It also needs an attractive image, competitive prices and effective promotion and sales. This marketing mix may also be adjusted according to the season of the year.

References

Doswell, R. (1997). *Tourism – How Effective Management Makes the Difference*, Butterworth Heinemann.

Hemingway, Ernest. (1964). *A Moveable Feast*. Penguin 1966.

World Tourism Organisation. (1993). *Recommendations on Tourism Statistics*.

chapter three
Visitors

This chapter starts by discussing who people are, what people need, what people think they need, and what people subconsciously need. It goes on to examine some particular travel motivations, and then discusses various types of ego benefits. It examines the relationships between popular culture and mass tourism. The chapter then discusses the concept of not meeting, meeting or exceeding visitor expectations, and explains how other tourists form part of the tourism product. It concludes by examining tourism communities and visitors' interpretations, and explaining the importance of visitor surveys.

An Initial Framework

One can look at people in four different ways: who they are, what they need, what they think they need and what they unconsciously need.

Who people are

To understand who people are, one segments societies into groups and markets. Each group unites people with common characteristics and wants. One can classify these in any way that makes the segmentation sharper. When developing and selling a product, one tries to understand everything possible about the target market segments.

People's nationality, age and gender are among the criteria used. So are their educational level, the kind of job they do, their income and where they live. Their civil status and stage of life also add to the picture; whether they are married, with babies or younger children, with school or university age children or already retired, or perhaps widowed. Their hobbies or sports are also an influence; where they normally spend their holidays and what they do with their spare time. Also their lifestyle, their behavioural patterns, and the way they choose to spend their available money.

What people need

Motivation theories have addressed two sorts of needs; basic and acquired needs. Basic physical needs include food, drink, shelter and sex. They also include the need to belong, human beings are social animals. Acquired needs cover individual preferences and are mainly cultural in origin. People want, for example, a particular kind of bed or food. Acquired needs, although they may change, are important to people.

What people think they need

These needs stem from particular cultural and social values. They stem from the need for social acceptance, recognition, prestige, and power. People use their values to determine what is important or not, or what is true or not, or how to respond to a given situation. For example, whether to buy or do something or not, or whether to go somewhere or not. What a thing or experience will do for them. These values go on being influenced during the first half of life. In later life they tend to become fixed.

Many of these needs are not strictly rational and are so subjective that people find it difficult to explain them. They bubble up from a mixture of thoughts to influence many buying decisions. People do what makes them feel good; what enhances their self concept and provides ego benefits.

What people unconsciously need

Sigmund Freud (1856-1939) added greatly to an evaluation of human nature. Freud split human thought processes into three levels; the id, ego and super

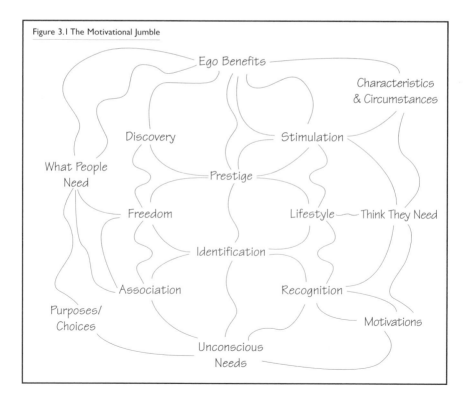

Figure 3.1 The Motivational Jumble

Ego Benefits

Characteristics & Circumstances

Discovery   Stimulation

What People Need

Prestige

Freedom   Lifestyle — Think They Need

Identification

Association   Recognition

Purposes/ Choices

Motivations

Unconscious Needs

ego (Stafford Clark, 1992). The id holds the biological needs concerned with the life and death instincts. From here come the sex drive, aggressivity and the primal driving forces.

The ego is the intelligent self; it harmonises the impulses of the id with the reality of the environment. It is oriented to the body and self preservation, and is without conscience or the restraints of moral codes or social norms.

It is the super ego's job to determine how to act within a particular cultural framework. The super ego regulates an individual's behaviour according to certain norms. People then adjust their behaviour to achieve given goals, seeking to gain love and respect in the process.

These concepts of levels relate to the conscious and subconscious mind; what we think we need and what we unconsciously need become confused. They all mix together to influence behaviour. The reaction to a tourist destination emerges from such a jumble of thoughts.

Travel Motivations

In Chapter 2, travel purposes were listed as leisure, recreation and holidays, visiting friends and relatives, business and professional, health treatment, religion/pilgrimages, and other. People travel for either pleasure or obligation.

Leisure travellers have a basic need for rest and relaxation. Travel provides a change of scene. It refreshes people's thinking and outlook. It enables them to recuperate their physical and mental well being. It is a cure for tiredness.

Other motivations for leisure travellers include the following needs:

Discovery

Travel can satisfy a person's curiosity to see other parts of the world. It can reveal the world's diversity, its beauty and attractions, and the way other people live.

Stimulation

Travel frees people from the humdrum and pressure of their daily lives. Travel relieves the monotony and breaks the routine. It provides an element of change and adventure, and can stimulate and revitalise people who have become dulled by sameness.

Freedom

Travel can provide a sense of liberation and detachment; of leaving one's responsibilities behind and becoming briefly more independent and anonymous. It provides a new setting with new rules; an escape from the limitations of day-to-day life.

One is motivated to fulfil a need. As noted, what people need, think they need, unconsciously need are multiple, varied and often complex. So are travel needs and motivations. Figure 3.1 illustrates this jumble of motivational influences.

Fear, of course, discourages people from travelling, e.g. fear of foreign cultures, of illness, of flying, of crime etc.

What Competes?

Choice depends first on whether one is travelling for pleasure or by obligation. Travelling by obligation, e.g. on business, a person generally has fewer choices.

What competes *within* leisure travel and tourism is the whole range of destinations, facilities and services – a variety of marketing mixes from which to choose. What competes *with* travel and tourism is anything which people may choose to buy instead. Any number of goods and services compete for a person's discretionary income. There is a hierarchy of needs which differs according to market segment; travel and tourism tend to rank highly.

Ego Benefits

Travel can makes us feel better about ourselves. Another important motivation. In this sense a travel experience can prove especially satisfying. Some of the elements in this are prestige/recognition, lifestyle/identification and association.

Prestige/recognition

Patterns of consumption bestow prestige and earn recognition. A combination of high price, exclusivity and relative inaccessibility make certain products and services difficult to attain. They represent symbols of achievement. Certain brands of wrist watch, models of car, and designer clothes are typical examples of prestige products. Particular destinations and resorts may also be highly prestigious.

In business travel, status, recognition and prestige are closely connected to the image of the traveller's employer or the company which he or she owns. The class of travel and the category of accommodation chosen are also a reflection of this organisation. To project a prestigious image for one's company means choosing a prestigious hotel, and flying first or business class.

Some products and services can become legends. They bestow classic status, standing for timeless and lasting prestige.

Lifestyle/identification

Lifestyle means the way people choose to live, their attitudes, values, preferences reflected in the things they do, clothes they wear, organisations they belong to, places they go, and people they know or emulate.

In this there is a process of identification with a particular lifestyle, and with the sort of people who seem to share it. Who else buys the product? For example, a person might see Barbados as the playground of the smart set; an image fostered by the gossipy travel writers.

Psychographic profiles try to place lifestyles and personality traits into clusters, characterising particular kinds of people and behaviour. These add to the more conventional ways of segmenting markets, helping to predict consumption preferences and buying behaviour.

Association

People go through life pleased by the happy associations which they find. Associations capture past happenings, holidays, people, experiences and other memories. Elements in a destination's core image may prompt such memories. They give a place a nostalgic appeal. People love a destination which stirs up these kinds of associations and "rings this bell".

Popular Culture and Mass Tourism

Mass tourism means the holiday and leisure travel enjoyed by the majority of people. However, it still lends itself to considerable segmentation according to different characteristics and needs. Minority tourism comprises the small market segments.

The twentieth century has changed many ordinary people's lives. In many countries, industrialisation, economic growth and modernity have created relative prosperity. This has marked a major shift in political power and social influence. However, the idea of a class system still persists.

High culture has traditionally been associated with the "upper classes"; the richer, more educated and more powerful sections of society. The "middle classes" are seen as middlebrow preferring a bland culture, usually judged as less intellectually and aesthetically satisfying. The "lower classes" are judged as enjoying a rough-and-ready culture, of little lasting value, vulgarly close to the melee of day-to-day life. Culture when given a broad popular appeal is described as "dumbing down".

F.R.Leavis, one of the twentieth century's leading British literary figures, feared popular culture's effect on high culture (Leavis, 1930). Ortega y Gasset wrote that, "The epoch of the masses is the epoch of the colossal. We are living, therefore, under the brutal empire of the masses" (Ortega y Gasset, 1932).

There is a fear of opening the floodgates and swamping high culture. Mass tourism, it is believed, is full of similar dangers. Foreign travel was historically an extension of high culture, whereas this century's rapid growth of tourism is an extension of popular culture. Growing and popular holiday-making is denigrated as mass tourism. In consequence similar sentiments and fears are expressed. "Mass tourism swamps and spoils destinations," people say. Krippendorf also sees much of contemporary tourism as superficial and vulgar, advocating a tourism of deeper human meaning (Krippendorf,1987).

People may not behave as others want. People respond to the world in which they move and decide their behaviour accordingly. There are always thinkers like Leavis, Ortega y Gasset and Krippendorf, who want people to want other things. They may exercise some influence but remain mostly irrelevant to modern marketing. Marketing identifies actual wants and needs and segments the market accordingly. It neither regrets what people want nor sets out to give them something else. One does not advocate either elitism or populism; one follows marketing principles.

However, governments may not leave the arts entirely to the dictates of the market. A government may act to foster certain cultural values, protecting, subsidising and supporting selected institutions and initiatives. Lionel Jospin, when French Premier, is noted for his yes to the market economy but no to the market society.

Government may even try to influence the development of particular types of tourism. Britain's Department of International Development has taken an initiative to support nature tourism in developing countries. "Nature tourism is a dynamic market," it points out, "…well placed to offer a viable source of income for rural communities…" (DFID, 1999).

Education can also develop people's thinking and expand their knowledge. It may modify their tastes and add to their wants and needs, even influence consumer choice in tourism. It is important to enrich the tourism product, adding dimensions that bring culture alive, enlightening and entertaining people at the same time. Tourism can also help to make high culture more accessible, providing crossovers to the main currents of populist attitudes and thought.

Increasing prosperity and educational opportunities blur many of the distinctions between high and popular culture. However, class, snobbery and exclusivity, as already noted, are important motivating factors in consumer behaviour.

Observations on mass tourism and popular culture have tended to come from the West. However, economic growth has created new generations of consumers in other parts of the world. Increasing numbers of non-Western tourists visit non-Western countries. This will produce forms of mass tourism modified to satisfy different sets of cultural needs.

Tourism can be a vehicle for high culture. But it does not have to be. It can also emphasise cultural discovery with a "people and nature" centred tourism. Destinations target particular market segments and develop their product accordingly. They may also choose a tourism which is lowbrow, equally sustainable and just as beneficial. Sound planning and management may make any tourism productive and harmonious, fully meeting social, economic and environmental objectives.

The Tourism Product Includes Other Tourists

A successful tourism destination always has tourists around, and lots of them during the high season. Part of the experience of the product includes seeing and being with other tourists. Other tourists add to the atmosphere. People seek people – the crowds of other tourists are part of the fun (Doswell, 1997). Travel advertisements often feature beautiful looking people and golden youth. And there are always enough glittering young people in St Tropez in August, for example, to validate this image.

Most destinations are full of tourists, it is part of the atmosphere. Tea at the Ritz is the enjoyment of late twentieth century tourism in a famous London setting. It may evoke, but cannot duplicate, a past era.

Tourism Communities

Some communities rely almost entirely on tourism for their economic and social well being. For example many Mediterranean and Caribbean resorts. Whole generations have been brought up in a tourism environment, most people work in tourism, and people live side-by-side with the tourists. Just as in the past one talked about mining and industrial communities, one now talks about tourism communities. Tourism's social impact is absorbed as part of everyday life, it is accepted as a norm. Tourism and tourists represent the life which everyone knows.

Visitor's Interpretation

The acts of reading a text, looking at a work of art or visiting a tourist destination all prompt a personal interpretation of the experience. However the text or work of art is invariable; only the interpretations can differ. In tourism the experience itself is variable and people may do and see different things. A huge number of different experiences and interpretations is possible.

However, we know that people of a similar background and profile arrive at similar ideas. The aggregate of their satisfactions is the same. Market segmentation succeeds in grouping together people with similar needs, wants and ways of seeing things. At the same time, within the same marketing mix, minimum standards of quality and service lessen product differences. People's interpretations, within any given market segment, may differ but not substantially.

Visitor's interpretations tend to differ only as widely as the number of different marketing mixes and the market segments which they serve.

Not Meeting, Meeting or Exceeding Expectations

Herzberg is renowned for his work on employee motivation. He showed that while poor working conditions could dissatisfy employees, good conditions did not necessarily satisfy them. Working conditions merely avoided dissatisfaction and were not in themselves a motivating force. The real satisfiers which motivated people were the things which enriched jobs, making work more challenging and fulfilling (Herzberg, 1966).

Venison acknowledged a parallel in the tourist experience. He saw that hotel guests were not fully satisfied by the provision of basic requirements alone. They were motivated by personal attention, care and that little extra, making them feel special and important (Venison, 1983).

Dissatisfaction is avoided if the tourist's expectations are met, but people are really happy when they are exceeded. This is particularly true of expectations attached to the intangible aspects of the tourism product; the welcome, human warmth and kindness which people receive. However, it is also true when any product element is better than expected. Figure 3.2 illustrates this meeting and exceeding of expectations.

Expectations may vary according to the destination and the marketing mix. A visitor may expect more in one country than in another. For example, expectations of a developed country may be higher than in a developing country. Visitors may be prepared to make allowances if certain basic requirements are not quite satisfied.

The tourist experience proves especially satisfying when standards achieved exceed expectations and overcome apprehensions. People tend to feel insecure and nervous when travelling abroad. They feel quickly reassured by a warm welcome, friendly people and good order and security.

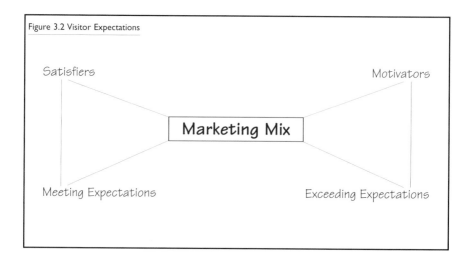

Figure 3.2 Visitor Expectations

Satisfiers

Motivators

Marketing Mix

Meeting Expectations

Exceeding Expectations

Visitor Surveys

It is important to maintain a flow of information about visitors, their profiles, motivations and satisfactions. Some of this information may come from desk research, advertising agencies, other marketing sources, tour operators and various branches of the travel trade. The rest of the information comes from visitor surveys.

Visitor surveys are usually conducted at the destination. Researchers use questionaires, sometimes linked to an interview. They collect and analyse data on the visitor profiles, characteristics, sex and age, occupation, marital status, preferences, and expenditure; tour operator/travel agency used, reason for visiting, other countries visited, length of stay, trip duration, package price and daily expenditure, return visits, places and attractions visited; the quality of tourist information, airline, accommodation, food and beverage, local transportation, and entry procedures. The precise data included can be tailored to the particular situation and market.

Visitors can also be interviewed at length, and asked to describe what was either good or bad about their holiday. When asked this question people tend to mention only those things which either exceed or fail to meet expectations. Anything else goes unremarked and can therefore be judged acceptable.

Visitor surveys help to generate some of the vital information discussed more fully in Chapter 8 – Market Research.

References

Department of International Development, Environmental Policy Department. (1999). *Changing (the) Nature (of) Tourism.*

Doswell, Roger. (1997). *Tourism – How Effective Management Makes the Difference*, Butterworth Heinemann.

Herzberg, Frederick. (1966). *Work and the Nature of Man, World Publications.*

Krippendorf, Jost. (1987). *The Holiday Makers*, Butterworth Heinemann.

Leavis, F.R. (1930). *Mass Civilization and Popular Culture*, Minority Press.

Ortega y Gasset, J. (1932). *The Revolt of the Masses*, George Allen & Unwin.

Stafford Clark, D. (1992). *What Freud Really Said*, Penguin.

Venison, Peter. (1983). *Managing Hotels*, William Heinemann.

chapter four
Product

This chapter considers the transition from destination to tourism product. It then examines the total product and its various components. It looks at diversification and the ever present element of change. It then examines the relationship of space to the tourism product and the concept of intangible components. The chapter goes on to explain the role of accommodation, and the product's predominant features. It then notes more fully the idea of completeness, and concludes with more information on the marketing mix.

From Destination to Tourism Product

A destination is not a tourism product until we think of it as a product. It can just be a place with a few hotels and some ancillary services. If no interrelated view is taken, it stays like this. The various components remain largely fragmented and uncoordinated. Some facilities and services may be absent or deficient, others may not match one another – either in quality or size.

The product has to be as complete as possible, fitting together harmoniously in a matching way and fully satisfying its various markets.

The overall demand for travel and tourism continues to grow. The market opportunities exist. But one has to have the right components and attractions, the right hotels, facilities and other services. To have a chance one has to have an appropriate tourism product. In this sense tourism is supply led.

The Total Product

The tourism product has components which are part of the country's natural resources and cultural heritage. These are its basic tourism assets. There are inherent features such as climate, landscape, scenic attractions and other natural resources. And there are cultural features which include the historical, archaeological and other attractions and the whole range of expressive arts covering both the visual and performing arts.

To be enjoyed, scenic areas and attractions need access. They also need conservation and protection. The historical and archaeological attractions can be enhanced through skilful and sensitive treatment, but they cannot be replaced or duplicated. Great art itself needs appropriate museums, suitable theatres, and concert halls. Both Great Britain and France, for example, have added new theatres, opera houses, concert halls, museums and libraries in recent decades. A great cultural heritage needs to be appropriately housed.

Once a destination takes stock that it is a place people want to visit, it should develop its overall tourism product. It should ensure that its infrastructure is adequate. It should open up and show off its cultural heritage. It should seek to both improve and develop the full range and choice of hotels and accommodation, food and beverage facilities, local transport networks and all the other services. And it should stimulate the development of all kinds of contemporary arts and cultural activities.

This does not only serve the development of tourism, it enhances the quality of life for the local population. Tourism, since it sells the place in all its dimensions, serves as a stimulus for many improvements.

The total product should get visitors:

to enjoy themselves more.
to stay longer.
to spend more.
to come back.

Product Components

There are two lines from a Paul Celan poem, "all things are less than they are – all things are more". This could sum up the tourism product.

The product, illustrated in Figure 4.1, brings together some or all of the following components:

Firstly the following inherent features:

- good climatic conditions;
- a variety of attractive natural resources – pleasant surroundings, good landscape, recreational attractions, and scenic attractions;
- a variety of cultural attractions including historical and archaeological sites;
- access to plentiful water supplies;
- a population with a culture inherently welcoming and hospitable;
- a location with potentially easy access from target markets, or with good sites to develop the necessary airports and harbours.

And secondly the following created features:

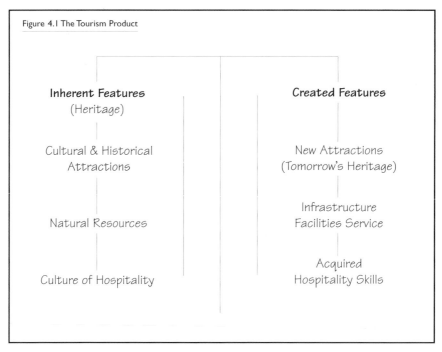

Figure 4.1 The Tourism Product

Inherent Features
(Heritage)

Cultural & Historical
Attractions

Natural Resources

Culture of Hospitality

Created Features

New Attractions
(Tomorrow's Heritage)

Infrastructure
Facilities Service

Acquired
Hospitality Skills

- good transportation links, with easy access established from other parts of the region and country, and serviced by an adequate existing airport;

- a selection of hotels, resorts, other accommodation facilities, restaurants, bars and catering services;

- a variety of sporting and recreational facilities within reach;

- a range of entertainment and shopping facilities;

- a mixed and already developed local economy able to supply and service the needs of tourism;

- well developed infrastructure with spare capacity, or capacity for easy expansion;

- well developed community services – e.g. police, fire brigade, health services, postal services etc;

- vibrant and wide ranging contemporary artistic and cultural activities;

- a local population able to supply a growing tourism labour force.

These are the features that come together to form the tourism product. Man-made features, of course, are either "old" (e.g. Notre Dame or the Eiffel Tower) or "new" (e.g. Disney World or Sun City).

Diversification

As a destination grows so it is likely to diversify both its products and its markets. It may not satisfy one market and one narrow range of tastes, but widens its appeal and diversifies its product accordingly. It is different things to many different groups of people.

A developed destination is multifaceted – the product includes a range of contrasting features and components. Visitors can PICK AND MIX to match a variety of different needs. As an expanding number of market segments is attracted, so the product diversifies in a matching way.

Change

Change is a recurrent theme. Like every other aspect of a place, the tourism product is subject to constant change (quite apart from planned change). The product alters as the result of the normal processes of economic and social development.

- the culture of a place changes all the time; attitudes and values cease to be exactly the same.
- new technology can produce major improvements, e.g. the introduction of air conditioning revolutionised the product in a destination like Florida.
- places grow or decrease in size; they seldom remain the same.
- the relative mix of old and new buildings changes. Some new buildings are added, some are renovated, others are demolished.
- the amount of money available for maintenance and upkeep varies over time, according to changing economic performance and prosperity.
- the security and stability of the place may change, there is more or less crime/terrorism than before.

A degree of quality control over the place and the product is possible. However, there is a danger that many changes may be random and uncoordinated.

In Chapter 1 we noted that the atmosphere of a place is influenced by the culture and way of life. We also saw that it is influenced by its government, its perceived social stability, and its economic performance. Major changes in these areas rebound on the tourism product.

Space

A large proportion of the tourism product is represented by space. Space in the hotel, the aircraft, the restaurant; the use of space for a period of time – a seat, room or, for example, space on a beach, tennis court or golf course.

Most of this space is offered for sale, if it goes unsold for any period that lost revenue can never be recovered. Space cannot be stored.

Different space must match. The number of people on the arriving aeroplane must match the number of available rooms. The number of tourists in a resort, the space on the beach. The number of golfers, the space on the golf course. The number of people dining, the space in the restaurant. Each facility or attraction can accommodate only a certain number of visitors at one time (the carrying capacity). If space is insufficient there may be overcrowding, long waits, dissatisfied visitors and damage to the buildings or surroundings.

Visitors may compete for space; the locals have to make room for them. Tourism is about space; you leave your space at home to take up space elsewhere. Some space you pay for – e.g. in hotels and visiting museums. Some you use free of charge – e.g. country trails and city streets. Tourism requires a series of spatial interrelationships. One sells space or buys space, borrows space, uses space, competes for space, makes space, and matches space.

The spatial relationships of various facilities, services and attractions, together with the movements of tourists, are important considerations in planning tourism.

The Intangibles

The tourism product is consumed on-the-spot in the destination itself. It is an amalgam of everything that happens while the visitor is there. It is a total experience which either pleases or displeases. Intangible factors which you cannot measure but only experience – e.g. a warm welcome, happy ambience and friendly people – add significantly to the enjoyment.

In any place we can get a good feeling just walking around. We feel wanted, relaxed and comfortable. If a place is unfriendly the reverse is true. These feelings add to, or detract from, the overall product.

As noted in Chapter 3 the intangible factors can help the product to exceed visitor expectations. It is the quality of the welcome which often surprises people agreeably.

There are strong traditions of hospitality and friendliness in some cultures but not in others. Some cultures may appear relatively unwelcoming and cold. It is possible to improve a host population's welcome, through public awareness and training programmes. However, one should encourage people to be themselves. Human warmth is mostly natural and spontaneous rather than taught or rehearsed, although social skills can be improved through training. The destination has to generate a good feeling not only for visitors but for its own people.

Accommodation

The accommodation chosen by a visitor, often included by a tour operator as part of a holiday package, is at the heart of the tourism product.

The basic purchase is a stay at the destination. This means buying transport and accommodation. The fact of being there opens the door to the complete experience. In general interest tourism the tourists themselves, given the choices and options, complete the product. Each stay or holiday becomes a very individual and subjective experience.

This reflects the stance of the tour operator, "We sell you this and the rest you decide for yourself". The main items are the room and the transportation – e.g. a hotel room and an airline seat.

The principal part of the tourism product traded by the tour operator is the room. The transportation, although important, is still secondary. Operators act as wholesalers; they buy rooms in bulk and add value by packaging them into inclusive holidays. They then promote and retail them to the consumer.

The room (or the place to stay) is sold as the core of the total product. It may be in a camping or caravan site, or on a boat, or in an self catering apartment, guest house, or person's home, hotel, motel or resort. Whatever the type of accommodation, however, this is the main item which people buy when they make the decision to stay somewhere.

Packages serving special interest markets may include other features as well as accommodation. For example, a golfing holiday may include the entrance and green fees to prestigious golf clubs. A diving holiday can have a range of organised dives, skiing may include passes to exciting ski slopes. The special interest itself is packaged by the tour operator, making the accommodation of relatively lesser importance. However, the accommodation still plays a pivotal role.

However acceptable a destination, poor accommodation ruins a holiday. The accommodation, further discussed in Chapter 5, is of central importance.

Predominant Features

Each product is characterised by its predominant features. In the Maldives, for example, the predominant features are the idyllic coral island settings, boundless fine white sand beaches, clear blue waters and tranquil lagoons and colourful and abundant marine life.

Fiji and the South Seas have the features of luscious tropical islands of both a coral and volcanic character. They also have the added popular conceptions of their widely known culture – rhythmic music, exotic dance, singing voices, garlands of flowers, happiness, charm and tranquillity.

Cities are characterised by their famous landmarks. Paris has, for example, the Eiffel Tower, London Big Ben, Rome St Peters, New York the Empire State Building and so on.

In terms of the tourism product these various features may assume different degrees of importance. In general interest tourism the accommodation used is a major feature, particularly among older people. They may spend more time in their hotel and comfort and services provided become especially important.

In a seaside holiday the quality of the beach is important; the space available, absence of overcrowding and nuisances, cleanliness, organisation, beach furniture, how safe the sea is, the way it shelves and the quality of the water. This is particularly true for families with young children. However, older people may have little interest in a beach – it is merely something to look at.

How people rank the various components of the product depends on their particular needs and preferences. People have their own way of ordering these, and it may differ according to each market segment.

In special interest tourism the main features are those which represent the holiday's principal purpose – the special interest itself. For a diving holiday, it is the quality of diving. For skiing the ski slopes. For golf the golf courses, and for white water rafting the river and its rapids.

A destination's predominant features are sometimes described as unique selling propositions. The reason is clear. They represent that part of the product which makes it stand out – important to emphasise in promotion and sales. This links the product directly with image, to be discussed in Chapter 9.

Completeness

Whatever the importance of intangible factors, or the accommodation used, or the destination's predominant features, the product is experienced in its totality. Everything counts. In this sense, no one feature can be separated from the whole. Leonardo Da Vinci talked about the totality of things, "Every part is disposed to unite with the whole, that it may escape from its own incompleteness".

Streets should look bright, clean and colourful, with plenty of fresh paint, flowers and greenery. Well designed signs help visitors to find their way, people speak their language and have all the tourist information they need. Attractive gathering places, esplanades, squares, open air cafes and beer gardens exist. Here visitors can look at, and mix with, other people. And they can always take pleasant strolls through attractive surroundings.

Chapter 3 indicated that the product includes other tourists. This is important in discussing completeness. They should fit with the product, enhance the image, and help create and sustain the right atmosphere.

Different market segments share some of the same components. For example, they share the place itself, its streets and shops, its scenic and cultural attractions, some recreational and entertainment facilities and various other services. The beach in coastal resorts is shared as are some sporting facilities and so on.

This concept relies on other people behaving in a way conducive to the product. But if they behave badly, drink too much, and become offensive and disruptive, they can fracture the product and change the image. In the formulation of a range of marketing mixes this is an important consideration. In jumbling markets together there has to exist a degree of compatibility.

The Marketing Mix

As already noted in Chapter 2, the product is a part of the marketing mix. The other parts are image, price, promotion and sales. They are all subjects of later chapters.

- the product reflects the idea of completeness – it includes all aspects including the intangibles.

- the image describes how the project is perceived and how we would like it to be perceived.

- the price indicates the positioning of the product, according to the other parts of the marketing mix.

- the promotion describes the actions taken to reach the market.

- the sales network describes the channels, outlets and coverage achieved.

The product as at the heart of the marketing mix, while accommodation is at the heart of the product. And effective promotion and sales are little use if one doesn't have the right product, image and price.

A destination generally has a diverse tourism product – it offers a variety of tourist experiences, at different prices, serving a number of different market segments. There is a marketing mix for each segment.

The overall marketing mix can be harmonised in the following ways, while still allowing for variations in the people comprising different market segments:.

- the product is differentiated to serve a range of market segments. Some components of the product remain the same – others vary (see Chapter 11).

- there is mostly a singular – core and brand – image for a plural product (see Chapter 9).

- the tertiary image targets specific market segments (also Chapter 9).

- the prices may vary but they support the main image projected (see

Chapter 10).

- the promotion may image-build for all markets but also targets specific segments (see Chapter 12).

- sales are mostly compartmentalised for each market segment, through the particular tour operators and channels chosen (see Chapter 14).

In conclusion, however, a destination usually has a mix of products, a mix of images or perceptions, and a mix of different prices, promotional approaches and sales channels. This means that there is a mix of marketing mixes. The tourist finds both sameness and diversity. Figure 4.2 illustrates this.

In some destinations, one can modify the marketing mix according to seasonality. Seasonal changes offer different possibilities e.g. in a ski resort. As part of this, the product, prices, promotion and sales can be adjusted.

Chapter 11 – Positioning – looks further at the formulation of a range of marketing mixes

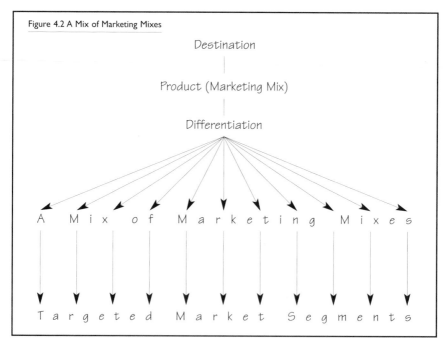

Figure 4.2 A Mix of Marketing Mixes

Destination

Product (Marketing Mix)

Differentiation

A   Mix   of   Marketing   Mixes

Targeted   Market   Segments

chapter five
Accommodation

The chapter starts by indicating the types of tourist accommodation listed by the World Tourism Organisation (WTO). It goes on to describe the size and characteristics of establishments, and the accommodation product's components and quality requirements. It then describes project feasibility, and explains how to shape a destination's accommodation and mobilise tour operators. The chapter then describes the similarities between a commodity – coffee – and the marketing of tourist accommodation. It concludes by highlighting, as a critical factor in tourism, the health of the hotel and accommodation sub-sector.

Types of Accommodation

As noted in the last chapter, the product is at the heart of the marketing mix. In a similar way accommodation is at the heart of the product.

The types of tourist accommodation vary greatly. They divide between accommodation offered commercially and rooms provided without charge by a visitor's relatives or friends. The World Tourism Organisation (WTO) classifies them as follows:

Collective tourism establishments

- Hotels and similar establishments
- Specialised establishments
- Health establishments
- Work and holiday camps
- Public means of transport
- Conference centres

Other collective establishments

- Holiday dwellings
- Tourist campsites
- Other collective establishments

Private accommodation

- Owned dwellings
- Rented rooms in family houses

- Dwellings rented from private individuals or professional agencies
- Accommodation provided without charge by relatives or friends
- Other private accommodation

Size and Characteristics Of Units

In most countries by far the largest proportion of hotels are small units (less than 30 rooms). There is usually a close correlation between the classification of hotels (e.g. one to five stars) and their size. As a general rule, 4 and 5 star hotels have over 250 rooms, 3 star from 100 to 250, 2 star from 50 to 100, and 1 star less than 50. There are always exceptions; a few small hotels may have four or five star standards, some large hotels may operate at the one and two star levels.

There are some exceptionally large "mega" hotels in various places, e.g. the casino hotels in Las Vegas.

A hotel classification system, if it exists, does not normally include the smaller operations such as home-stay units, bed-and-breakfast operations and small guest houses. These may have their own classification system, as may other categories of accommodation such as apartments and self catering facilities.

Registration means merely registering the details of the enterprise, licensing normally requires the fulfilment of certain minimum criteria, and classification means the designation of a grade according to the level of quality and range of facilities provided. Classification and grading systems, described in Chapter 21, can include all three steps.

For the purposes of registration, licensing and classification, hotels are often defined by the relevant legislation as having a minimum number of rooms (e.g. ten rooms), with the provision of some catering facilities and services. However there are exceptions; in Fiji, for example, hotel is used as a generic term for all types of tourist accommodation. The act to provide for the licensing and control of hotels (Act No. 27 of 1973), defines hotel as a boarding-house, lodging-house, guest house, and any building, vessel, premises, structure, caravan or house on wheels (or any part of them) used or occupied for the business of receiving guests or travellers for hire or reward of any kind.

The Accommodation Product

The accommodation product consists of location, facilities and services.

Location is also discussed in the next chapter in relation to transport and access. It is accommodation's key component and, in this sense, is similar to retailing and many other services. The location is unchangeable unless the accommodation is mobile, for example boats or caravans. Even then, they have to be moored or parked in specific locations. The location's ease of accessibility is important, as is its proximity to the major attractions or centres which represent the purpose of the visit. For example, if a business hotel is near the business district or if a resort hotel is situated on an attractive beach. Freedom from noise or nuisances, and the attractiveness and appeal of the location are also important considerations. It is an advantage if the location is particularly evocative of the destination's image. For example, the Ritz in London is situated in Piccadilly and borders on Green Park.

In a hotel or resort the facilities include not only the accommodation itself, but the restaurant, banqueting, entertainment, shopping and recreational outlets. The type, size and themes of these various facilities contribute significantly to the total product.

The type and style of service reflect the image and category of the operation; the formality or informality, the speed, friendliness and efficiency, the personal touch and degree of individual attention given, and the helpfulness of staff in responding to special requests. The opening hours and availability of services according to the time of day are also important. The provision of other services such as laundry, valet, business and secretarial services, and car parking complete the product.

A customer survey prepared for the UK's Department of National Heritage and the English Tourist Board in 1995 (The MVA Consultancy, 1995), identified the following as the most important hotel features, irrespective of the particular category of establishment:

- ✔ high standards of cleanliness throughout;
- ✔ high quality bed, mattress and linen;
- ✔ attractive and pleasant bedroom;
- ✔ quiet bedroom, no disturbance;
- ✔ lighting in room and at bedside good enough to read by;
- ✔ high quality well maintained bathroom with good fittings;
- ✔ efficient, easy booking service;
- ✔ prompt, efficient check-in and check-out;
- ✔ attentive, efficient staff.

These results reflect, not unexpectedly, the main aspects of acceptable service: cleanliness and good hygiene, acceptable standards of comfort, courtesy and attentiveness, an appropriate speed and rhythm of service without unnecessary delay, and an absence of any nuisance e.g. noise, smells, or an excessively hot or cold room temperature.

The tourism product's intangible factors described in Chapter 4 are equally important in hotels; a warm welcome, happy ambience and friendly people. Nigel Massey, hotel consultant, is quoted as saying, "Hotels are in danger of introducing too much high-tech at the expense of the human-service element. I'm fed up speaking to voice mail. I want to speak to a person. Does anybody speak English? Does anybody speak?" (New York Herald Tribune, 12, March, 1999).

For each type of accommodation the product (location, facilities and services) will come to form part of the marketing mix together with the image, price, promotion and sales.

Project Feasibility

A study is required to determine whether a proposed hotel, or for that matter any other type of project, is feasible. It has three dimensions – marketing, operational and financial.

A study depends first on an analysis of demand and the market needs, segment by segment, and the choice and formulation of the project concept and marketing mix. The corresponding revenues are then calculated, how many customers spending how much money. Second is the development of an operational plan and an analysis of projected levels of profit.

Finally the capital budget needs double-checking, to ensure that the project can be built and equipped for the amount planned. The sources of funds, cost of capital, repayment schedules and cash flows all need analysis, together with the debt service coverage and rate of return. The success of the overall feasibility exercise depends on the rigor and skills of the analysts.

The novel "Hotel" highlights the skills of an analyst, "He possessed an extraordinary ability to enter any hotel and, after a week or two of discreet observation – usually unknown to the hotel's management – produce a financial analysis which later would prove uncannily close to the hotel's own figures" (Hailey, Arthur, 1965).

Figure 5.1 shows the project feasibility study's main criteria.

Figure 5.1 Project Feasibility	
Marketing	Choice and formulation of the project concept and marketing mix.
Operational	Operational plans – staffing and cost structure. Projected performance, costs and revenues.
Financial	Project profits and cash flows. Loan finance and debt service. Returns on investment.

Factors Influencing a Destination's Accommodation

A destination's market stems from the hotel and accommodation marketing mixes. If it has only low priced, modest accommodation, it attracts the people for this type of product (plus a few people from other markets willing to sacrifice their usual needs). If it has some fine up-market five star hotels and resorts, it can be expected to attract a share of the top end of the market. The product range influences the rest of the marketing mix, and consequently the type and mix of visitor.

All product development should be market led. Anybody opening a business must have some idea about its potential customers and their needs. However, many businesses fail to analyse the marketing opportunities sufficiently. They don't know who their customers are going to be.

Since hotels in most societies represent private sector initiatives, each one decides its own marketing mix and positioning. A destination's total accommodation product, therefore, is the aggregate of these individual decisions which are usually taken in an unrelated way. Accommodation's final mix – its totality – is more random than planned. The number, size and types of hotel and accommodation facilities, and the locations, images, facilities, levels of service, and prices result from different interpretations of free market forces.

However, the relationship between the investment, the market and the operating costs constrain the type of accommodation added to the existing supply (either new or renovated properties). For example:

- The number of suitable hotel sites available influences land prices. The structure of a hotel investment generally requires that land should not exceed 25 per cent (this is high) of total capital costs. It can go even higher in some cases but excessive land prices mean that only some types of up-market hotels are feasible.

- Fitting out, furnishing and equipment costs influence a project's level of capitalisation, and the returns needed to make it a safe financial proposition. High capital costs require a relatively high average room rate. This means that up-market segments have to be targeted – there is no other choice.

If business conditions are not favourable, entrepreneurs may not invest in hotels nor banks provide loan finance. This can give governments a problem.

The structure of local operating costs may make it difficult to achieve the necessary levels of profitability, given the targeted markets and room rates. Costs such as labour costs, public utilities, and real estate taxes may be on the high side.

Operational expertise may be lacking in some destinations, principally in developing countries. There may have been insufficient time and opportunity for enterprises and personnel to gain the necessary knowledge, skills and experience.

An old rule-of-thumb states that the average room rate achieved should be equivalent to one thousandth of a hotel's total capital cost; e.g. US$100 for a hotel costing US$100,000 a room. This gives a broad and arbitrary indication only. The actual ratio depends on various factors; e.g. the number of food and beverage and other facilities, and the volume of business and occupancy achieved. Room rates together with other prices, though they must be reconciled with costs, are influenced mostly by market forces.

Shaping a Destination's Accommodation Mix

As noted above a destination's final product mix is often more random than planned. This is why the government tourism administration (GTA), working together with the private sector and other interests, can coordinate and agree a product development strategy. This sets out the size, categories and locations of new facilities needed, together with desirable improvements to existing facilities. Once this strategy is agreed, measures can be taken to guide its successful implementation. For example:

- Discussions with potential investors to explain the agreed guidelines.

- The tying of zoning and approved sites for hotel development, to specific minimum requirements on size and category of facility. Planning permission is only granted accordingly.

- A system of grants and, or, tax incentives tied to the building or renovation of only selected categories of accommodation

One can influence the type of accommodation provided by a destination or leave it to chance. The free market, it is said, reacts appropriately to the realities and opportunities. It is argued that one does not interfere with the entrepreneurial prerogative. However, development may not take the form wanted or go where it is needed. Sometimes, governments choose to intervene. In the UK in 1994 a local authority made it clear that it wanted a four star hotel with conference facilities on a particular site, and not a budget hotel. This was despite being told by the owners that all four and five star operators had rejected the site as inappropriate (National Planning Forum, 1998).

Many argue that government should exercise leadership, on behalf of the sector and society at large. It should coordinate the development of strategies and see that they are implemented. Whatever the case, it does this to some extent. How far it chooses to go is a question of political judgement. The management tools exist (see Chapter 15) to influence the nature of future development.

The shaping of a destination's accommodation is discussed more fully in Chapters 16 and 17.

The Role of Tour Operators

Inbound tour operators – as the name denotes – handle incoming groups, outbound operators handle outgoing traffic. Some companies handle both inbound and outbound. And inbound operators work with the outbound operators from other countries.

Tour operators are responsible for a large proportion of sales. They should therefore be closely involved with the development of a destination's marketing strategy, fully supporting product development categories and standards.

A tour operator, when contracting hotel rooms, develops its own marketing mix for a country. This should reflect, and not conflict with, the destination's marketing strategy. The tour operator knows how it wants to sell the country, the kind of packages to include, how many of each and in what numbers, in what price range, and with what appeal and image. This is examined more fully in Chapter 14.

The tour operator then buys the accommodation which best fits with these needs:

✔ appropriate location;
✔ category, image and quality of facilities;
✔ availability, range and level of services, quality of food and beverage,
✔ cleanliness and hygiene, courtesy and attitudes;
✔ acceptability of the price and contractual conditions.

A Commodity

A tour operator buys hotel rooms or units of accommodation in a similar way to a commodity. Comparing coffee with accommodation, for example, one can note many similarities.

Some 90 per cent of the world coffee crop is produced in about 40 developing countries, while 80 per cent is still consumed in the United States and Western Europe. For a country to do well it has to produce the grades and quantities which are needed. Prices on the international market respond to current supply and demand.

The coffee purchased, however, is not a final product in itself. Enterprises, mostly transnational, undertake the processing (usually including roasting), packaging, promotion and distribution of the coffee as a final high value added product. The price paid for the green bean is a cost in this process. It is estimated that 15 per cent of the final retail value goes to the producing country (Barratt Brown, M. & Tiffen, P., 1992).

Through acquisitions and mergers, the coffee markets have become dominated by just a few transnationals. A high proportion of trade is controlled by Nestlé, the Kraft Jacobs Suchard group, and the Sarah Lee group (which includes Douwe Egberts).

Better grades, the Arabica coffees, may be processed and marketed mainly as a roast and ground product. The Robusta coffees, which are cheaper, are used mainly for the soluble/instant brands. With the increasing international division of functions, dictated by a rationalisation of costs and opportunities, coffee may be processed in one place, packaged in another, and distributed and sold in yet another.

Each coffee-producing country attempts to coordinate production in accordance with world market needs. It reviews the qualities and quantities of coffee produced, the yields per hectare, and the trends in consumption and demand. It tries to gear the production to the needs, and to optimise the economic return for the overall coffee crop. In this it may offer a range of government subsidies, grants, training and technical support to assist the growers to achieve the best possible return.

A country may produce the wrong grades and quantities of coffee. If so it may be handicapped by unavoidable production constraints, or it may have overlooked or disregarded key marketing information. The need to match the product to market needs is a constant struggle.

After coffee has been produced and sold, ships and/or other means are found to transport it. Similarly given the accommodation contracted by tour operators, transport is found to carry the tourists (assuming that there is no transport shortage). Transport, as is noted in Chapter 6, can be shifted to different routes as the needs arise.

The Hotel Room as a Commodity

A destination is marketed because of everything it offers, but the tourism product is not traded as a total item. What one buys and sells is a hotel room or accommodation unit for a given number of nights, often together with space on the transport to get there. What are traded are rooms and seats.

For the price of the accommodation and transport, people can visit a destination. Once there they buy and use additional services and attractions according to their wants and needs. According to their spending power, they construct their own particular travel experience.

Unlike green coffee beans the room or accommodation unit is a comparatively finished product. However, it is still treated by a tour operator as a component to be packaged, promoted, distributed and sold as a final composite product and marketing mix. Figure 5.2 illustrates this. The principal constituent in a bottle of instant coffee is the coffee itself. In a tour operators package holiday it is the hotel room or other accommodation.

The percentage of the tour operator's final package price received by the hotel varies. It depends, among other things, on the number of nights in the package, whether meals are included, and the cost of transportation. The amount usually ranges from 30 to 50 per cent.

As noted, the make-up of the overall accommodation by grades, types, size and location of units, determines the marketing opportunities and the economic benefits obtained. As with coffee the rooms must match the market needs in the most advantageous way. If not the mix in the types and categories of rooms has to be adjusted.

Figure 5.2 The Room as a Commodity

Travel Trade Interests
Tour Operators & Retailers

↓

Rooms as a Commodity

↓

Selected, Contracted & Packaged

↓

Promoted and Sold

Many hotel rooms, like coffee, are produced in one country but packaged, promoted, distributed and sold in another country. Tour operators fulfil a similar role to a manufacturer. They buy a basic product, combine it with other elements, package, promote and sell it. They buy the accommodation most in keeping with their own mix of marketing mixes. Tour operators stamp their own brand image on the destination just as coffee manufacturers stamp their brand on coffee. For example, Maxwell House as compared to Thomson Holidays.

Tourism markets change all the time. Hotels and accommodation providers constantly modify their product to try and meet the needs. Some hotels change hands, some fall into disuse, some are renovated, some deteriorate and drop in category, others improve, others cease to be competitive, and some new hotels are added. It is a constantly changing situation; the hotel and accommodation sub sector ceaselessly modifies and develops its structure and composition.

The Health of the Hotel and Accommodation Sub-Sector

It is easy to see that the well being of the tourism product depends on the health of the hotel and accommodation sub-sector.

Hotels that do not perform adequately go bankrupt. Bankrupt properties can be acquired and operated by new owners. They may even be purchased for a figure below their replacement value. New owners may then have a reduced capital base and lower debt service commitments. They may also be able to operate a hotel more efficiently. And they may be able to modify the product to serve the needs of a different and more feasible segment of the market.

The standards and well being of the total accommodation product should be constantly monitored. Hotels in financial trouble tend to cut maintenance costs. This drives down the quality level. As a product deteriorates it can lose customers. It can also change customers; a poorly maintained product commands lower prices. The destination can fall into a downward spiral with declining occupancy and room rates, deteriorating buildings and interiors, and worsening operational standards.

References

Barratt Brown, M., Tiffen, P. (1992). *Short Changed*, Pluto Press.

Collis, R. (1999). *The Frequent Traveller – High-Tech Hotels of the Future*, New York Herald Tribune, 12 March, p.11.

Hailey A. (1965). *Hotel*, Pan Books.

MVA Consultancy. (1995). *Crown Scheme Customer Evaluation for the Department of National Heritage and the English Tourist Board*, MVA, MVA House, Victory Way, Woking GU21 1DD, U.K.

National Planning Forum. (1998). *Planning for tourism – Report of the NPF working group*, NPF Secretariat, Local Government Association, London.

chapter six
Transport

This chapter considers transport and starts by examining all aspects of access. It looks at transport's marketing mix, its interrelationships with tourism, and the concept of the journey as a travel experience in itself. It also discusses the technological development of transport and its influence on tourism. It then explains the concepts of location, macro-access and micro-access. The chapter goes on to describe the characteristics and development of air, road, rail, sea and waterway transport and their impact on tourism. The chapter concludes with a list of key points.

Access

Transport ensures access to a destination (Figure 6.1). One talks of how well located a destination is, how accessible it is, and how well served it is by transportation networks and systems. One has to be able to get there and back. Different forms of transport require:

- the infrastructure – the ports, airports, railways, and roads able to handle transport in a sufficient volume and an acceptable time.

- the associated services which permit acceptable standards of use and operation.

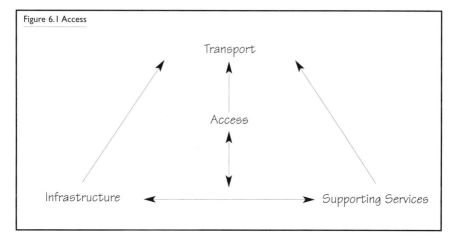

Figure 6.1 Access

Transport

Access

Infrastructure ◄────────────► Supporting Services

The development of transport has served as a key factor in the history of tourism. By making destinations accessible, transport opens up new markets.

Transport for tourism falls into three main types (these accord to the three types of tourism destination shown in Chapter 2):

- The main destination; transport to get there and back and transport to get around when one is there

- The secondary destination; transport to move on from the main destination by road, air or even rail.

- The multiple destination – a series of different places – a tour. The journey is the holiday.

E. M. Statler when asked to describe the three most important factors in the hotel business, replied – "location, location and location" (Podd and Lesure, 1964). One might equally well say access, access and access.

Change

The location of any facility is good or bad depending on access. Access tends to change as time goes by and circumstances change. At the macro level location applies to a destination as a whole. At the micro level it refers to a specific location (for example, for a hotel or restaurant) at the destination. Location generally improves or worsens, it seldom stands still.

Macro-access can improve due to:

- better transport infrastructure, improved transport equipment (e.g. improved aeroplanes or motor vehicles), better connections, more frequent services, faster travel times, and lower costs and fares.

and can worsen due to:

- infrastructural changes and technological developments which make it possible to bypass existing destinations. This makes them less accessible. For example, as indicated in Chapter 2 new motorways speed up traffic and bypass towns, new jets can travel further and start to overfly certain places.

Micro-access can improve or worsen due to:

- the policies governing circulation – infrastructural changes (e.g. motorway improvements), a rise in traffic and traffic pollution, the designation of one-way systems, the availability of parking, pedestrianisation, the capacity of public transport systems, and the growth or decline in types of transportation.

In feasibility studies for hotels, restaurants and other tourist attractions and services, location and access are the first aspects to be evaluated. One studies the existing situation as well as the likelihood and impact of future changes.

As noted above, improvements mean that transport can travel farther without stopping. This makes access cheaper, quicker and more direct. Older destinations can lose out to the competition this creates.

Generally, all destinations are becoming more accessible. Air and other forms of transport are improving everywhere. Better airports , roads and railways, as well as deep water harbours create the capacity to bring more people. And, given an attractive marketing mix, operators are not slow to provide the needed transport services. For example, the right marketing mix in some of the Caribbean's smaller destinations should remove any need to subsidise inbound air services.

The Travel Marketing Mix

Each type of transport has its own marketing mix based on its market research and related strategies. This will include the product it offers – type of train, plane, craft or vehicle, the related services, the relative journey time, comfort and convenience – the image and the way it is seen, the prices, promotion and sales. Like accommodation, transport contributes to all the components of the tourism marketing mix (product, image, price, promotion and sales). For a marketing mix to meet the needs of a particular market segment, the transport components have to match in both quality and quality. For example, the volume and quality of inbound transport seats should match the number and category of accommodation places at the destination.

The image of the transport should be compatible with the overall tourism experience, the price should be complementary, and promotion and sales should be appropriately linked.

Travel is more than a question of access. As also indicated in Chapter 2, the form of transport chosen and the journey itself form an integral part of any tourism experience. Transport is included when considering a particular marketing mix. For example, the Eurostar train for a weekend in Paris travelling from England, the private motor car for a camping holiday in Brittany, the aeroplane for a business trip to New York or a holiday in Bali. Some tourism combines different forms of transport; for example, fly and cruise, fly and drive, take the train and then drive, or take the train and then bicycle.

International Links

Trade, tourism and economic cooperation between countries, can lead to efficient international transport links. However transport policies are often impeded by incompatible systems, for example trains that have different loading gauges. They are also impeded by the undue protection of national enterprises, for example road hauliers and national airlines. In Europe some airlines are still government-subsidised with authorities reluctant to expose them to the full impact of deregulation and free market competition. Deregulation benefits the consumer but shakes up the sector. It creates competition and adds risk. New partnerships and alliances occur and tariffs and costs are cut. However, safety standards can be compromised and the continuity of services disrupted.

Europe has embarked on the creation an integrated transport network. It should provide Europe with an operating network of high speed trains, more efficient air traffic control systems, airports and ports, the extension and improvement of motorways, and some new or redeveloped inland waterways (EU, 1998). As other regions choose to harmonise their transport systems, similar interlocking systems may be expected to develop.

Road Transport

Road traffic causes most pollution. For example, in the European Union transport is responsible for some 30 per cent of energy consumption. Of this road transport accounts for 84 per cent, and 75 per cent of the CO_2 outputs that make up the "greenhouse" global warming effect.

By switching transportation, emission levels should decrease. Freight should rely less on roads and more on rail. Cars are being made cleaner, while measures are being taken to reduce car use. Public transport should offer attractive alternatives. For example, it can enhance the tourist experience with scenic bus and train rides. Coaches or buses are important in tourism. Apart from transfers to and from the airport, they are also used for excursions, sightseeing and overland tours. New vehicle designs have improved comfort and service. Park and bus ride schemes have proved effective in keeping cars out of city centres.

However, the car's success is due to the freedom it gives. People go where they want, when they want, for as long as they want. Once at the destination the car continues to provide the same freedom of movement. Urban planning and development worldwide have also tended to serve private car use.

Railways

Railways are a quick and clean form of transport. They can carry large volumes of people, and are particularly efficient for transporting commuter traffic into urban centres. High speed trains have brought cities closer together, providing a smoother and more comfortable ride. Railways have adapted to tourism by offering various tours and excursions, and by putting automobiles on a train they offer the rail/drive option. Many special trains – including steam trains – have been revived, some with luxury sleeping and catering facilities. They enable people to recapture the past romance and excitement of railway journeys.

Railways can also bring people easily into a city centre. Congestion and parking restrictions make this difficult for cars, while airports are usually located well away from the centre.

Air Transport

The Chicago Convention in 1944 resulted in the freedoms of the air governing the various rights to pick up and put down passengers, mail and cargo. However, the air services between two countries have been regulated through bilateral negotiation and agreement.

National Airlines and Privatisation

National airlines – the flag carriers – are not only transport companies, but also symbols of national identity and prestige. To operate a national airline also seems to reassure governments about sovereignty and national security. Traditionally governments have protected and subsidised their airlines, and many still do. Additionally the interests of the national airline are often put before those of the tourism sector itself. This has cost countries dearly – when planeloads of tourists have been turned down to protect the national airline's interests. However, with the general swing away from government ownership some privatisation has occurred. For example, British Airways.

Privatisation tends to result in better use of resources, and a more competitive business climate with more consumer choice, better service and lower prices. And it can help to counter protectionism, price controls, and restricted services.

However, tourism should remain vigilant. Air transport should serve tourism and not vice versa.

Deregulation

The EU indicates that air transport has been characterised by state intervention and bilateralism. Although a certain amount of competition between air carriers existed, there was also control of fares, market access and capacity sharing. These were enshrined in restrictive bilateral agreements between Member States (EU, 1994).

This kind of state intervention and bilateralism was common everywhere. However, deregulation in the USA has now been followed by deregulation in Europe. This has influenced a general liberalisation of air traffic around the world.

Deregulation generally means to break down the protective walls built up around public sector monopolies. It allows any enterprise to enter the market, free to decide its own marketing mix. However, it does not mean total deregulation in terms of standards. Airlines continue to be regulated in terms of safety and consumer protection.

Deregulation in Europe allows any European airline to fly any route in Europe including domestic routes. Increased competition and the low-cost fares, which demonstrate the price elasticity of travel demand, have appeared to boost the growth of overall air traffic. New airlines entering the market have tended to use the secondary airports where slots are not scarce and charges are lower. This also results in the better distribution of passenger flows and ground handling. There is also a switch to direct sales and the use of electronic sales outlets. This creates a speedy and efficient booking service while it also cuts out the payment of commissions.

Aircraft and Distance

As noted, transport's technological advances have speeded up journeys and made distances seem shorter. Air travel has done this while reducing, on most routes, the cost per kilometre flown. In terms of buying power the price is much less. Distance seems to enhance a destination's image – "the further away it is, then the more one succeeds in getting away from it". For example, Bali has one image to Europeans but a different one for nearby Australians. Distance denotes setting oneself more apart, escaping from the familiar, getting to another world with a different feel, a different look. It is escapism measured in time zones, with nowhere more than a day away (Doswell, 1990).

The Boeing 747-400 series is the most effective and profitable large long haul aircraft. In response, Airbus was developing the 600 seater A3XX. However, due to insufficient airline support, this has now been deferred to sometime in the future.

Chartered And Scheduled

All or most of a charter flight is block-sold to tour operators. In principle, flexible pricing and sales strategies mean that planes sell out and fly full. Tour operators tend to sell a total package rather than just transport. The package itself is more important than the day and time of departure.

However, the day-of-the-week and departure and arrival time remain important considerations. A weekend departure and return is usually more popular, and is priced accordingly.

Similarly the regular airlines market their schedules emphasising frequency, convenience, and connections. These are the features which sell seats. However, the difference between scheduled and charter operations has narrowed. On particular routes the scheduled airlines also now block-sell space to tour operators in advance. The feasibility of a route at a certain level of frequency depends on a mix of markets; people travelling for different reasons, at different prices, through different booking channels and modalities. On the other hand, charter airlines now sell a proportion of their seats to individual travellers who make their own arrangements at the destination.

Both charter and scheduled airlines may promote their in-flight comfort and service. But charters may generally have tighter seating and lower costs. In-flight passenger care is of more competitive importance to scheduled airlines. It is a question of the relative marketing mix and value for money – high-cost versus low-cost..

Airline companies are diversifying into both charter and high and low-cost scheduled services. These represent distinctive marketing approaches.

Leisure and Business

The most profitable business for the established high-cost airlines is upper-market business traffic (as little as 20 percent business traffic may produce more than 50 percent of profits). The economy business traveller has tended to switch to low-cost carriers. This creates a sharper differentiation between low-cost and high-cost carriers, one streamlines service and the other embellishes it. It has created a more marked segmentation of the airline market according to purchasing power. A two tier system has emerged – the "frills" and "no-frills" markets.

The frequency of flights has facilitated the ease of travel and access. This features strongly, together with the avoidance of airport hassle, in a traveller's choice.

The Transfer Market

The proliferation of alliances between airlines is an indication of the globalisation of air transport. It is important how airlines interconnect to facilitate rapid transfers and quicker, easier onward journeys.

Long haul routes tend to operate from hub to hub. Hubs may therefore serve an international market. In Europe, for example, London, Amsterdam, Paris and Frankfurt all act as hubs. In South East Asia Bangkok, Kuala Lumpur, Singapore and Hong Kong act as hubs. Passengers fly from somewhere in a region to a hub, they then fly point-to-point to another hub, they then transfer onto a flight to their final destination. Airports and airlines develop the quality of their services to be more hub-competitive in comfort, convenience and price. For example, somebody Spanish from Madrid, to get to a particular place, might decide to "hub" either through Frankfurt or London. British Airways and Lufthansa would compete for his or her business.

Marine Transport and Inland Waterways

The cruise ship, it can be said, offers a multiple destination holiday but is a complete resort in itself. It is a floating resort – a floating destination. It moves from one place to another with its ports of call serving as secondary destinations. The main holiday experience is what happens on board – it is the ship itself. It is like any holiday spent within a resort, with the occasional excursion outside to visit an attraction. However, some cruises also emphasise the natural and, or, cultural attractions visited. With the cruise ship one has the additional product elements of the sea and the associated romance and escapism. It is a tourism sub-sector which has increased its appeal and rate of growth.

As the cruise ship business has prospered and expanded, marketing has become more diversified. From a similar product in similar areas of the world (e.g. the Caribbean and the Greek Islands), new experiences have been added. Ships of varying standards and types of comfort have been brought into service, the facilities, culture and entertainment offered have become more differentiated, the price range has widened, and new areas of the world have been introduced. For example, South East Asia and the South Pacific, and cruises up the Norwegian and Alaskan coasts. There is now something somewhere to attract different segments of the market.

Visas and Facilitating Entry

Visa requirements are usually linked to questions of internal security and immigration control. However, foreign policy tends to view them as reciprocal – "we give as good as we get". Requirements are put in place unthinkingly on a tit-for-tat basis, and visa fees are sometimes seen short-sightedly as an additional source of government revenue. The results can be counter productive, inhibiting demand and seriously impeding the development of potential markets. It is acknowledged that one has to counter the dangers of illegal immigration. However, it seems contradictory for a government to promote tourism while making entry to the country overly difficult.

Key Transportation Points

The following points, in linking transport with tourism, are important:

- Treat transport not as ancillary to the tourism product but as part of it. Integrate the transport marketing mix within the total tourism marketing mix.

- Make sure that airline interests are at the service of tourism and not vice versa.

- Provide adequate transport infrastructure to keep pace with tourism.

- Link the transport companies to tourism development strategies.

- Match transport capacity to the rest of the tourism product's capacity.

- Try to keep transportation costs in balance with other costs.

- Encourage transport companies, as appropriate, to combine or integrate with other travel trade interests – e.g. other forms of transport like rental cars, hotels, and tour operators.

- Ensure that transport terminals such as airports include, as far as feasible, a complete range of services – e.g. hotels, catering, telecommunications, postal, medical, hairdressing, shopping, and recreational.

- Interconnect diverse transport services to create complete national and international networks – air, rail, bus, taxis etc.

- Lobby the government transport and civil aviation authorities, so as to keep tourism's needs at the forefront.

- Maintain close relations with the transport private sector (and any public sector enterprises), seeking marketing mix compatibility and joint promotional and sales efforts.

- Ease immigration controls and visa requirements to stimulate tourism growth.

References

Doswell R. (1990). *New Destinations for Developed Countries. Horwath Book of Tourism (M.Quest, ed.) pp. 35-45*, The Macmillan Press Ltd.

European Commission. (1998). *Transport policy statements.*

European Commission. (1994). *Directorate General of Competition, Application of Articles 92 and 93 of the EC Treaty and Article 61 of the EEA agreement to State aids in the aviation sector (94/C 350/07).*

Podd G. and Lesure. J. (1964). *Planning and Operating Motels and Motor Hotels*, Ahrens Book Company.

chapter seven
Cycles

The chapter starts by examining the general concepts of cycles and change. It goes on to discuss the product life cycle and its relevance to tourism. It then refutes the idea that all destinations follow a particular evolutionary pattern, and lists the various types of change which can occur. It describes the proximity of markets as a major development factor, and highlights the importance of sound planning and control. The chapter then discusses the nature of obsolescence and concludes by emphasising the need to anticipate change.

Cycles in General

Places change, they grow or shrink, they develop and improve, they decay and deteriorate. They never stand still. When we live somewhere we never tend to notice the day-to-day change. Everything that enters our routine life gradually tends to go unnoticed. Most people hardly see or think about what is happening around them.

The cycle of birth, life, death and re-birth characterises all aspects of human existence. Everything starts over. The cycles of earth, sun, moon, stars and seasons reflect renewal and influence beliefs.

Economic and business cycles are fluctuations within a trend; things tend to go well, then badly, then well again. In developed countries, at least, the long term growth trend moves forward in this fitful way. The jerkiness of growth and development – the stops and spurts – is a fact of life. The cycle normally repeats every five years or so and passes through four stages: expansion, peak, recession, and trough.

Tourist accommodation supply also tends to follow demand in a jerky, uneven way. A scarcity of rooms is followed by a number of new projects and this produces an oversupply. It takes time for demand to catch up, eventually it overtakes supply again, then another period of scarcity follows. Major new hotel and accommodation projects can take 3-5 years to complete. They also depend on the overall economic and business cycle. These influences create time lags in matching supply with demand.

The idea of cycles and the inevitability of change dominates much of our thinking and approach to life. T.S.Eliot wrote "In my beginning is my end" and followed it with:

> *In succession*
> *Houses rise and fall, crumble, are extended,*
> *Are removed, destroyed, restored, or in their place*
> *Is an open field, or a factory, or a by-pass.*
> *Old stone to new building, old timber to new fires,*
> *Old fires to ashes, and ashes to the earth.*

(T.S. Eliot 1944)

Sustainability, echoing Eliot, is often a misused term. Much that is man-made has a given life. It does not last forever. However, the world itself must be sustainable – looked after, enhanced and enriched. Sustainable relates to heritage and the environment, it means adding, protecting and conserving. But not everything. Some things are better renewed or replaced.

Product Life Cycles

The concept of the product life cycle was first formulated by Theodore Levitt in 1965 (Levitt, 1965). It is based on the premise that the market's response to a product changes over time. Product sales grow, mature, level off and eventually decline. At this last stage the product has lost its appeal and ceased to be competitive. It may also have been overtaken technologically. The product was developed to satisfy the needs of a certain market at a certain point in time. As time goes by it must keep up-to-date, change according to market needs, possibly realign itself to market opportunities, and stay fresh and relevant. Figure 7.1 illustrates the concept.

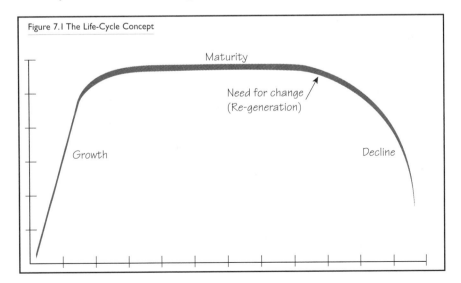

Figure 7.1 The Life-Cycle Concept

Maturity

Need for change
(Re-generation)

Growth

Decline

Restaurants are particularly prone to a life cycle (however, a few notable exceptions achieve classical status). Pick a place and take 20 restaurants at random from a past year, and check how many remained 5-10 years later. Sometimes restaurant life cycles are even shorter. Mariana Pages-Palenque, a restaurant owner in Punta del Este, Uruguay, is reported as saying, "Lots of the restaurants (here) are like film sets, they build them and tear them down." (Newsweek, 1997)

The product life cycle does not usually apply to a total tourist destination for the following reasons:

- a tourism destination is generally not one product serving only one market. A destination is usually diversified, offering a range of products at different prices to different market segments. As noted in the last chapter, it has a varied marketing mix.

- a destination may have assumed classic status as a part of global culture. Its overall image, while slightly different according to the perceptions of each market, is not likely to wane. For example, London is London whatever changes it undergoes.

- part of a destination's product can include heritage sites and attractions. As a part of national and world heritage they have an indefinite life. Places with a great cultural heritage or extraordinary natural beauty (e.g. Angkor Wat, Niagara Falls or Ayres Rock) do not have a life cycle. They are enduring, enjoy classical status, and remain magnetic and timeless.

The world's great cities also assume classical status. They may become too expensive, or unsafe – something may happen in the short term to produce a decline in visitors – but there is no life cycle as such. Just the normal ups and downs due to economic and social factors.

A diverse destination with more than one product cannot have just one product life cycle. However, a single-product destination – with narrower marketing objectives and common image and environmental problems – can suffer a product life cycle fate.

The component entities within any destination – a hotel, restaurant, night club or any other facility – may each have its own product life cycle. So can an international chain; by the mid-1990s the Club Med group (the international chain of popular holiday resorts organised as clubs) was in decline, recording big losses. New management started to make some major conceptual and operational changes.

In Chapter 2 we looked at demand-side descriptions of destinations. On the supply side there are also differences between types of destination. For example:

- established places, with medium to large populations and mixed economies, which have developed tourism as an important additional sector, e.g. many major cities.

- established places where tourism has grown up over many years, is one of the largest economic sectors and has now more or less levelled off, e.g. many seaside destinations.

- resort complexes, developed in an integrated way on a new site which include hotels, other accommodation, restaurants, recreational, entertainment and related facilities and services, e.g. Nusa Dua in Bali and Cancun in Mexico.

- new destinations where tourism has created a mono-economy, and rapidly changed a small community into a large community, e.g. Benidorm and Ibiza in Spain.

- small destinations which represent communities serving tourism alone, and offering a single product to one narrowly defined market segment, e.g. very small island destinations such as Mana Island, Fiji, or Bandos Island in the Maldives.

- destinations which serve either mainly or exclusively various types of special interest tourism, e.g. ski destinations, deep sea diving centres and mountaineering resorts.

- micro destinations, such as villages or other rural centres, serving small specialised markets, such as communities specialising in farm, nature-based or ecotourism holidays.

The seven categories above are generalised and many overlaps can exist. Destinations can learn from one another as they pass through the various stages of development. However each destination, in its particular marketing mix and targets, is likely to be distinctive. It is likely to have reached a different stage of development in terms of the built environment, ranging from overbuilt, highly built to building-free or virtually building-free. Here we can list four stages:

- Fully urbanised environments – major cities and large coastal centres – such as Honalulu, Acapulco or Miami. These are so built-up that there is little possibility of expansion. The major needs concern urban renewal and regeneration.

- Partially urbanised environments often representing recently expanded coastal centres. They have already been substantially developed, but there remains major potential for further expansion.

- Small resorts and resort towns with a limited built environment. They are of roughly two types; either tight controls permit only limited projects and prevent further extensive building, or the resort is at the embryonic stage awaiting further major investment and expansion.

- Building-free destinations, or with only minor building, serving special interest tourism. Tight restrictions either prevent all building or allow only limited and carefully controlled development.

Problems vary depending on which stage a destination has reached or stopped at. At one extreme there are the problems of urban decay, at the other the struggle to protect the environment from development. In the middle there is generally the challenge of maintaining and improving what has gone before.

Tourist Destinations Can Fall Away

Tourist destinations may not follow a precise product life cycle, but they are certainly subject to change and decay.

Tourism itself acts as a change agent. Sometimes it builds up slowly bringing about gradual change; sometimes it expands quickly causing quite immediate and dramatic change. The physical environment and local culture change, as do the product and the market. The act of expanding the tourism product changes it and can, in so doing, change its markets. Such change may not be detrimental to a destination; it depends on how well tourism development is planned and managed.

There is an idea that destinations move through an evolutionary scale; that they follow a particular pattern of development and eventually fall away. Still off the beaten track they are first of all discovered by adventurous international travellers, often backpackers. They have few facilities and little development, and can be enjoyed for their tranquility, uncrowded nature, unspoilt beauty and traditional ways of life. Once they are more discovered, they open up, become more accessible, start to expand, attract more investment, and bring in more visitors. Better accessibility and proximity to markets may lead to discovery and development. Fully developed the environmental quality suffers, there is overcrowding, migrant workers move in, and the local community changes. Mass tourism takes over and there is an air of stagnation. Nothing works very well; local people are richer (not all) but unhappy. This general idea of tourism growth coupled with degradation has been discussed in various ways by a number of authors (e.g. Butler, 1980. Doswell,1979. Plog, 1973)

There are different kinds of destination and many have not passed through this kind of evolutionary development. The main reason for destinations to expand quickly is because they are in easy reach of major markets. However, some do start out in a small way, e.g. a coastal fishing community which becomes a major seaside resort; or a small alpine village which grows into a booming ski resort.

Backpackers may be among the first to discover an out-of-the-way new destination; but a potential destination close to major markets will be discovered anyway. The rate of a place's development depends first on its proximity and accessibility to these markets. Destinations then develop according to attractiveness, competitiveness, investment conditions, the availability of sites, the potential labour market and the capacity of the construction sector.

Negative outcomes are avoidable. Two general rules can be counterposed:

- Where similar mistakes are made similar outcomes are suffered.
- When development is well planned and managed, similar successes are recorded.

Sensible planning can also anticipate change, set objectives, establish action steps, and predict outcomes. Sound management can make things happen as planned.

Some say that the external pressures created by emergent and voracious global forces are now irresistible, e.g. the power of foreign investors in controlling capital flows, and airline and tour operators in controlling markets. However, this is a cynical and tired viewpoint. The right partners respect sensible policies.

In pluralistic societies development may always be contentious. Decisions are usually characterised by trade-offs; something is gained and something lost. People place a different weight on the various outcomes.

Changeability

A destination is subject to constant change:

- The quality of the physical environment may deteriorate through overcrowding, inadequate infrastructure, poor quality buildings and the absence of sensible planning and building regulations. The upkeep and maintenance of the environment in general may be neglected.

- The product changes as the destination expands. It can become more diversified and its size and range can change its character, feel and atmosphere.

- Tourism requires a large labour force and often necessitates the use of migrant labour. It also brings alternative employment, usually better paid, to the traditional occupations. All this changes the patterns of employment and the labour market. It also changes local culture.

- Tourism growth brings many external influences which change the local cultural characteristics. Economic well-being also improves people's health and education, and this brings many changes. Greater prosperity also changes people's expectations and the way they live.

- Competing destinations may start to displace more business, by better accessibility and a more attractive marketing mix.

- The destination simply becomes outmoded and loses its appeal.

- Currency exchange rates change resulting in significant price increases, suddenly making a place poor value for money and less competitive. Or, conversely, making it cheaper and more competitive.

- Changes in the range of aircraft, or improvement in roads or railways change transport patterns.

- The place may also become unsafe and dangerous with a major increase in crime.

Proximity to Major Markets

Any attractive destination which sits close to major developing markets, tends to plug into the mainstream chunk of these markets. As a result it enjoys a rapid initial growth in the number of visitors. Since the 1950s this has been particularly true of Spain, the South of France and Italy. Their Mediterranean coastal destinations are a short flight away from the Northern European concentrations of population. As people acquired more time and purchasing power they travelled south on holiday. Other Mediterranean destinations, e.g. Greece and Tunisia, have followed a similar pattern.

In the 1980s the South East Asia major demand generating markets enjoyed fast economic growth and a new wave of prosperity. Although they suffered setbacks in the 1990s, they will revive and stimulate the regional destinations within easy access.

At the end of the 1950s Benidorm in Spain was still a fishing village with a smattering of visitors. It is now an urban beach resort with a population of 50,000 permanent residents 148 hotels, 35,000 hotel beds and approximately 175,000 to 200,000 apartment beds. The total population (including visitors) now averages 125,000; in August it rises to 300,000.

Ibiza is also a popular destination in the Mediterranean. However, a 1925 commentary stated, "it is fairly safe to prophesy that the smallest and most picturesque of the Balearic Islands (Ibiza) will never become a resort" (Goldring, 1946, p.182). With the transportation system as it was in 1925, Ibiza seemed a remote and undiscovered part of Europe.

Florida has a similar relationship with much of America, lying within easy reach of its major markets. Cuba's proximity to the United States and these same markets, link its future inevitably to American tourism and make it Florida's main potential competitor.

As pointed out, any destination which has notable tourist potential and sits close to major developing markets, will expand its tourism product quickly. This depends however on the availability of land and the controls on development. If land is plentiful and cheap, with only a sketchy planning policy and regulatory framework, development will be especially rapid.

Under the circumstances in Spain at the time, the rapid development of destinations like Benidorm was left unimpeded by planning regulations. The country was in need of rapid economic growth and tourism promised to make a significant contribution. Almost anything anywhere was permitted.

Opportunism is a characteristic of free markets. It has a connotation of impulse, a speedy response to an apparent market need and a rush to seize the chance offered. Suitable sites are available and construction costs and capacity are within acceptable limits. The market feasibility is supported by some tour operators who see the potential profitability; and governments are anxious to push economic development and employment creation. They believe that strict planning policies and codes might be a hindrance to progress. The desire for rapid economic development obscures the need for careful planning and control. These tendencies, rather than any evolutionary pattern, have determined the development of most new destinations.

Obsolescence

The reasons for obsolescence are listed above. Obsolescence means to be outmoded or out-of-date. Any product, of course, can be made obsolete by technological advance and new competition. In Europe, old northern seaside resorts failed to compete with new ones in the South. As noted in Chapter 6, motor vehicles travel farther in a day and planes fly farther without refuelling. Transport technology makes stopover destinations obsolete.

A place can also lose its attractiveness to a certain type of visitor. Low levels of occupancy can push hotels and other facilities into decline.

If a destination falls seriously into disrepair, its marketing can collapse completely. The road back to prosperity seems impossible. This situation seems to give the destination a life cycle. It prospered once but eventually died.

Places that rely on a particular economic sector for their well-being, can find themselves seriously affected by social and economic events. Industries too can be made obsolete by technological advance. Output may no longer be competitive. For example, coal-mining became uneconomic in Britain. The places concerned cease to fulfil needs appropriately or competitively. Similarly industries can move away or close down and depopulation follows. A place's prosperity depends on its economic relevance. It has to provide what the world wants at a marketable price.

Any place declines if one of its main sources of economic life dies or falls away. Such a place has to find alternative economic activities.

Tourist destinations may also lose business, deteriorate physically, or become too expensive and out-of-fashion. Customers die off and are replaced by new ones; markets are generational. New needs, new leisure pursuits, new ideas and new values take over.

Staying Alive

Destinations – even though they may not experience a life cycle as such – must weather normal business cycles. They should respond to change; stay relevant to market needs, retain their competitiveness, discard obsolescent elements, and continue to maintain, update and improve their marketing mix (Figure 7.2).

Figure 7.2 Staying Alive

Destinations

Maintain, Update and Improve the Marketing Mix

Stays Relevant to the Market Needs

Stays Competitive with Other Places

Discards Obsolescent Elements

References

Butler, R.W. (1980). *The Concept of a Tourism Area Cycle of Evolution: Implications for Management of Resources*, Canadian Geographer 24 (1): 5-12.

Doswell, Roger. (1979). *Further Case Studies in Tourism*, Barrie and Jenkins.

Eliot, T.S. (1944). *East Coker in Four Quartets*, Faber and Faber.

Goldring, Douglas. (1946). *Journeys in the Sun – Memories of Happy Days in France, Italy and the Balearic Islands*, MacDonald.

Levitt, T. (1965). *Exploit the Product Life Cycle*, Harvard Business Review, November/December.

Newsweek. (1997). 17 February.

Plog, S. (1973). *Why destination areas rise and fall in popularity*, Cornell Hotel and Restaurant Administration Quarterly, 55-8.

chapter eight
Market Research

T his chapter discusses the objectives of market research, and looks at the factors which influence the current business climate. It then considers structure and complexity of markets, and goes on to explain the main components of market research: tourist statistics, desk research, intelligence work and visitor surveys. The chapter then discusses market research on tour operators, the concept of management information systems and the dissemination of information. It concludes by relating market research to the evaluation of tourism results.

The Objectives of Market Research

Market research is fundamental to all of the topics discussed so far. It is the acquisition and interpretation of information concerning market behaviour, needs and preferences. The right marketing mixes attract and satisfy targeted customers. Research answers the questions to make this possible. It creates the basis for future marketing strategies; how to develop the product, sharpen the image, set prices, and ensure effective promotion and sales.

One can't just pretend to know, one really has to know. This timeless idea of needing to know was echoed by Marcuse, "Artisan and merchant, captain and physician, general and statesman – each must have correct knowledge in his field in order to be capable of acting as the changing situation demands" (Marcuse, 1972).

Market research involves collecting, collating and analyzing statistics and information from primary and secondary sources. It uses travel statistics, desk research (including studies undertaken by travel and tourism research companies), intelligence work and field surveys.

One can conduct market research at two levels:

- on behalf of the sector, providing an overview of tourism trends and prospects, and serving as the basis for future tourism policies and strategies.

- by the individual entrepreneur, as he or she wrestles with a range of decisions relating to product development, marketing mix and marketing and financial feasibility.

The Business Climate

Tourism takes place in a particular business climate. This climate is influenced by political and social trends and events, economic performance and prospects, and technological change. Market research monitors what is happening and gauges its impact on tourism.

A SWOT analysis (strengths, weaknesses, opportunities and threats) which also includes an approach to PEST (political, economic, social and technological change), brings these considerations together (Doswell, 1997).

The following list outlines the various influences:

- the government's support for tourism, its stated policies and plans, measures and action steps, and its commitment to the further development of the sector.

- the current travel trends to the country in question, and to the particular region or cluster of countries. With international tourism, a country does not so much generate new markets as increase its share of existing markets.

- in relation to the above, the trends in transportation and access. Whether transport services have increased, and whether they are cheaper, more comfortable and quicker.

- whether the destination's various tourist markets are stable and growing.

- the effect of the country's own economic performance on the growth of domestic tourism, both internal and outbound.

- the pace of investment and the availability of capital, on feasible terms, for the realization of both infrastructural works and hotels, resorts, and other facilities.

- the measures to facilitate, and stimulate private investment in the sector, both domestic and foreign. The attitudes of the banks and financial institutions towards the tourism sector.

- the current exchange rates and the level of prices compared to the competition.

- sufficient physical and human resources to support tourism development. For example, qualified management and skilled personnel, adequate infrastructure and the capacity of the construction industry.

- social and political stability and the absence of tourist related crime.

Structure and Complexity

To study a market it has to be structured in a systematic manner, according to particular segments and marketing mixes. These follow the criteria discussed in earlier chapters. Market research confronts a multiplicity of factors. These have to be sorted and sifted, relationships established, connections made, and assumptions agreed. Even so, many factors in many situations remain unknown or linked in unidentifiable ways, full of contradictions and discontinuities.

The approach to adopt obeys the following steps:

- **Exactly what happened?** This requires the complete collection and thorough analysis of all information related to past performance and trends. It also requires an assessment and explanation as to why it happened This needs to be done not only for the particular country and region but also for global tourism.

- **What exactly is happening now?** This means the monitoring of current developments and trends. What is happening and why? Who is going where? What are the product trends and the range of marketing mixes currently on offer? What are the trends?

- **What may happen in the future?** This requires an analysis of the available forecasts, trends, changes in market share, switches in short and long haul travel, the growth of particular segments, and the general development of the business climate. One should be clear about why certain things are expected to happen.

These assessments are of two types:

- **The objective** – this is essentially the factual approach. Data are collected, processed and analyzed. The country's tourism statistics are presented both quantitatively and qualitatively (using tables, graphs, pie charts and diagrams) with a written explanation of the results and conclusions. Additionally all sources are consulted about various aspects of national and international tourism. Data are combined and synthesized, compared and assessed.

- **The subjective** – this is the conjectural approach. It addresses the interpretation of past events and future outcomes. It involves the subjective assessment of all factors, trends and developments. Judgments are reached, sometimes by consensus, risks are assessed and people give rein to their insight and intuition. Alternatives can be presented with different assumptions and a range of possible outcomes.

This dichotomy anticipates the process of entrepreneurial decision making. Entrepreneurs take all available statistics and research, review the results and findings, make their own studies and reach their own conclusions. The objective and subjective fuse. They become inseparable – integral. One weighs all conclusions, all assessments.

For the tourism sector as a whole, market research has the following four objectives (Figure 8.1):

- identifying needs and opportunities.
- fulfilling needs and opportunities through the marketing mixes.
- monitoring performance.
- adjusting to changing needs.

The role of a GTA is discussed in Chapter 13. The extent to which a government should coordinate and steer sector-wide development policies is an open question. It depends on views about what governments should or should not do. A GTA can merely point to, and make recommendations about, perceived trends and opportunities. Or it can take more of a leadership role, using a combination of management tools to push development in certain directions.

In any event, a GTA's statistical department produces statistical data on arrivals usually covering such information as visitors' age, marital status, means of

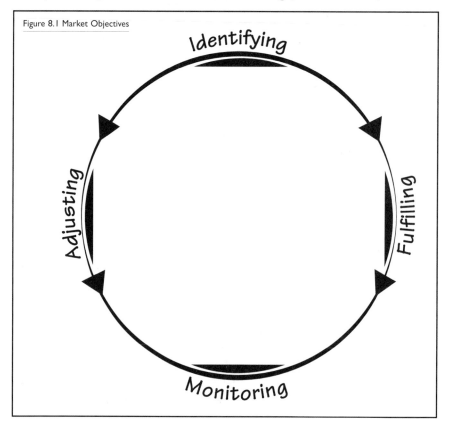

Figure 8.1 Market Objectives

Identifying

Fulfilling

Monitoring

Adjusting

transport, transport networks and gateways, gender, occupation, date of entry and length of stay, nationality and country of residence, type of accommodation used, and number of previous visits. Statistics should follow the basic recommendations and definitions of the World Tourism Organisation.

Statistics are collected at ports of entry or through visitor surveys and sometimes hotel and accommodation guest registration procedures. Visitor surveys augment previously collected data; e.g. they add information on preferences, likes and dislikes and expenditure.

Desk Research

Desk research aims at monitoring all aspects of travel and tourism related to the interests of the organisation in question. Researchers consult all published material; public and private sector publications, reports, newspapers, magazines, and statistical bulletins. The Internet has also become a major desk research tool, acting as an important source of data.

Desk research should not be structured too rigidly; an unforeseen source may contain important and relevant data. A lot of valuable information is available from national and international associations and organisations, e.g. the World Tourism Organisation (WTO) publishes tourism statistics, market trends and global tourism forecasts, with information broken down by region and country.

Not all information is free or obtainable for just the cost of a publication. Work is also undertaken by commercial research companies who sell their resulting reports and findings. This effectively shares the cost among a number of clients, which usually includes both public and private organisations.

These research companies produce work on a wide range of travel and tourism topics; particular markets, sub sectors, countries, regions, and trends and developments. This permits some economies of scale; the research expertise is pooled and costs are shared between a number of users and subscribers. As tourism continues to grow, these companies add to the topics they research. Users, either GTAs or commercial companies, find it surer and cheaper to buy these services than to try to undertake the research themselves.

Travel and Tourism Intelligence (TTI), in London, and the European Travel Monitor in Munich are examples of independent tourism research companies.

Intelligence

The term intelligence simply means knowing what's going on, and goes beyond just desk research. To know, for example, what people are worried about, what difficulties they're having, who is doing what, who is planning what, what the competition is doing, and what the future trends are likely to be. This relates to the second market research step – what exactly is happening now – listed earlier in the chapter. One monitors everything which affects the market – keeping a finger on the pulse, an ear to the ground.

Good intelligence is based on constant and well informed feedback. This doesn't happen automatically; it needs a network of well established relationships. For example, one should:

- not only read the travel trade press but also talk to the journalists.
- maintain contact with the leading tour operators and travel agencies.
- talk to leading hotel companies and airlines.
- consult regularly with the trade and consumer associations.
- talk to the leading travel writers.
- keep active in international travel and tourism organisations.
- attend national and international tourism conferences and meetings.
- maintain contact with university tourism departments and other centres of study.
- keep in touch with other destinations, comparing statistics and trends.

Information reaches us in a fragmented, unstructured way, like the pieces of a jigsaw thrown on a table randomly. The information has to be sorted, fitted together, analysed and thought about. Good intelligence leads to new ideas and propositions.

Tourism marketing specialists build up their intelligence networks over a period of time. They work at it, keep in touch and keep listening.

Visitor Surveys

Visitor surveys were discussed in Chapter 3. They are a part of the flow of information about visitors, their background, motivations and satisfactions. Usually carried out at the destination they analyse the visitors' background, experiences and levels of general satisfaction.

The GTA can conduct surveys itself or employ the services of specialised research companies. The private sector, e.g. tour operators, airlines and hotels, tend to organise their own surveys.

Surveys can be structured to separate specific market segments. There are marked differences between people of different nationalities, ages, culture and spending power. All surveys need to be based on a carefully structured sample with respondents targeted accordingly.

Other types of survey may research buying choices, marketing appeal and motivation. Such research tends to work with small samples, in-depth interviewing, panels and group discussions. This is a part of the work normally carried out by specialised market research companies.

The Performance of the Tour Operators.

Market research plays an important role in monitoring the performance of the tour operators. One tries to assess the part they play and the volume of traffic they generate. This applies to both the foreign operators and any local inbound operators working with them. To obtain this information requires the collaboration of the local hotels, normally through the hotel association. One takes the following steps:

- Estimates the number of rooms (beds) contracted by each tour operator according to the market segments in which they operate.

- Assesses the contractual conditions under which these arrangements are made.

- Questions whether any guarantees are in place (rooms are paid for whether used or not), and for how many rooms, for what periods of the year? Otherwise what cancellation clauses exist, particularly those permitting the operator to cancel without penalty?

- Estimates the number of aircraft seats contracted by each tour operator, or seats on any other means of transport, e.g. overland. Again assesses the likely contractual conditions, and whether the number of seats available to the tour operator balances with the number of contracted rooms (beds). Also assesses the contractual commitment to the seats booked, and the cancellation provisions likely to exist.

- Assesses whether sufficient seats into the destination have been contracted, to achieve targets and to fill the optimum number of room nights available. Evaluates the likelihood of contracting additional seats, at short notice, if they become necessary

- Assembles full details of each tour operator's offer to the market, and the relevant marketing mix. These can be collected from the tour operators catalogues and brochures. Builds a profile of the market segments to which these marketing mixes appeal.

- Assesses the prices, the positioning of the destination, the support given to the image, and the comparisons with competing destinations.

- Compares the image as projected by the tour operators, with the image agreed by the sector and disseminated through the destination's own promotion.

- Assesses the operators' marketing punch and the impact of any promotion additional to the catalogues.

- Evaluates the operators' sales networks and their market-wide coverage. Tries to establish in which geographical areas of a country the destination appears to sell better.

It is not always possible to assemble all of the above data. It depends on the size of the destination and the corresponding volume of tourist traffic. Where there are many different tour operators from many markets, contracting a wide number of hotels and other accommodation, it is difficult to collect complete data. In this case, one should concentrate on the major operators (e.g. the leading ten producers), using the resulting data as an indication of the overall picture.

The general opinions of the travel trade given verbally, together with commentaries from the trade publications, also help to construct an assessment. Local and foreign operators and airlines should also be questioned about the strategies they intend to follow.

It should be possible to monitor the performance of the local inbound operators; how many packages have been placed in the various markets, how many have been sold, the problems encountered, and the results achieved.

Information Systems

In tourism the new advances in intelligence gathering link tourism statistics, with the tourism assets inventory and other aspects of market research These all tie together to form an integrated tourism database or tourism information system.

The information system (administered by the GTA) has usually developed from the department of statistics. It normally includes background and economic data, an inventory of tourism assets, relevant tourism statistics and the results of visitor and other surveys. It should have, at least, the following data fields: background data, economic data, tourism assets, access and transportation, national development perspectives and projects, current patterns of tourism, marketing information, new developments and future trends (Doswell, 1997).

A tourism assets inventory (a compilation of product components) is also essential. It can be structured as follows: natural resources, cultural and historical attractions, other tourist attractions, sports, recreation and entertainment, services, infrastructure, accommodation, restaurants and other facilities.

An information system can also be given the facility to map data. A geographical information system (GIS) uses specialised software and provides a valuable tool for tourism planning. Various data can be correlated on the same map; for example, weather, population, visitors, tourist facilities and attractions. By overlaying data on the map, the various spatial interrelationships can be illustrated. Proposed planning solutions can also be tested, and refined or discarded accordingly.

The economic analysis of tourism should be an ongoing part of the information system. It should show the contribution of tourism to foreign exchange earnings and the balance of payments, income generation and gross domestic product, regional development, employment creation, and government revenue. Such a model should allow for the disaggregation of the sector according to particular categories of product and corresponding marketing mixes and market segments. The model should update the estimated economic impact on an annual basis, and should also allow for the measurement of domestic tourism's contribution. One cannot monitor the sector effectively unless this economic overview – and year-to-year comparison – exists. One has to establish tourism's contribution, its trends and its potential for growth and development.

Disseminating Information

The traditional scope of tourism statistics provides only a partial view of tourism. Market research and a tourism assets inventory provide further important information. As already noted, this all ties together to form an integrated tourism database or tourism information system.

An annual report should be produced, based on all available information, with quarterly or semi annual updates. The purpose is:

- give an overview of what happened on the demand side – how many visitors from where – identification of trends – analysis of particular markets. Comparisons with last year, last quarter etc. Overall analysis of market performance. Purpose of visit, length of stay, area visited etc.

- give an equal overview of supply. Closures or additions to the supply of facilities and services. Trends in the structure of the sector – facilities and services; numbers, categories, geographical distribution. Sectoral performance. Occupancy rates, average room rates achieved.

The typical users are:

- the media – newspapers, radio, TV – enabling them to produce newsworthy items about tourism performance.

- other government agencies – particularly those involved with economic planning – also Ministry of Information.

- the sector itself – wanting to monitor its own performance – how well it is doing.

- potential developers in need of data on the characteristics of demand – some operational analysis – all important sources in the conduct of feasibility studies.

- other Ministry of Tourism departments – an important data source for decisions on markets and marketing, and product development and analysis.

- other persons e.g. scholars, the university, students, schools, embassies and aid donors (partners in development) – all with a particular interest in tourism sector performance.

Given this wide demand, the report is best published and sold. If so it should be a part of the wider availability of studies and reports. For example, an annual digest of tourism statistics or the results of any visitor surveys. Plus an annual supply side study – giving details of the various facilities and services – and the structure of the sector, categories of establishment, geographical distribution etc.

Given the above demand for information – publications should be made as useful as possible. To do this, one must be aware of the needs of the users.

Just ask the question – What would I need to know? For example:

- If I were opening a new restaurant?
- If I were working on a hotel feasibility study?
- If I were forecasting the future performance of the sector?
- If I were writing an article on tourism performance?
- If I were teaching a class on tourism at a University?
- If I were studying the country's economic performance?
- If I were commenting on the Ministry of Tourism's current marketing strategy and budget?
- If I were giving a career talk on tourism to the local high school?

Evaluating Results

Sales targets should be developed (also see Chapter 14) according to the marketing mix and market segment; numbers of visitors, length of stay, average daily expenditure, country of origin. These should be reconciled with occupancy forecasts for each type of accommodation. They can also be reconciled with airline passenger forecasts.

For the medium and long term, one cannot forecast tourist flows to a particular destination without taking into account the specific product to be marketed. A destination may lack rooms of the right type, serving the appropriate market segments. In this case, one can assess the demand based on an assumption of having certain numbers of rooms of a given category and price. When one assumes this, there should be firm evidence that the necessary capital will be forthcoming, the investments made, and the rooms added. If not, the assumption may be unrealistic and there will be no significant addition to supply. If this is so the forecasts are mistaken. Yet governments may be asked, based on these mistaken forecasts, to provide infrastructure, train staff, and make other provisions. With all forecasting, governments should exercise caution. And politicians should resist the temptation to exaggerate future prospects.

The matrix at Figure 8.2 shows the results of market research as used to monitor the performance of the sector as a whole. It shows how objectives correlate with research methods, results and verifiers.

Most destination's sales results are not disaggregated but lumped together. This does not permit an evaluation and comparison of the different sub sectors. One should know, for example, how well the small

Objectives	Methods	Results	Verifiers
Identifying opportunities	Reviewing trends, success of competing destinations, growth of particular market segments. Existing strengths.	Existing marketing mixes. Capacity for diversification and improvement. Action steps. Market forecasts.	Desk research; trends and forecasts. Travel trade response and feedback. Trends. Local support - sectoral consensus.
Fulfilling needs through the marketing mixes	Target market surveys. Visitor feedback. Study of all competing destinations; competitive advantages.	Assessment and development of the product, image, price promotion and sales network. Re-engineering – improvement, re-positioning, diversification and expansion.	Statistics and trends. Acceptance in the market place. Travel trade/tour operator offers and advertising. Visitor surveys.
Monitoring performance	Up-to-date statistics. Market information. Desk research.	Achievement of sales forecasts. Anticipation of problem areas. Contingency plans. Damage control.	Statistics and trends. Sales performance. Strong and weak segments. Economic reviews and commentaries.
Adjusting to changing needs	Consensus on adjustments; what needs changing, how, where etc. Industry-wide consultation. Short and long term change	Improved marketing mixes by segment. One or all components. Agreement on feasibility, resources and means.	Feedback from visitors and the travel trade; surveys. Global statistics and trends. Competing destinations.

Figure 8.2 Approach to tourism market research

guest houses are doing as compared to the four and five star hotels and resorts; or how well the camping sites and holiday apartments are performing. Or how well the special interest markets, for example diving and golfing holidays, are doing. And in which market segments and which countries these marketing mixes are achieving, exceeding or not achieving sales targets. In Chapter 11 the position matrix does go a step further, breaking down information by marketing mix.

References

Doswell, Roger. (1997). *Tourism – How Effective Management makes the Difference*, Butterworth Heinemann

Marcuse, Herbert. (1972). *The Affirmative Character of Culture in Negations, p.88*, Penguin University Press.

chapter nine
Image

This chapter starts by describing what is meant by image; core image, brand-image and tertiary image. It then describes the idea of a place's ethos and discusses some contemporary viewpoints and the overall tone and brand-image of a destination. It then examines romance, familiarity and intimacy as three stages in image-formulation. The chapter goes on to examine the significance of sign systems and concludes by considering ideas about fiction and reality.

The Image of a Destination

The image refers to the feelings, ideas and reactions which the name of a particular product, person or place evokes.

If a place is well known its name will generate a host of ideas and associations. If it is not well known it may prompt only the vaguest of notions. At worst, it will suggest nothing at all.

The overall tourism image changes therefore according to the viewer and the viewpoint. The British may have a different way of viewing France than, for example, the Italians or the Germans. They may see some things in the same way and others not. Part of an image is shared by one or more countries while other aspects are seen differently.

The prior knowledge or ignorance of a place is a major consideration. The typical American may have lots of ideas about Ireland, but know nothing about Fiji. The British tend to know more than the French about India, but less about North Africa.

The image of a place may also depend on how well read or educated, or how well travelled, a person is. It changes according to the market and people's backgrounds and characteristics.

A tourism destination wants to attract people and tries to project its image in the most favourable way possible. It takes a collection of ideas, builds it into an overall picture and then tries to enhance it. This image, while it promotes tourism, has spin-off benefits for other sectors. The place itself – everything it stands for and produces – is viewed more favourably.

The tourism image, to make more sense, needs to be broken down (see Figure 9.1) between:

- the core image which attaches itself to a place regardless of tourism. What does it conjure up?

- the brand-image which comprises the core image but emphasises the factors which create most tourism appeal.

- the tertiary image which comprises the additional factors linked to each particular marketing mix and market segment. This does not change the brand-image, it merely slants and differentiates it in various ways. For example, for cultural tourism it stresses the development of the arts, for ecotourism the remarkable characteristics of countryside settings, for scuba diving the exceptional qualities of the waters, or for golf the outstanding range of courses. There may be as many brand-images as there are marketing mixes and market segments.

Figure 9.2 shows a matrix which takes London as an example, and lists contributions to the core image, brand-image, and tertiary image (using a British history special interest market segment as the example). As can be noted, the core image only changes as old events, features or personalities

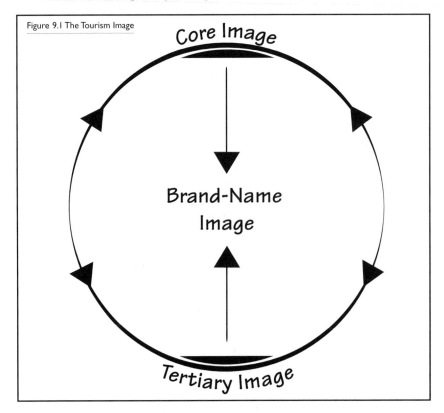

Figure 9.1 The Tourism Image

Core Image

Brand-Name Image

Tertiary Image

Type of Image	Ideas Evoked
CORE IMAGE What we think about the place.	Hub of the former British Empire. Big Ben. BBC World Service. The Tower of London. The Thames. The Queen. Buckingham Palace. Princess Diana. Fog. Sherlock Holmes. Charles Dickens. Parliament. Harrods. The Guards. Piccadilly Circus. Pubs and parades. The Beatles. Shakespeare.
BRAND-IMAGE What we think of the place as a destination.	Friendly welcome. Good service. Dining out. Value for money. Plenty to do and see. Things to buy. Swinging London. Lasting memories. Fun and enjoyment.
TERTIARY IMAGE What we think of the place for a particular special interest. For example, British history.	Lots of museums. Easy access to books and information. Well organised tours. Historical sites and attractions. Good tourist guides. Supplementary lecture programme.

Figure 9.2 The Tourism Image – The case of London (British History)

are dropped or new ones added. The brand-image emphasises those aspects of the core image likely to promote tourism in general while, in the case of special interest tourism, adding more specific factors.

As noted, the image changes according to each market – sometimes slightly and sometimes markedly:

- The core image is differently known, according to each culture. For example, the Brazilians and the British would have some different ideas about France.

- The brand image is adjusted to each culture, each audience. It tries to make each set of viewers see things in the best possible light. It appeals – "Hey! This brand is for you".

- The tertiary image adds the special interest factors – the things of particular interest to specific users. It adds to the appeal "Hey! And furthermore we offer this, this, this and this!".

The Core Image

The core image tends to comprise those factors which withstand the test of time. These are the predominant features which were discussed in Chapter 4. People think of the famous landmarks and historical attractions, links in literature, certain cultural traits, particular music, traditional modes of dress, famous hotels and restaurants, street-markets, parks, and the weather, landscape and atmosphere.

Part of this image is formed through stereotyping – the unthinking reliance on fixed and standardised ideas about the way things are. For example, the

British are this – the Japanese are that. Or Amsterdam is this – Bangkok is that.

Some of the image always consists of myth. Oscar Wilde blamed Turner, the artist, for giving London a fog-bound image. Foggy London – made famous in songs and films – is now a stereotypical idea of the city, full of wistful connotations. And it has become part of the city's core image. It doesn't matter that London is no longer foggy.

Derek Walcott refers to a French place on the sea, without naming it, in either Normandy or Brittany and paints a decidedly French image:

> *...it trembled with summer crowds, flags, and the fair*
> *with the terraces full and very French, determinedly witty,*
> *as perhaps all Europe sat out in the open air*
> *that was speckled and sun-stroked like Monet that summer...*

(Walcott, 1997)

Core images are about places, regions and countries; sometimes all three at the same time all mixed up. For example; Quimper in Brittany in France; Marbella on the Costa del Sol in Spain; Kuta in Bali in Indonesia.

The place itself usually has its own image but shares something with the region and the country. Each shares in the same core image but each has something of its own. And in the case of each, something is always changing but something always remain the same.

Places themselves also change as we have already noted in Chapter 1. New buildings and monuments, changing road systems, and newly pedestrianised areas.

Each generation throws up its leading personalities – artists, musicians, politicians, actors, actresses, singers, entrepreneurs. Contemporary culture also produces new theatre, music, art. Changing fashions also produce new modes of dress, new hotels, bars, restaurants and shops. People's lifestyles, preferences and tastes change. People do different things and go to new places. They look, think and behave differently.

Everything can change. The image of Japan in the United States was notably different in 1995 to 1955, simply because the intervening 40 years marked a prominent series of historical events and trends.

In Great Britain the Beatles were a post 1960 phenomenon as was Carnaby Street in London. As a place itself changes and develops so does part of its core image. The European Union has listed the first five things which it thinks spring to mind for each European country. For example, for Italy they are Rome, Pasta, Shoes, Art and Pavarotti. For Spain, Barcelona, Paella, Bullfighting, Art and Juan Carlos. For France, Wine, Paris, Gerard Depardieu, Food and Fashion. And for Britain, Shakespeare, London, the BBC, the Royals and the Beatles (EU, 1996). However, one should never lose sight of the main objective – to get people to conclude, "Hey! This is a nice place to visit".

Some destinations in some markets do not really have a core image. They mean nothing to people and provoke no reaction. For example Fiji is still unknown in many markets so is Eritrea. Such places start off with a clean slate, they have nothing to build on but nothing to live down. They are a blank sheet, one builds a brand image almost from scratch.

The Brand-Image

A brand-name is the name given to a particular product, or range of products. This brand-name is promoted to emphasise particular meanings and attributes. In turn, these evoke the brand-image. Attached to the name are logos, colours, slogans, music – they are part of the brand. They help to conjure up distinctive messages and meanings. The brand-name – for example, Bali, Biarritz or Tonga – should conjure up a clear brand-image.

Different marketing mixes may enjoy the same brand-image. It represents therefore a mostly singular image for a plural product. Reference is made to this singular image in both Chapters 4 and 11.

As already noted, the brand-image does add tertiary image factors to improve the appeal to a specific market segment. This reflects people's special interest. For example, an image of golf in Ireland or deep sea diving in the Caymans.

Ethos

A place's ethos was among the characteristics mentioned in Chapter 1. It is the spirit of a place which communicates itself firstly through the image. It describes an interpretation and conclusion – the way one feels about the place and reacts to it – both before visiting and after visiting. It's the soul of the place, and the magic which one either finds or not.

The Spanish have a way to describe this quality. It is "tener duende" – which means to have a magical and haunting quality. It is a subjective response – a feeling. It attracts people to a place, it enchants them when they are there.

Promotional material tries to capture the idea of ethos but often fails, the words and phrases used often sounding superficial even banal.

The Contemporary Viewpoint

As noted, there are elements in the image of a place that are lasting. They are passed on from generation to generation and form a part of the core image. But there are also contemporary happenings. For example, one has mentioned changes in the leading personalities. In a British newspaper article on Barbados Belinda Edwards tells us that Mandy Allwood, Mark Gardiner, Michael Winner, Andrew Neill, Robbie Williams and Nicholas Parsons go there not to mention the Island's earlier associations with Ronald Tree, Sir Anthony and Lady Bamford and Robert and Sue Sangster (The Daily Telegraph, 1997). These are names which may mean something in the 1990's British market but they would mean nothing in, for example, Germany or France. They are also names which will probably have no meaning to future generations in Britain.

The above article also mentioned Luciano Pavarotti. Pavarotti, by contrast with the others, is a name with worldwide appeal likely to be remembered for some time to come.

What people write and say about the destination and how it appears in the current scale of things may differ from market to market and generation to generation. There is a great element of fashion in this – each generation has its preferred styles and modes and its ways of expressing itself. Each generation has its smart set and its favourite destinations.

Setting the Tone

A key part of the tourism product tends to set the tone of a destination. Particular hotels and resorts exercise a major influence on the overall brand-image.

These flagship operations tend to be of two types:

- the great classic hotels of the world. These are the famous old hotels that have been renovated or maintained over the years and have achieved classic status. They have often become famous institutions in the places where they are located. They symbolise the place itself, standards of excellence and a clientele of the highest standing. Examples are the Oriental in Bangkok, Raffles in Singapore, the Plaza in New York, Claridges in London, the Ritz in Paris and the Sandy Lane Hotel in Barbados.

- the leading transnational operations which also symbolise a discriminating market and excellent product standards. For example, Hilton, Hyatt and Sheraton.

Projecting an image is a question of getting into people's minds. The flagship operations help to do this. They get high media exposure and provoke glamorous and upbeat ideas.

Romance, Familiarity and Intimacy

The brand-image held by a person at any point in time is at one of three stages: romance, familiarity and intimacy (Figure 9.3).

Romance

Before people visit a place there is the stage of romance. People nurture some ideas and image of a place. They may have an ample core image, knowing about the destination from what they have read, seen or heard. They may have even assimilated a multitude of knowledge and impressions.

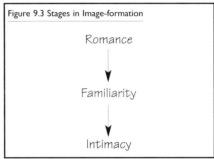

Figure 9.3 Stages in Image-formation

Romance

Familiarity

Intimacy

This gives the destination a compelling image and it brings a person to say, " At least once in my lifetime I have to visit this place."

As noted, the brand-image builds on the core image and is reinforced through advertising and promotional programmes. Particular people, pieces of music, commentaries, visual scenes and places may be used to support and strengthen this image. They look for the response "Hey, I really have to visit this place"

Familiarity

People may not enjoy their visit. If so, they feel misled by what they were told – by what the advertising and promotion promised. As a result, they change their thinking about the brand-image. However, they may still cling to much of the core image. This may even persuade them, in later years, to give the destination another chance.

Once people have visited the destination the image changes. This is the stage of familiarity. People complement their first ideas with memories of their own. If they liked the place, they will add to their ideas based on all the positive things that happened.

Intimacy

When people return to a destination a few times, they reach a stage of intimacy. There is a feeling of belonging; they identify with the place, defend it and make allowances for it. If they become regular repeat visitors, the place assumes a growing importance in their lives. They become involved with a wide range of local friends and acquaintances. The image is now based mainly on personal experience, but remains tinged with the ideas from the first core and brand-name images. They also build up the image for other people by talking about the place.

Sign Systems

Images are triggered by signs. This falls into the area of semiotics or semiology – the production of meanings from sign-systems, linguistic or non-linguistic. In the UK it is now difficult to hear Bach's `Air' without associating it immediately with Hamlet cigars. Other examples are:

- The sound of Big Ben generates a cluster of ideas about Britain and London.
- The shape of a Coca Cola bottle is unmistakable and the sight of it, even empty and discarded, may bring to mind a particular cluster of agreeable ideas.
- NIKE, in many advertisements, uses its symbol alone.
- The glimpse of a map – the shape of a continent or country – immediately generates a flood of ideas.
- The sound of a gamelan may remind people of Bali. Or a steel band Trinidad. Or castenets and a guitar Andalusia.
- A logo, a shape, a combination of colours or sounds, a key word or phrase are all signals to trigger the mind.

Transnational business and marketing continue to spread a huge commercial sign system with increasing global reach.

Fiction and Reality

A part of the core image is fictitious. Much of it is handed down from myth; for example, fairytales and storytelling, old photographs, paintings, legends, films and novels. And some of it is from the media; radio, television, travel books, magazines and newspapers. People's imaginations pick up these ideas and make something of them. The image keeps updating itself in their minds, and keeps adjusting to new impressions and inputs.

Other Ideas of Reality

There is an immense degree of subjectivity in our interpretation of people, places and events. Truth becomes whatever we choose to think. Magic realism is the literary term for mixing fantasy with normal happenings. It adds a magic and fairytale dimension in a matter-of-fact way. One believes in what happens – guesses at what made it happen.

Surrealism also means something which goes beyond conventionally realistic interpretation. It creates a dream world, the jumbling of fact and fiction, myth and legend. It draws its own truths from fancy and imagination, from hidden meanings, symbolism and flashes of insight.

Virtual reality comprises the seemingly real life situations and experiences created through the computer screen. The computer simulates reality with increasingly accurate results. Anyone using up-to-date flight simulation software, knows that flying an aeroplane seems like the real thing. As technology advances the computer will permit people to enter different environments and see and sense things as if they were real.

Also as digital applications perfect the three dimensional and holographic imagery, what one sees will seem even more real. Virtual reality can enable people to experience destinations. Our image of somewhere becomes sharper and clearer, our feeling for the reality of the place more concrete.

The Unfinished Image

Image exists in the mind – it is formed and held there. It always remains unfinished. As unfinished as the product itself.

People tend to fantasise. They buy the product to be part of its image. They want to step into the advertisement and be like the people portrayed as buying and enjoying it. The reasons for this were listed in Chapter 3.

The meaning of a cluster of things and ideas is an elusive concept. People interpret everything they hear, read or see according to who they are and how they think; their occupation and social status, cultural and educational background, nationality, age and sex, and the values of the society in which they live. The interpretation is always changing; things change, ideas change and people change. Nothing is ever quite the same.

References

Edwards, Belinda. (1997). Goodbye Paradise, Hello Hello!-on-Sea. *The Daily Telegraph*, 8 January.

Office for Official Publications of the European Communities. (1996). *Exploring Europe*.

Walcott Derek. (1997). *The Bounty*, Faber and Faber.

chapter ten
Price

This chapter starts by explaining prices, receipts and tourism's economic impact. It goes on to discuss leakage, reducing leakage and the price elasticity of demand. It then examines the relation of price to image. It looks at currency exchange rates, the factors influencing them and the introduction of the EURO. The chapter goes on to discuss anti trust and monopoly controls and the dangers of two-tier tourism pricing. It concludes by listing key pricing criteria.

Prices and Tourism Receipts

Price is a part of the marketing mix. This gives it, quite rightly, a marketing focus. However, cost-plus pricing techniques are still found. Pricing of this kind, without reference to marketing criteria, is perilous. One recognises that prices always need to be reconciled with costs and returns but, in the first instance, one should be sure of their marketing feasibility. The prices for a destination's facilities and services have to meet the following criteria:

- be compatible with the image and accord with people's perceptions of the product's category and value.

- permit a given volume of sales. There have to be enough people able and happy to pay these prices.

- be competitive when compared with the destinations offering a similar product.

- if the product is unique there are no direct competitors, but it still competes for its share of people's money. Holidays compete with all forms of discretionary spending.

- be at a level to capture the targeted shares of particular markets.

- permit a minimum level of profitability and return on investment, both for the enterprises within the destination and for the tour operators selling it.

A destination doesn't offer one tourism product at one price. One offers a mix of marketing mixes and prices to meet a range of purchasing power. Different marketing mixes, which were discussed at the conclusion of

Chapter 4, give a destination a broader more diversified appeal. The factors influencing the mix of marketing mixes which a destination offers, together with its overall market positioning, are discussed in Chapter 11.

Tour operators usually try to capture interest in a destination by featuring its starting price – the lowest and most aggressive – known as the "lead-in" price.

The prices paid at a destination, not only for accommodation but for all the optional items, result in the average daily expenditure per visitor. This, based on the length of stay, the WTO defines as "the total consumption expenditure made by a visitor or on behalf of a visitor for and during his/her trip and stay at the destination" (WTO, 1994).

The WTO definition of international tourism receipts, generated by inbound tourism, also includes payments to national carriers for international transport. And the definition of expenditure on outbound tourism includes similar payments to foreign carriers.

Tourism's Economic Impact

Chapter 8 has already indicated the importance of the economic impact and the need to measure it. Tourism adds to incomes, creates employment, generates government revenues, stimulates regional development and foreign exchange earnings. As expenditure works its way through the economy, it has a multiplier or knock-on effect. This varies according to the type of tourism and particular marketing mix.

Economists should create models to measure the impacts of these tourist expenditures across the economy. As noted – whatever the modelling approach used – impact studies should recognise that different types of tourists use different accommodation and spend their money on different things. For example, locally owned small tourism enterprises may have comparatively low income with a higher proportion of it spent locally. By contrast a large international style resort may have a high daily expenditure but much lower local content. The sector should be disaggregated to measure the relative impact of these different kinds of operation. An economic model establishes the typical structure of revenues and costs – it examines linkages within the economy and identifies leakage. This enables the impacts to be measured on an ongoing basis. As also noted in Chapter 8, the model becomes an important part of the information system monitoring sectoral performance.

Tourism is not an industry in itself but a multisectoral economic activity. It therefore defies the conventions of national economic accounting. This makes it difficult to analyse tourism as a sector. The adjustment of input-output models to measure the impact of tourist expenditure can also be misleading and unreliable. The simple calculation of economic multipliers based on collected sample data may provide more reliable results.

However, there are international initiatives afoot, at the beginning of the twenty first century, to measure more completely the economic impact of tourism e.g. domestic tourism is seldom figured. This will establish a tourism satellite account designed to go beyond the simple reporting of international arrivals and foreign receipts, to create a comprehensive national tourism economic accounting system.

To calculate gross foreign exchange earnings from tourism one simply asks visitors how much they spent. Visitor expenditure surveys do this. However, as noted above, visitors should be disaggregated according to market segment and purpose of visit. Different kinds of visitor spend different amounts of money. Surveys, safely representative of traffic, should take these differences into account.

When governments are hungry for additional revenue, tourism is a tempting target. However, tourism already boosts government revenues. To directly tax inbound tourism is like taxing an export. Similarly outbound tourism may also be taxed; a country may introduce departure taxes to limit the number of its citizens travelling abroad. This is equivalent to a tariff on imports, it is protectionist by nature and can provoke retaliation. It also undermines the concept of open markets and inhibits international trade.

Leakage

Leakage (how much leaves the country) for the purchase of various goods and services is also the subject of surveys. Again the tourism sector needs to be disaggregated; different sub sectors have different patterns of consumption and some rely on more imported items.

The items which are imported to support tourism fall into the following categories:

- construction equipment, materials, and even the management and labour force sometimes used to build new hotels and tourism facilities.
- furniture, fixture and equipment.
- food and beverage, and other operating supplies; e.g. paper supplies, spare parts and engineering supplies etc.
- advertising and promotional expenditures outside the country.
- the costs of any foreign management and labour. A proportion of the wages and salaries paid to these personnel usually leaves the country.
- any fees paid outside the country; e.g. design fees, management fees,

marketing fees or fees to purchasing companies, maintenance companies, and training companies.

There are the expenditures related to the creation or improvement of the tourism facilities (capital costs), and the expenditures related to the operation of these facilities (revenue costs). Capital, both equity and loan finance, may come from outside the country. This requires the repayment of capital and the payment of dividends and interest.

Reducing Leakage

Some leakage should be treated as the economic cost of doing business, not as an undesirable by-product. To maintain quality there may be certain essential import components in both construction and operational costs. For example, foreign marble or imported wines. However, it is important to know the comparative local economic content and impact of various kinds of tourism project.

It may be possible to reduce leakage without handicapping the product and the marketing mix. For example:

- local construction methods and materials can be used more extensively. This may only be possible if it does not change the concept of the product.

- lower construction costs may mean that the necessary capital can be found locally.

- more furniture, fittings and operating equipment may be manufactured locally. This may depend on capacity, markets and economies of scale.

- it may be possible to substitute local items for imported foodstuffs and other supplies.

- it may also be possible to use and develop local design and other consultant expertise.

- with expanded training opportunities, local personnel can replace foreign personnel.

Each existing or new facility should operate strictly according to its marketing mix; short sighted attempts to reduce leakage can damage the product and wreck results. They do not always lead to increased economic benefits. One tries to favour local products when they are as good as, or of an acceptable quality, and will achieve satisfactory results.

Local products should be given a fair chance. Also the development of new regional trading blocks has opened things up and extended the concept of "local". One should also remember that open markets promote world trade. In developing a balanced approach, one bears all these considerations in mind.

Elasticity of Demand

If sales are sensitive to price changes, demand is price elastic. If not, it is price inelastic. Even small changes in some prices affect demand, while substantial changes in others have little or no effect. Holiday travel tends to be price elastic; business and other obligatory travel tend to be price inelastic.

Cross elasticity may occur between one destination and others. Prices can rise to such a point (through inflation and/or changes in the exchange rate) that demand drops and is displaced to other more attractively priced destinations. A surge in a currency's exchange rate favours imports (outbound tourism) and hurts exports (inbound tourism).

The tendency to cross elasticity can be part of the marketing strategy, trying to use price cuts to achieve bigger market shares.

Space (e.g. rooms in hotels and seats on aeroplanes) is perishable. As pointed out in Chapter 4, it has to be sold for today – it cannot be stored. Late price cutting can fill up leftover space, making an important contribution to revenue. This strategy, common in tourism, exploits the price elasticity of demand. However, as already noted, price is a part of the image. To cheapen the product can cheapen its image.

Pricing requires flexibility and speedy responses to changing market conditions and circumstances. To make this possible, one needs a steady flow of up-to-date market information (see Chapter 8). To respond, one needs to know what's happening. One changes a price to get better results. For example, one can change prices according to the season.

Price Related to the Image

Published or "sticker" prices are important in marketing. They help to position a destination in the market. Correct pricing supports the image; wrong pricing undermines it.

Destinations tend to fall into price categories and this is discussed more fully in Chapter 11 on positioning. Prices convey ideas about desirability and exclusivity, part of the destination's image.

Many products and services, particularly those considered as luxuries, bestow the types of ego benefit discussed in Chapter 3. Using the product or enjoying the particular service can make one feel good in a number of ways. Paying a high price contributes to the perceived value and adds to the satisfactions. "It's expensive but it's worth it", one says. This is sometimes called the Chivas Regal effect, after the marketing of this brand of whisky.

As with hotels and airlines it is tempting, for example, for a school or university to cut prices to sell unfilled capacity. This exploits the price elasticity of demand but may damage the image. Cutting prices can be seen as cutting quality. It is also upsetting to people who have already paid a higher price.

As a general rule different prices can be charged for the same thing, if disguised by wrapping the prices into an overall package. A strict comparison of prices, item by item, is then impossible.

Quite apart from image, higher prices sometimes generate more demand. An initial increase in revenue enables an improvement in the marketing mix (better product and more effective promotion and sales). As a result, the market responds positively and – even with higher prices – demand continues to increase.

A Giffen good means that a rise in price of cheaper, basic items forces a re-ordering of spending priorities. This releases funds to buy more of these items, so although price rises so does demand.

Currency Exchange Rates

For many holidays, accommodation and perhaps meals are paid in advance. People then change money or use credit cards for their discretionary spending at the destination. Credit card spending appears less sensitive to exchange rates. However, the money which visitors change at the destination has more immediacy. It determines how much people get for local spending. If they can buy and do a lot of things, this is more likely to attract them back for a return visit.

Differing rates of inflation cause changes in exchange rates, and compensating price adjustments are needed to maintain the status quo. Apart from this, there are other factors which influence exchange rates:

- increases or decreases in the rates of interest, set by the country's central banking institution as a part of its monetary policy. High rates of interest attract capital inflows and strengthen the currency.

- relatively poor economic performance leading to substantial foreign debt, a large trade deficit, and government overspending, can weaken a currency.

- alternatively, sound and disciplined macroeconomic management can strengthen a currency.

The prices of currencies, as they are bought and sold, tend to fluctuate. Market forces react to the above indicators, changing the relative value of currencies. Many people buying the same currency push its value up. A run on the currency, with everybody selling it, pushes it down. Governments tend to intervene and buy or sell currencies to counteract what they see as an undesirable market trend.

The control of inflation is a major objective of economic policy. Low inflation helps to maintain a currency's value. It creates economic stability and a climate of greater certainty and predictability.

Currencies are of two types; first those which are freely traded on the open international money markets. The market determines the current value of one currency against all others. A little less than one third of currencies currently float. Other currencies may be pegged in value by the country's central bank, or tied to the value of a major freely traded currency or a basket of currencies.

In entering into contracts for aircraft seats, hotel rooms or local ground transportation, tour operators are careful to avoid exchange rate risks. They hedge against fluctuations in the exchange rates by buying futures, contracting to buy currencies at an agreed price at some future date. Contracts can be negotiated in any currency, prices agreed, and risks eliminated.

The Euro

As pointed out by the European Union the single currency, the EURO, eliminates the risks and costs of currency fluctuations. It also facilitates intra-Community trade by reducing the transaction costs. As a result it is expected that the EURO will produce greater trade and stimulate integrated markets. Greater price transparency should also enable quicker price comparison between member countries. A a result, increased competition should produce a downward convergence of prices (European Commission, 1998).

Saving the exchange charges imposed on currency transactions and enabling visitors to feel comfortable and "at home" with local prices, should help develop inter-European tourism. It means that visitors do not need to adjust to different currencies or bear high exchange costs.

Anti Trust and Monopoly Controls

The advantages of competition are undisputed. Anti trust and monopoly regulations prevent the restriction of trade and ensure that markets are kept open. Sellers cannot collude to fix prices, and neutralise the free market.

There is an advantage for operators to disclose their prices, revenues and operating results. It permits industry-wide comparison. Operators can perceive the general framework of prices and revenues within which they must compete. There is competition but there is transparency. One can see where and how the sector as a whole is positioning itself.

A lot of this depends on the size and complexity of the destination. In a large destination there may be hundreds of hotels selling their rooms. This ensures diversity and competition. With only a handful of hotels an oligopolistic market exists. Each hotel represents an important part of the destination's product. However, there should be no price-fixing and hotels should compete with one another. Altogether there can be:

- **Trust and togetherness** – openness in the sharing of information.

- **Freedom of action** – prices set freely within a framework of complementary marketing mixes.

- **A common strategy** – competition but coordination within an agreed strategy.

The sector combines not to fix prices but to maintain an agreed overall strategy. However, the sector often agrees (or looks the other way) on two tier pricing for locally purchased goods and services. One price for locals and another price for visitors.

Two-Tier Pricing

Two-tier pricing in tourism for locally produced goods and services is common. One price is charged for locals and a higher price for foreign visitors. It is based on the foreigners' perceived purchasing power and the belief that (i) they can afford to pay more, and that (ii) given their system of values they don't mind paying more. However, this is seldom true. When charged more for the same thing people feel "ripped off". Yet the practice continues, e.g. it was reported that the Czech Ministry of Finance still supports the idea of charging foreigners as much as they will pay (Daily Telegraph,1999).

Differences in spending power and the prices people pay when at home or away, are one of tourism's traps. However, it is these differences which give a competitive advantage and remain an important promotional element. People may choose to go somewhere partly because prices are low. Rather than just charge visitors more, it is better to justify a higher price by adding value. For example, a night at the ballet in St Petersburg can become ballet and a candlelit supper. A museum entrance can include a guided tour, refreshment and an illustrated lecture.

Yield Management

Yield management is the term applied to the management of prices so as to maximise revenues and returns. It has become particularly important in the marketing of space – e.g. airlines and accommodation. How much you get per unit and how many you sell, e.g. average rate and room occupancy achieved. One weighs all the variables discussed – e.g. marketing mix, day-of-the-week, seasonality, special events, price elasticity, numbers travelling, frequency of travel etc – and one sets the prices. At the micro level, yield management remains one of the owner's or manager's major responsibilities. At the macro level – for the sector as a whole – it remains key in maximising economic benefits.

Key Pricing Criteria

Price is interdependent on the other four components of the marketing mix; it cannot be treated in isolation. The following list serves as a useful reminder of key tourism pricing criteria:

- One is not talking about one price but many different prices. Prices are not fixed but fluid, always able to respond to the market.

- A lead-in price is an effective promotional price, it offers exceptional value for money and is intended to capture the potential customer's interest. It's designed to penetrate the market. A restaurant menu has lead-in prices, as does a tour operators catalogue.

- Price must always be assessed against the competing prices of alternative products and destinations. Also alternative ways of spending one's money.

- There are as many prices as marketing mixes, as seasons, as special promotions and circumstances. In worldwide tourism, the passing of every hour sees thousands of price changes.

- In the short term, prices may be juggled as a part of sales tactics, e.g. buy and pay now to get a 15 per cent discount, come out-of-season for a 50 per cent discount, come next month and bring your spouse free. These tactics exploit the price elasticity of demand.

- The price elasticity of demand can also be used effectively to sell last minute unsold or leftover capacity. For example, hotel rooms or airline seats.

- There should be a sense of price integrity, customers should have confidence in the price they have paid. Price cutting can damage the image.

- In any destination there is an idea of price which attaches itself to, and supports, the accepted image. Price can add ideas of exclusivity and prestige.

- In turn, the development of the image, full of intangible factors, is aimed at adding value and delivering enhanced satisfactions in the customer's mind. The successful elevation of the image may justify an increase in the price.

- In the long term, prices are set to support the marketing mix, to reflect the image and value for money, and to win market acceptance.

- The price of a tour operator's package takes into account all component costs, e.g. transportation and transfers, accommodation, taxes, perhaps some food and beverage and other costs, and promotion. In this, for example, the price of the hotel becomes a cost. The price to the consumer is the price of the package.

- The influence of currency exchange rates on prices may be unforeseen. If this happens prices may need some correction.

- The hotel rack rate, or the published air or train fare are the "sticker" prices; they are subject to the payment of commissions to booking agents. "Sticker" prices are also subject to substantial quantity discounts.

- Price increases can be used to decrease demand when the carrying capacity of a place or attraction is exceeded.

Yield management weighs all relevant criteria and sets prices to maximise revenues and returns. As noted, acceptable levels of pricing lead to targeted revenue generation. They are about money, something never far from mind.

References

Shadbolt, P. (1999). Czechs may play fair. *The Daily Telegraph*, 13 March, T.2.

European Commission. (1998). *XXVIIth Report on Competition Policy 1997*, Foreword by Mr Karel Van Miert, Commissioner with responsibility for competition policy, EU-Brussels.

WTO. (1993). *Recommendations on Tourism Statistics*.

chapter eleven
Positioning

This chapter starts by describing the importance of positioning, and its relationship with the product, brand-image, pricing and marketing mix. It then goes on to look at the positioning of "classics". It examines the formulation of the marketing mix range, and the introduction of balance and proportion. The chapter concludes by explaining the use of a positioning matrix and the criteria used in its construction. This includes examples of a matrix at both the macro and micro levels.

The Importance of Positioning

Positioning is the way in which a destination is perceived and ranked in relation to other destinations. It is where the market chooses to place a destination in relation to the competition. The destination may target the position it wants, but it is the market which decides where to put it.

One promotes a destination to distinguish and differentiate it. People then rank destinations on an imaginary list of preferences. They put them high or low – among the best, in the middle, or among the worst. Once a person positions a destination it is difficult to change.

Each destination consists of a range of products and a mix of marketing mixes. One markets from the top down in the following way:

- Chapter 9, on image, describes a destination's core image – the established ideas about the place and what they conjure up. It then describes the brand-image – what promotional programmes choose to say about the destination. Finally it refers to the tertiary image – the additional factors and spin aimed at different market segments.

- The brand-image helps to position the destination in an overall way. In its range of marketing mixes there is a lead or flagship marketing mix (particular hotels or resorts) which both contributes to, and reflects, this brand-image. Starting from this, one then has several different marketing mixes serving different segments.

- Tour operators often choose to market from the bottom not from the top. They feature firstly the "lead-in" price based on the cheaper, more economical categories of accommodation. In smaller destinations this can damage the overall brand-image and positioning. Tour operators should agree their promotional strategies with the destination beforehand. The GTA should make this clear.

- Much of a tourism product is shared regardless of the market segment, e.g. the atmosphere, landscape, sites, streets, attractions, shopping and many other services. Other visitors to a destination are also a part of its product. What differentiates products and their customers (the marketing mixes and market segments) are the different quality and price categories, e.g. the types and category of hotels, resorts, restaurants, clubs and other facilities. However, the mix of mixes has to be compatible and not risk upsetting a particular category of visitor.

- How many different products and marketing mixes a destination can have is a major consideration. If the range is very wide, too many products can jar against one another. They have to be in tune with one another – there has to be harmony.

- The overall positioning and brand-image benefits the entire range of products and marketing mixes. It does not matter how much you pay, or where you choose to stay, you are attracted by the same brand-image. This what a mostly singular image for a plural product, discussed in Chapters 4 and 9, means. For example, Barbados has a clear "island in the sun, playground of the rich" type of image. Yet it has many small medium priced hotels, patronised by modest visitors. The destination is known as one thing for certain people, but it is enjoyed by many other types of people. One marketing mix leads, and the others follow. The famous Sandy Lane, for example, contributes to the island's overall positioning which also benefits the many small locally run hotels. Similarly Cable Beach and Paradise Island contribute to Nassau's positioning but also benefit its smaller operations.

- A destination tries to secure its positioning by sending out a fresh and special message. It promises particular attributes, certain experiences and a distinctive appeal. Something that makes people pick this destination over others. Something that sells the ideas that sell the destination.

- Once people have visited the destination and like it, they modify the brand-image according to their experiences. They build it up and enhance it, change the emphasis and personalise it. And based on their ideas and conclusions, they recommend the destination to other people.

- The image does not portray the reality of a place. This does not mean that it is false, merely that interpretations of reality are elusive. The reality is what people see, what they feel, and what the product does for them. This has some relation to the product's intrinsic characteristics and its measurable quality, but it is mostly to with perceptions. The important thing is how people see a tourist destination.

First, one establishes an overall market position. One then tries to secure a position for each marketing mix in each market. Competing destinations may decide to pursue the same market segments. Each aims at the same visitors, competing to increase its market shares.

A destination might decide to concentrate on being the leader in one special interest segment (e.g. diving), while obtaining a lesser share in other markets. Once one achieves the desired positioning for all marketing mixes, the promotional programmes and everything else seek to maintain it.

Figure 11.1 shows the general approach to positioning.

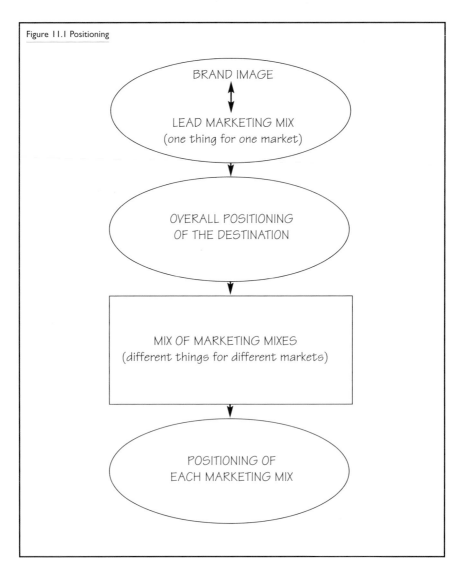

Figure 11.1 Positioning

BRAND IMAGE

LEAD MARKETING MIX
(one thing for one market)

OVERALL POSITIONING
OF THE DESTINATION

MIX OF MARKETING MIXES
(different things for different markets)

POSITIONING OF
EACH MARKETING MIX

The Positioning of `Classics'

As noted in Chapter 9, some parts of the product such as grand old hotels and restaurants appear to enjoy classic status. For example, The Plaza or St Regis in New York or The Savoy or Claridges in London. Now regarded as institutions, they don't seem to have to sell themselves. This is deceptive. Although such hotels have achieved a special position, they must still stay relevant to contemporary needs. They must still compete. If they ever cease to meet the expectations of their customers, they will be in trouble. The concept of the product may be timeless, but all other aspects of quality, service and hospitality must continue to satisfy today's needs.

To be an institution, a hotel is:

- part of the myth and legend of the destination.
- historically widely known and acclaimed – almost synonymous with the destination itself – and a distinguished place in the destination's past development.
- able to bestow status on the people who use it.
- maintained in keeping with its traditional standards.
- priced at a level compatible with its status and image.
- seen to be recognised and patronised by the personalities of the day; people who enhance its image.

If all of these conditions are met, it means that:

- its quality is maintained.
- it stays relevant.
- it stays competitive.

People are sometimes misled into thinking that their product has achieved classic status. Club Med, already mentioned in Chapter 7, believed that it had become an institution and didn't have competitors. It was wrong. In the 1990s it slipped into difficulties, its product and standards out-of-date.

Formulating the Marketing Mix Range

One usually sees, in a given destination, a mix of different facilities, locations, sizes, categories, types, prices and standards. They have not normally come about through a carefully conceived plan, but are the result of independent private sector initiatives based on different financial, marketing, and operational assessments. To make sense of what there is, one must categorise and structure them according to their marketing mixes. The result will reflect the actual marketing strategy. One sees what one has and what it is all aimed at achieving. One can note what is doing well and what is doing badly, and how one objective is either helping or hurting another.

One is more or less stuck with the range of products and marketing mixes one inherits. It is only with relatively new destinations that one can plan from the beginning. However, some change may be possible and this is discussed in Chapter 16 on regeneration and re-engineering.

In the case of a company, too extensive a product range tends to confuse and dilute a company's main focus. The company may lead the field in a particular thing or things and becomes tempted to sell more products under the one successful brand name. However, it expands its range and blurs its image. Buyers become confused about what the company does, what it sells, and in what markets. They are no longer clear about its positioning. It is a long-standing dictum that if one mixes markets the overall market finds the lowest level. This is the danger unless one keeps emphasising the brand-image and keeps the lead marketing mix to the forefront.

A destination's singular image can be threatened by a plural product. This can happen if the lead market segment is lost altogether, or if it starts to be swamped by a lower market segment. As noted, one must keep a balance in the overall mix of market and product segments.

One stamps a destination according to its lead or flagship marketing mix. As noted in Chapter 9, this sets the tone and typifies the singular image. Everything else moves under this one umbrella. This lead marketing mix can cohabit with other marketing mixes if certain conditions are met:

- that the brand-image is always projected from the top.

- that notable zoning has occurred so that the different types of facilities, serving different market segments, are separated spatially. This is likely to have come about through the relative prices of land. It may also result from a selective granting of planning permission (if this is policy). This allows only certain categories of facility to be constructed in certain areas. It means that, in the geographical distribution of the facilities, one type and set of people should not crowd people of another type or set. For example, in Barbados the south coast tends to have a different type of tourism to the west coast.

- that the mixed use of certain optional recreational and entertainment facilities is discouraged by the high prices charged. Price levels create a degree of exclusivity. The free market usually takes care of this. It figures our what product and appeal to provide, for what segment at what price.

- that the use of shared amenities such as streets, shopping areas, squares, public gathering places, conforms to certain standards of public behaviour. For example, no hordes of drunken louts or street prostitutes. This needs careful monitoring and concerted action. One can discourage undesirable demand by controlling the product.

- that there is no overcrowding of shared amenities including places like the airport, post office etc. This means that the general carrying capacity of the destination and its various services is sufficient.

- that each market segment is well served in terms of the total product designed for its use. This tends to hold people within certain areas and orbits. It is not how many people there are, but where they are and what they are doing at any one time.

- that there are continuing quality improvement programmes aimed at more customer satisfaction.

These criteria, and the ability of a destination to mix market segments harmoniously influences the formulation of the marketing mix range. There is no formula to specify the precise proportions of each category of facility. There are too many differences between destinations. Each destination has to sort this out for itself, bearing in mind the guidelines listed above.

It should be noted that the creation of up-market products is discouraged by an existing predominance of lower positioned products. In this case the destination may have already taken on an overall lower-market brand-image. However, down-market facilities do not tend to be discouraged by a strong existing up-market product. On the contrary, something good can seem to be sold cheaply. Issues of this kind can represent important considerations in regeneration, re-engineering and expansion decisions (see Chapters 16 and 17).

It is critical that each enterprise understands the destination's marketing rationale, and how it fits into the overall picture. This requires the effective coordination of the whole sector, and plenty of discussion and consultation. This is helped by joint, sector-wide promotional programmes.

The Positioning Matrix

The positioning matrix should be prepared at two levels:

Macro

This is prepared for the sector as a whole. It segments the overall market – domestic and international – and indicates the approximate proportion of business obtained from each segment – both in numbers of visitors and earnings. Similarly it shows each main type of product (product segment), indicating the market segment which it serves. It indicates the level of occupancy, or the percentage of its capacity, under which it is currently operating. Access, because of its importance, is looked at separately. The matrix also indicates current performance, opportunities and future targets. The rest of the marketing mixes are analysed – image, price, promotion and sales. The competing destinations are examined, and current positioning described. Opportunities for future positioning and yield management are identified.

Micro

This is prepared for each product and marketing mix designed to satisfy the needs of a particular market segment. A market segment for a particular product differs according to the nationality of the visitors, and may need to be sub-segmented. For example, as noted in Chapter 9, the Japanese perceive a product, image and price in a different way to the French. For this reason a product's position may vary from country to country. A micro positioning matrix should therefore be developed for each product and sometimes for each market sub-segment, e.g. not only for the dive market as a whole but also for the British, German, Japanese and US dive markets. The matrix also looks at distance and ease of access, and follows the other points listed in the macro-matrix. However, the micro level adds one more item to this breakdown – the relationship to the total product. This indicates how the particular facility, attraction or service fits in with the total product, indicating its importance and contribution. The matrix, as with the macro, concludes with overall positioning. A product may be the leader in one market but of lesser importance in another, and this should be indicated. The matrix also points to opportunities for future positioning and yield management.

Each matrix is broken down according to the following system of headings:

- Market segment/s. The characteristics and the profile of each market segment served.

- Product segment/s. The product or products designed to satisfy the identified markets.

- Access. How you get there and the ease and characteristics of access.

- Image/features. The core image and predominant features. The brand-image. In the case of the micro product – the tertiary image – how this relates and how it adds particular "spin".

- Price. The price range, discount policies, and relationship to competitors

- Competing products. The major competitors. What they offer – product, image, price? Advantages/disadvantages through their promotion and sales.

- Promotion. Current approach. Main focus. Techniques used. Budget and results obtained.

- Sales network. Current sales patterns. Tour operators. Airlines. Retail agencies. Hotels. Group and individual travel

- Position. Current position according to the various markets. Main strengths and weaknesses.

As noted the micro-matrix also includes the relationship to the total product. As also noted, the positioning matrix is prepared for each product for each major market (country of tourist origin), including the domestic market. There is no alternative to this approach. Each product in each market has particular characteristics and should be analysed accordingly. This means disaggregating or segmenting the overall product, according to its different types and categories. One can do this based on the accommodation product. For example, in a typical resort destination (e.g. in the Caribbean or South Pacific), it might break down as follows:

- Main island beach hotels and resorts. Four and five star properties.

- Main island beach hotels and resorts. Two and three star properties.

- Main island locations – beach and other – mainly small hotels and guest houses. One star or unclassified.

- Boutique small island resorts. Located on the outer islands. Four and five stars.

- Other small island resorts. Mainly economy operations; unclassified.

- Inland resorts. Small, economy and mainly unclassified. Ecotourism, special interest, nature tourism and community development projects.

- Main town area. Small business hotels. One and two star or unclassified.

- Bareboat yachting. Yachts chartered without crew; cruising holidays.

While accommodation is only a part of the product it can be used to disaggregate the sector. In the matrix, under market and product segments, other product components together with visitor motivations can be included and analysed. However, a matrix could also be prepared for a number of tour operators' packages, or a particular type of special interest holiday. The product can be disaggregated in any way that makes marketing sense.

There are sub-products (components) which make up a destination's total tourism product. For example, particular tourist attractions and things to do and see. Each one of these can be positioned in relation to the main product. Each attraction, for example, a museum or famous country house, has a marketing mix. It is a useful exercise for everyone to complete a micro positioning matrix. A matrix should also include any seasonal modifications to the marketing mix.

Figure 11.2 illustrates the approach to a positioning matrix for the macro level. Figure 11.3 shows it for the micro level.

Positioning – the **Macro** Level

Criteria	Assessment
Market segment/s	Describe the market appeal for this destination and its tourism products – and the market segment or segments targeted. Detail each segment: who makes it up – profile and characteristics. Length of stay, interests and motivations. Spending power. What do these people seek in the product? What do they seek in relation to the tourist trip as a whole – the total product? What's the experience – what do they want to see and do? Describe the performance of each market segment, number of visitors, economic impact etc. Indicate growth opportunities and future targets.
Product segment/s	Describe the products – for each of the market segments indicated. Indicate the type of experience – mainstream or special interest – and the type of holiday sought. Describe to the product for business trips or other purposes. List the various facilities, services and attractions – e.g. hotel, guest house, restaurant, cultural attraction, recreational facility, place of entertainment, retail shop – each product's specific components. Indicate the completeness of the product – and opportunities for additions and improvements. Describe the destination's features and attractions shared by all of its products. For example, the urban environment, scenic and cultural attractions. List any seasonal adjustments.
Access	Describe the access to the destination – by road, sea, waterway and air, from the markets indicated? What are the transport marketing mixes? Are they sufficient, comfortable, priced competitively, promoted effectively and easy to book and buy? What people come alone or in groups? Are they organised by a tour operator?
Image/features	Describe the destination's core image and brand image in relation to each product and market segment. Indicate how these are adapted through the each product's secondary image. Also indicate how they are given particular "spin" – e.g. for a special interest markets such as diving or golf. Describe the use of ·slogans, logos and other devices. List any seasonal adjustments.
Price	Describe the daily visitor expenditure – and its breakdown – for each type of visitor – each market segment. Are prices competitive with other destinations? Are the local services – e.g. restaurants, recreation, entertainment – reasonably priced in relation to all inclusive package holiday prices. What is the overall pricing strategy – yield management? List any seasonal adjustments.
Competing products	One competes with the same or similar destinations. One may also compete with other products, e.g a holiday may compete with a new television. One competes for the discretionary spending. Make a list of the products which compete with this destination. – similar product, same market. Indicate the influence of key tour operators. Shares of the market. Competitive strategies.
Promotion	Current promotional activities; this destination, these products, these market segments. Describe the consumer and trade promotion. Assessment of past and future effectiveness. List any seasonal adjustments.
Sales networks	Ease of purchase. Advertising. Public relations. Direct mail. Other promotional activities. Sales and reservations outlets. The internet. Tour operators. Influence of retail outlets; geographical coverage. Organised travel. Companies selling packages including this product to this market. Current programme; future perspectives. Number of packages. Promotion. Sales networks. Sales performance. List any seasonal adjustments.
Position	This describes, after an assessment of all the above factors, the position of the destination and its products as against other competing destinations and products. Total tourism potential from all markets for each product. Current numbers received. Market shares. Future perspectives.

Figure 11.2 The Positioning Matrix – the Macro Level

Positioning – the **Micro** Level

Criteria	Assessment
Market segment/s	Describe the market appeal for this product – the market segment or segments targeted. Detail each segment: who makes it up – profile and characteristics. Length of stay, interests and motivations. Spending power. What do these people seek in the product? What do they seek in relation to the tourist trip as a whole – the total product.
Product segment/s	Describe the product – e.g. whether it is a hotel, guest house, restaurant, cultural attraction, recreational facility, place of entertainment, or retail shop etc. Describes its facilities, service, opening hours and attributes. Is it one of the destination's major features – like Harrod's in London, the Prado in Madrid or the Plaza in New York? Is it famous for particular items or experiences – e.g. pressed duck at the Tour d'Argent in Paris, or a Singapore sling at Raffles or a Daiquiri at the Floradita, Havana. List any seasonal adjustments.
Relationship to the Total Product	Describe how this particular product – e.g. a hotel, restaurant, tourist attraction fits in with the total product. What kind of total product and experience does this market segment or segments enjoy when visiting the destination? What contribution does this product make to total satisfactions? If the product is optional – the local museum – to whom does it appeal and why is it important?
Access	Describe the location of the product? How well located is it in relation to the rest of the product? How accessible is it to its markets? Do people come alone or in groups? Are they organised by a tour operator?
Image/features	Describe the destination's core image and brand-image in relation to this product. Indicate how these are related to the product through the tertiary image. Also how this is emphasised through particular "spin". Describe the use of slogans, logos and other devices. List any seasonal adjustments.
Price	Describe the range of prices and likely average spend. In a hotel list the average room rate achieved, the length of stay and the rate of single/double occupancy. Indicate sticker prices and the discount and promotional pricing. Show the pricing in relation to the competition. Disaggregate spending by type of service e.g. in a museum entrance charges, and spending in the museum shop, restaurant and snack bar. What is the pricing strategy – yield management? List any seasonal adjustments.
Competing products	One competes with the same or similar products, e.g. a hotel with other hotels. One may also compete with other products, e.g. a good dinner out may compete with buying a locally produced painting. Make a list of competing products – in the same destination, in other destinations. In particular list the competitors – similar product, same market. Influence of tour operators. Shares of the market. Competitive strategies.
Promotion	Current promotional activities; this product, this market. Consumer and trade promotion. Assessment of past and future effectiveness. List any seasonal adjustments.
Sales networks	Ease of purchase. Advertising. Public relations. Direect mail. Other promotional activities. Sales and reservations outlets. The internet. Tour operators. Influence of retail outlets; geographical coverage. Organised travel. Companies selling packages (including this product) to this market. Current programme; future perspectives. Number of packages. Promotion. Sales networks. Sales performance. List any seasonal adjustments.
Position	This describes, after an assessment of all the above factors, the position of this product in relation to competing products. Total outbound tourism. proportion in this market. Current numbers received. Market share. Future perspectives.

Figure 11.3 The Positioning Matrix – the Micro Level

chapter twelve
Promotion

This chapter starts by examining where promotion fits in, indicating its importance to image-building and positioning. It then lists and describes the various promotional techniques and approaches. It goes on to examine public and private sector roles and the possibility of clashes through duplication, distortion and contradiction. The chapter then lists the different levels of promotion, and examines joint public and private sector initiatives. It explains indirect promotion and concludes with a discussion of promotional budgets.

Where Does Promotion Fit in?

Marketing underlies all aspects of a business. It is based on customer needs and the development of marketing mixes which satisfy them. Promotion helps to build and reinforce the brand-image and secure the destination's overall positioning (see Figure 12.1)

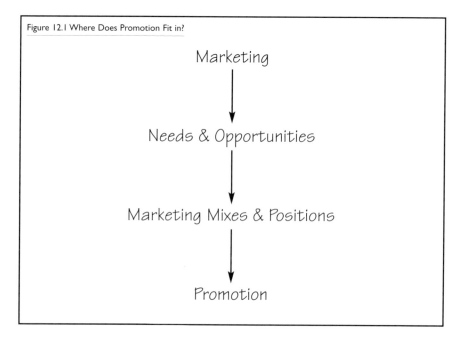

Figure 12.1 Where Does Promotion Fit in?

Marketing

Needs & Opportunities

Marketing Mixes & Positions

Promotion

Promotion lets people know that their needs have been filled. It persuades them to buy within an appropriately priced product range. It can also adapt readily to changing priorities. It can be adjusted, reduced, or even discontinued. Given adequate lead time, promotion is easy to change.

Chapters 8 and 14 discuss setting sales targets, disaggregated according to each market and product segment. Chapter 11 discusses the positioning which underpins these targets. The mix of marketing mixes comes together to form a marketing strategy aimed at certain results. Promotion makes no sense as an activity unless it is evaluated against the results achieved.

What Does Promotion Consist of?

Promotion is designed to tell or remind users that there is a marketing mix which can satisfy their particular needs better than anything else. One relays this message in a number of different ways, using different approaches and techniques. Effective promotion depends on how well one expresses the message, where one says it, whether it reaches the right people, whether they understand it clearly, and whether they act on it.

Promotion can consist of one, more or all of the following approaches and techniques:

- **Advertising.** This is a non personal form of communication using a wide variety of media – printed (newspapers, magazines, travel agency manuals and information booklets etc), radio, television, and billboards. It is normally paid and can be aimed at consumers or the travel trade itself.

- **Printed material.** This covers a wide variety of material: brochures, posters, leaflets, promotional manuals or catalogues, postcards and other collateral material such as pens.

- **Direct mail.** This is anything promotional sent directly through the mail. It can consist of brochures, single page announcements, regular newsletters, bulletins and up-dates. Any of these may be accompanied by a letter. It is always based on a well prepared mailing list, targeting particular people or companies.

- **Direct sales.** This takes the form of personal sales calls either through visits or telephone calls by a salesperson. Seldom used by a destination itself, it might be used by hotels, resorts and tour operators.

- **Internet.** This is already put to wide promotional use, particularly through destination web sites which project the image and provide complete product information. They can also allow for bookings and sales transactions.

- **Audio visual material.** This material usually consists of videos, film, recorded items, and multimedia compact discs.

- **Travel writing.** This is any kind of travel writing from daily newspapers to magazines and specialised publications. It may also include books of various kinds, particularly guide books.

- **Familiarisation trips.** These are complimentary trips offered to prospective buyers (usually travel agency staff) to visit a destination, and experience the product firsthand.

- **Trade shows and exhibitions.** This is where destinations mount a stand, organising at the same time a programme of activities. This acts as a focus for its various private sector operators (particularly inbound tour operators and hotels) to do business with foreign tour operators and the travel trade.

- **Special promotions.** These may consist of any activity organised to promote sales. For example, they could consist of special festivals, international competitions, or sports events.

- **Representative offices.** These are offices aimed at promotion rather than sales. They are there to provide an information service and a point of contact, to distribute printed material, handle local public relations, make sales contacts and support the overall promotional programme. They are usually the government tourism administration's (GTA) offices overseas either staffed and organised directly, or contracted out to a local company. Offices also have an intelligence and data collection role that contributes to market research. Airlines, large hotel, resort and other companies may also operate sales and representative offices.

- **Public relations.** This includes any other activities aimed at disseminating the brand-image and the destination. It can include radio and TV shows, fashion and the arts.

The above list applies to promotion irrespective of whether it is undertaken by public or private sectors.

Public and Private Sector Roles

Institutional promotion is public sector coordinated or led. It is normally carried out by a destination through the GTA, working in collaboration with the private sector. Its main purpose is to promote the total destination in a general but forceful and striking way. It projects the brand-image clearly and powerfully, but may modify it slightly according to the particular needs of each market. In this, it provides comprehensive, persuasively communicated information on every aspect of the product. It also supports the image and product with price range information. It answers the question – how do I go there? – by giving clear indications about tour operators, airlines and sales outlets.

Private sector promotion is carried out by each particular tourism enterprise.

The extent and nature of the promotion depends on the size and type of operation. It also depends on the management's marketing commitment and promotional know-how.

Large outbound tour operators situated in the major markets have considerable promotional expertise. Similarly an international chain of resorts and hotels also commands considerable promotional punch. By comparison small guest houses or camping sites may have little idea about promotion, buying only a listing in one or other tourist facilities guide. However another kind of small hotel may belong to a marketing cooperative, benefiting from an extensive and shared promotional programme. Many other hotels rely on the tour operators to sell their rooms (see Chapter 5).

Institutional promotion communicates most of all the image and appeal of the destination. It captures peoples' imagination, excites them, and gives them all the information they need. It persuades them to come and see for themselves. Or if they've already been, it persuades them to come again. It does not promote particular facilities, programmes or package holidays. However, it does act as a signpost pointing buyers in the right directions.

Private sector promotion follows up where the public sector stops. It sells the specific programme – the seat, the room, the actual experience. It makes the visit possible. However, the private sector also projects an image and gives information.

The dividing line between public and private sector roles is sometimes fuzzy. There can be problems of duplication, distortion and contradiction. This is the danger.

Generally public sector led promotion has the following scope:

- *it advertises the product* – through posters and printed material and possibly in the consumer and trade press. Also through other media – TV, radio, direct mail etc.

- *it exhibits the product* – at trade exhibitions and trade fairs.

- *it provides an experience of the product* – through travel familiarisation trips.

- *it writes about the product* – through travel writers and other editorial copy guide books, travel books.

- *it talks about the product* – through public relations activities, talk-ins, presentations etc.

- *it shows the product* – through video, film and audio visual presentations.

- *it draws attention to the product* – through festivals, competitions and special promotions.

These various promotional activities and approaches link together through integrated promotional programmes. Each message builds upon the previous message, while establishing the foundation for the next message. Promotion always links forwards and backwards. It is incremental; it adds and explains more, "we told you this before – now let's tell you this". Promotion keeps the product prominent in the eyes of its potential users. It keeps the destination's image sharp and the product's appeal fresh. It explains how much it costs and where and how to buy it.

Public and Private Sector Disharmony

Private sector enterprises tend to develop their promotion independently, without sufficient reference to parallel initiatives. The clashes between public and private sector promotion may be as follows (see Figure 12.2):

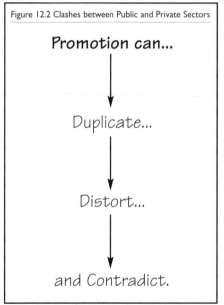

Figure 12.2 Clashes between Public and Private Sectors

Promotion can...

Duplicate...

Distort...

and Contradict.

• **Duplication.** Some repetition helps to get a message across; unnecessary duplication is a waste of money. Public and private sector promotional material and copy should be looked at together, as part of the same well coordinated programme. Each piece or item should build on the other in a harmonious way. For example, if the public sector has produced a good tourist map of the city the private sector has no need to duplicate it.

• **Distortion.** There should be consistency in the message which a destination sends out. For example the image of the place may revolve around ideas of elegance, tranquillity, restraint and restfulness. To portray it as one of the "liveliest and swingingest spots on the coast" is therefore a distortion. Foreign tour operators often do this. They get the message wrong and project the image in a mistaken light.

• **Contradiction.** There can be contradictions of both a quantitative and qualitative kind. One brochure can say there are five golf courses while another lists eight. One says that there is an abundance of well manicured gardens. Another says that most gardens were seriously damaged in the last hurricane.

These dangers can be avoided by sound coordination between private and public sector interests.

The Different Levels of Promotion

Some promotional activities are conceived as long range reach, designed to promote a destination internationally or inter-regionally. Some are medium range reach, within the same region of countries or within the one country. Some are short range reach, concentrating on promotion within the region or locality.

Promotional programmes are therefore developed and organised at four different levels:

- **Internationally.** Governments may link together on a regional basis to develop a joint promotional programme. For example, the countries of the South Pacific have a joint initiative as do many of the world's regions. The private sector, through either multinational companies or marketing cooperatives, also have internationally organised promotional programmes.

- **Nationally.** The GTA coordinates the promotion of the country as a whole abroad and at home. This promotes both international inbound and domestic travel. On the private sector side a chain of hotels or a marketing cooperative, for example, promotes a nationwide product.

- **Regionally.** The tourism office of a particular region of the country may have its own promotion. For example, a region such as the Loire Valley in France or the Lake District in England. A major city is best equated to a region; for example, London or Amsterdam. Some of these programmes may promote the region or city internationally, projecting and reinforcing the image; some may promote it domestically. Some of it may have a short range reach, promoting activities and attractions within the region. Private sector companies with a significant regional presence may also give their promotion a particularly regional focus. A high proportion of such regional promotion may be medium reach and domestic in its focus.

- **Locally.** Municipalities and local resorts may also undertake promotion. Long range reach may be confined to brochures, posters and information leaflets sent on request. In the case of a substantial integrated resort complex, such as Cancun in Mexico, there may be more extensive promotional activities. Other promotion may have a short range reach, designed to promote activities and attractions to visitors already there. Local hotels, resorts and restaurants and other facilities, may also undertake short range reach promotion within both the locality and the region.

Joint Public and Private Sector Approaches

The public and private sectors may form a joint marketing organisation, at any or all of the above levels, to coordinate their promotional approaches and programmes. This can range from a consultative committee at the local level, to a national statutory board, council or corporation set up with its own powers to raise and spend money. Whatever the organisational form chosen, it should be able to have the following objectives:

- To review the tourism policy, future directions of tourism, present development strategy, marketing mix and the regeneration, re-engineering and expansion of the sector.

- To discuss and agree the sector's sales targets, in the light of past performance and future perspectives.

- To agree the annual promotional programme, monitoring its subsequent execution and effectiveness.

- To review and agree the promotional budget, earmarking any private sector joint funding and in-kind contributions.

- To coordinate closely with all private sector interests promoting the destination, including airlines, foreign tour operators and hotel or resort companies, to try to maintain brand-image consistency. This should avoid the dangers of duplication, distortions and contradictions already noted.

Large tourism enterprises – particularly hotels, airlines and tour operators – often try to increase government's promotional expenditure so as to lessen their own. In some developing countries there are even astonishing examples of aid donors using public money to pay for pages in tour operators' catalogues.

Small enterprises have less promotional expertise and small budgets and need advice and assistance. This is where the public sector can help.

The promotional results expected should be expressed in measurable terms and supported by a list of activities to be undertaken. The GTA can act as the secretariat to any committee or board, coordinating activities, preparing reports and providing the administrative back-up. Promotion can be divided into the six following areas for planning purposes:

- advertising including direct mail
- printed material and audio-visual material
- the Internet
- travel trade shows and exhibitions
- familiaristion trips; travel agencies, tour operators and travel writers
- special promotions and other activities

Promotion informs people, educates them, entertains them, stimulates interest and captures their imagination. These elements tend to be mixed together in every promotional activity.

Indirect Promotion

Indirect promotion is usually unplanned and just happens, as the destination's image, reputation and quality become widely recognised. This promotion is at no cost to the destination, and can be greatly beneficial. For example:

- writing and talking favourably about the destination e.g. in newspapers, magazines, television, radio, and the media in general.
- other favourable mentions of the destination in various contexts.
- people's personal recommendations made to their friends, relatives and colleagues.

Other indirect promotion may also be initiated by various parties but is not without cost. The destination may be invited to participate on a cost sharing basis. Proposals are usually made sufficiently in advance for activities to be included, if agreed, in a marketing plan. For example:

- publications may plan editorial copy on the destination, but require (or reasonably request) that some advertising space be taken.
- a holiday in the destination is provided as a prize in media run competitions e.g. in the press or television quiz shows.
- the destination is used as the setting for a fashion shoot.
- the destination is similarly used as the backdrop for the marketing of related services or products. This is particularly true of various luxury brands. A credit card company may promote the use of its card by advertising a particular type of holiday.
- the destination is linked to airline promotion.

The Promotional Budget

There are three main sources for funding tourism promotion;

- the destination's public sector budget,
- the aggregate of national private sector expenditure (e.g. the hotels, resorts and inbound tour operators),
- the aggregate of international private sector expenditure (e.g. the multinational hotel and resort companies, and foreign tour operators).

The mix and make-up of total expenditure (combining these three sources) differs from country to country, destination to destination. In most countries it is possible to estimate it, based on the researched ratios of promotional expenditure to revenue. In many destinations, total private sector expenditures dwarf those of the public sector.

Unfortunately, governments tend to allocate funds based on guesses, broad estimates and last year's figures. One should ask whether the amount requested is really necessary? Is it well spent? What would happen if the money wasn't spent? Unfortunately, there may be no close evaluation of expenditures and results achieved.

Comparisons between the promotional expenditures of different countries may be misleading. A country with a large and successful tourism sector may get more money allocated to it, whether it needs it or not. Various promotional expenditure ratios may also be misleading; e.g. promotional expenditure per international visitor, or the number of pieces of promotional material per visitor.

Advertising agencies and promotional specialists are in the business of spending money not saving it. They all tend to make extravagant claims for their proposals. Promotional expenditure should be treated with scepticism. The best advice – always doubt – never stop questioning – ask for data – introduce rigour – remain hard to convince. Effectiveness per dollar spent, according to type of promotional activity, is also an important consideration.

As we have already noted, public sector promotion should project the correct image constantly and consistently. It should keep the destination at the forefront (e.g. through trade shows, familiarisation trips) and it should support the private sector with material (printed and audio visual items). Budgets should not be based on how much do we have to spend, but on how much should we spend. How much should we spend should be based on a clear understanding of the public sector role. Some initiatives jointly funded by the private and public sectors ensure that the sector acts together.

Any joint public and private sector promotional body should monitor the success of its activities. Transparency is essential; effective control is only possible if everything is out in the open. There is usually plenty of evidence; from the results achieved, travel trade feedback, visitor surveys, and published information.

However, many countries have no basis to evaluate their promotional expenditure and its effectiveness. As noted, they justify promotional expenditures by comparing them to last year, or with other destinations, or with any tourism growth and increased earnings. If the trends are up it's because of promotion, they say. If they are down, because of lack of promotion. Yet these things may tell us very little about promotional effectiveness. One should look for better evidence and ask for the proof.

A marketing professional's status tends to be dictated by the size of the budget he or she controls. There is a natural tendency to ask for more money. It is important to be aware of this and to justify all expenditure. A GTA should work with the private sector and match funds or make contributions, playing a supporting and catalytic role. One should build the image, help to promote the country but let the private sector promote itself.

section two
the implementation

chapter thirteen

Governance

This chapter introduces Part II of the book. It starts by explaining governance and the normal range of government responsibilities. It then describes the composition of the tourism sector and lists the parties involved. It goes on to discuss the management needs and continues by explaining the role of a government tourism administration (GTA). The chapter then looks at the words and concepts used to describe this role, including the relative meanings of planning, policy and strategy. It also explains management and tourism development plans. The chapter concludes with consensus building and the development of an agreed sector-wide strategy, illustrating – as an example – the Delphi technique.

Looking at Governance

The World Bank defines governance as, "The manner in which power is exercised in the management of a country's economic and social resources for development". (World Bank, 1994)

With a freely elected government, policy represents the majority view. It sets out guidelines for the development of strategies and action programmes. However, politicians have to know:

- What's possible in terms of resources and capacities. Is it possible to do certain things?

- What people want. Will they give their support?

- What constraints are imposed by international agreements and treaties. Is one free to act?

A government is effective according to how it organises itself, motivates its personnel, obtains help and advice, exercises its authority, and centralises or decentralises. There is normally constant interaction between the following parties:

- **the politicians** – they try to maintain party unity, fulfil their mandate, justify the confidence shown in them, establish a record of achievement, and make bold claims about the future.

- **the civil servants** – they implement the policies and strategies emanating from the politicians, while ensuring the effective functioning of government.

- **the consultants and advisers** – they counsel politicians and civil servants – sometimes about what to do – but mostly about how to do. They recommend what activities to undertake and what systems and methods to use.

- **the professional and trade associations and institutions, the consumer organisations, interest groups and lobbyists** – they must be consulted and listened to – their points of view noted and assessed – their support solicited and mobilised. They lobby accordingly.

- **the trade unions and organised labour** – their viewpoints are also noted and assessed.

- **the media** – monitor government's performance and either endorse and support, or oppose and criticise, its actions and efforts.

- **the major corporate entities** – these are the companies sufficiently large and important that they are consulted on matters of industry-wide importance. They lobby accordingly.

- **the rest of the industry** – everybody is consulted, particularly the mass of small hotel and tourism enterprises.

- **international organisations and bodies** – particularly intergovernmental – are consulted. Information is shared, common standards agreed, and international treaties and conventions signed.

Managing the Tourism Sector

The sector is made up of a variety of activities: the airlines and other transport companies, hotels, resorts and other accommodation units, restaurants and catering outlets, shops, tourist attractions, recreational and entertainment facilities, travel agencies and tour operators, booking and information services. It also includes ancillary services; for example, the police, health, education, postal, religious and banking services. Also included are government agencies which either have regulatory responsibilities related to tourism, or provide infrastructure or support services; e.g. the agencies responsible for finance, transport, labour, education, public works, economic affairs, planning and the environment.

All of the private sector enterprises pursue their own policies and objectives. While they must conform with the law, they run their own affairs and make their own decisions. However, to bring these together there is a need for coordination. A need to look for, agree, and share a sense of purpose. Government departments should share a similar sense of purpose. They should liaise to avoid duplication of effort, contradictory strategies, and the wasteful use of resources

The private sector combines its strengths through various trade and professional associations. It can then speak with a single voice. It may also believe in the advantages of certain joint training, purchasing and marketing initiatives. It also tries to generate a positive image with the general public, enlisting its sympathy and support.

Many GTAs still think of their role as "regulation". However, a GTA doesn't just regulate – it coordinates an assortment of autonomous businesses and organisations. As a government agency it doesn't rule over the private sector, it is answerable to it.

If the GTA did not coordinate tourism-related decisions, other government agencies would be forced to make their minds up by themselves. For example, immigration authorities on work permits, public works on infrastructure, planning authorities on land use, education authorities on training, civil aviation on air transport, and finance on fiscal policies. They are best guided within the framework of a comprehensive tourism development strategy.

Approaching Tourism Sector Management

How does a government tackle tourism? The government's idea of managing the sector may be confined to three main areas:

- The government wants to see the sector prosper and improve, making its expected contribution to the economy. To do this the government checks that its fiscal and economic policies create encouraging conditions. It may also choose to establish special incentives for businesses in particular development areas. It monitors, through its system of information and statistics, that sectoral performance is satisfactory.

- In particular, it wants to see the sector generate income and sufficient government revenue. It also wants the sector to create a certain number of jobs, and contribute to social and economic development in general.

- The government also wants to ensure that the legal framework governing the conduct of the sector is appropriate and adequate. Such a framework is likely to cover the payment of taxes, the safety of the consumer, employment of staff, adherence to fair business practices, certain planning and building regulations (including minimum hygiene and fire prevention standards) as well as the satisfaction of some minimum quality standards.

In fulfilling this role government will normally establish a series of consultative committees, boards, or councils, enabling it to liaise with the private sector.

The private sector will agree that the above actions lie within the normal scope and responsibility of a government. However, it could add other areas such as product development, marketing, human resources development and public awareness programmes. Government can play a strong role, even take the lead, in coordinating an industry-wide approach to all four of these areas. It can choose to:

- Incorporate a product development approach within its planning, land use and zoning regulations, determining how the marketing mixes in various areas can best be regenerated, re-engineered or expanded (see Chapters 16 and 17).

- Link government and private sector marketing, possibly funding and leading a joint marketing organisation. This possibility was discussed in Chapter 12. It can raise a special levy to help fund such an initiative, developing an integrated industry-wide marketing plan.

- Coordinate the development of occupational skill standards, liaise with educational and training institutions, review curricula and accredit programmes, participate in testing and certification, and require minimum numbers of properly trained staff (see Chapter 22).

- Coordinate a programme of public awareness about tourism to encourage the participation of the local community and keep it informed (see Chapter 15).

The Secretary General of the WTO has pointed to changes throughout the world in the balance of tourism responsibilities: e.g. disengagement of certain governments from tourism, reduction of public budgets, privatisation and partnership modalities, and decentralisation (WTO, 1999).

Government should take on its management responsibilities while not acting alone in an interventionist manner. While the private sector could possibly handle the product development, marketing, human resources and public awareness programmes, it is better to work with government. Private sector bodies tend to lose sight of the overall sectoral view and often act quite narrowly. Also the private sector has no single organisation capable of taking on the management and coordination of the sector as a whole.

One can argue that pluralism, the explosion of initiatives by the private sector, creates a multiplicity of approaches and solutions. Out of this a destination remains more competitive, more attuned to the market. One does not want to choke this process – to stifle private sector initiatives. Out of the plurality of alternatives, competitive market forces bring the best to the top – keeping the sector relevant and up-to-date.

However, government should help to channel this creativity, not choke it. It can play a central role, through the GTA, acceptable to the component sub-sectors. However this is only possible if the GTA can field a team of trained and experienced tourism professionals.

The GTA should not be what it alone decides it wants to be. It should try to be what the private sector wants it to be. It should not impose its role on the sector. Instead it should play a role which responds to the sector's needs and wants.

The Role of the Government Tourism Administration (GTA)

Effective management is the only way to avoid tourism's abuses and excesses. For example, the wrong things built, poor marketing, inadequate training, and bad economic, social and environmental mistakes. It is the only way to develop tourism to meet a country's needs and expectations. This is not a simplistic position which ignores the influences of globalisation. Good management establishes resolute criteria by which to balance and reconcile all the different sets of needs.

GTA is the preferred term for the government's organisational arrangements for the management of tourism. It includes any international offices and is an appropriate term to cover all levels of government in all parts of the country, at national as well as regional and local levels.

Each government decides how to organise tourism bearing in mind local practice, preferences and political considerations. For example, a single ministry is made responsible for tourism – either alone or together with other responsibilities. A board, corporation or other type of semi-autonomous body may then be established to carry out the day-to-day responsibilities.

One can also establish more than one body to achieve objectives. For example, establish a separate joint marketing board to undertake promotion and coordinate sector-wide marketing. Or establish a joint venture corporation to manage the development of a particular area, tackling the site planning, infrastructure development, and investment promotion. Or establish an organisation to handle industry-wide training.

In many cases the GTA, as a part of the conventional civil service, may lack sufficiently qualified and experienced people to take an effective lead role by itself. For example, government bureaucrats in many third world countries are often poorly paid and motivated. They are also switched frequently from sector to sector. Bureaucrats in general may be mainly interested in personal status, job security and career advancement, all of which may have little correlation with technical knowledge and expertise. And the GTA itself may have little impact beyond the administration of regulations and the collection and publication of tourism statistics.

However, staff can be separated from the strictly government service into semi autonomous bodies (the QUANGO – quasi autonomous non governmental organisations). These bodies can be more able to recruit, develop and retain career specialists. They can also recruit from the public or private sector, seeking the most experienced and knowledgeable people available. They can also retain the services of expert consultants more easily. They can also borrow specialists on secondment from the private sector. They can also take their funding from wherever feasible, and act in private sector ways. Such bodies or boards have tended to be favoured in many countries.

The tourism sector needs to be represented at the highest level. What does one do for tourism? – What does tourism do for us? – are important political questions. Tourism policy is therefore placed at ministerial level. A senior member of government represents tourism, explains it, and makes a case for it. However, if a complete Ministry of Tourism is established for this role alone, there is a danger that it will duplicate the functions of the tourist board (QUANGO). This sometimes happens. It need not – a Ministry can be streamlined with a small staff and a clear and specific mandate. It represents tourism at central government level, while coordinating with the provincial governments. It also submits its annual budgetary requirements, providing all the supporting arguments. Alternatively, tourism can be included in an existing ministry – usually the Ministry of Trade – to play the same role.

Figure 13.1 uses a matrix to illustrate the functions which need to be incorporated at the various levels of government. It is important for a GTA to reflect all the functions listed in its organisation chart, its job descriptions and work plans. It is equally important that these jobs are filled with well qualified personnel.

In managing tourism, the public sector joins with the private sector to form an effective partnership. The GTA may use a variety of joint committees, advisory boards, and consultative bodies. It has to find ways to cover all interests and opinions, from all branches of the sector.

Words and Concepts

This chapter indicates two basic choices on tourism management:

- one leaves the sector hanging loosely together – mostly uncoordinated and poorly informed – lacking the power of concerted planning and action;

- or, one welds it into a more effective entity – coordinated and aware – keeping it moving forwards in the common interest.

The second option is clearly preferable, with the following kinds of words most frequently used:

Level of Government	Responsibilities & Functions	Executive or Consultative Mechanisms
MINISTERIAL (national government – cabinet level).	PLANS, POLICIES & STRATEGIES - related particularly to the economic, social and legislative frameworks and developmental needs.	MINISTRY OF TOURISM – or a ministry responsible for a number of sectors. Plus A NATIONAL TOURISM COUNCIL or consultative committee at the highest level.
TOURISM ADMIN (at the national level). Overall management of the sector. Establishment of clear implementation plans and guidelines in each major sphere of development. Coordination with the private sector, and the development and refinement of the necessary management tools.	IMPLEMENTATION (at the national level) – in each sphere of development: product development (regeneration, re-engineering and expansion), marketing, human resources development, research and statistics (information system) and publications, regulation, public awareness, international relations, industry liaison, tourist information and services, international offices and regional and local representation.	A statutory board/QUANGO responsible for tourism management. Possibly some separate statutory boards, development agencies, or other bodies established – for areas such as marketing, training, and development. Joint initiatives with the private sector and various consultative or advisory committees.
REGIONAL, LOCAL AND MUNICIPAL LEVELS. Regional, local and municipal development, acting on the established guidelines and using the management tools effectively. Close working relationships with the private sector.	REGIONAL AND LOCAL IMPLEMENTATION – in the same spheres of development. Responsibility for certain functions may be combined together, depending on the size and complexity of tourism.	REGIONAL, LOCAL AND MUNICIPAL GOVERNMENT The implementation of land use planning and the administration of regulations in general, are usually a part of local government. The GTA at this level may also be incorporated within local government. However, some functions may be jointly organised with the private sector – particularly, tourist information and marketing. Various consultative and advisory committees.

Figure 13.1 Government Tourism Administration

- **liaise** – to ensure cooperation and concerted action;
- **consult** – to seek advice and opinions; to exchange views and information;
- **coordinate** – to combine in a harmonious interrelationship;
- **collaborate** – to work with one another;
- **integrate** – to incorporate into a cohesive whole.

These words all contain the same idea of building a unified approach. Similarly, words such as combine, join forces, bring together and mobilisation contain the idea of strengthening this sense of unity.

The term strategy is often used interchangeably with policy and plan. However, strategy is best used selectively to describe aspects of the overall plan. First it is used to summarise the plan's main proposals and directions, in the form of an agreed tourism development strategy. This can usually be published as a concise document of 25-40 pages. The term is also used to summarise particular areas of responsibility such as the marketing strategy, product development strategy, and human resources development strategy. While all chapters act as a basis for the plan, policies and strategies, the checklist detailed in Chapters 23 and 24 serves as a comprehensive aide memoire.

- Planning is a function of management. It includes policy and strategy formulation. A tourism development plan is not something done now and then, planning is an ongoing part of management. Performance is monitored, and the plan is constantly reviewed and adjusted.

- As noted, policy means the agreed underlying values and the corresponding guidelines which should be followed. For example one of the policies might read – `to use tourism to conserve the uniqueness of the country's heritage, its history, and its culture'. Policies indicate what a country

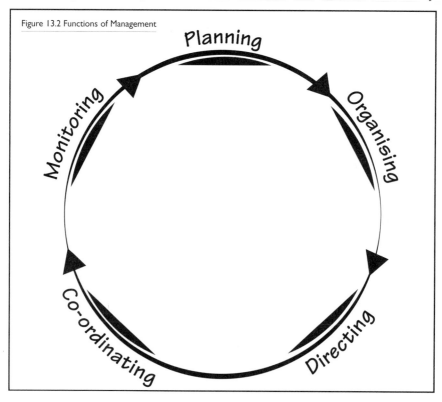

Figure 13.2 Functions of Management

Planning

Monitoring

Organising

Co-ordinating

Directing

wants tourism to be, contribute and achieve. A full list of example policies is included in Chapter 16.

- Contained within the plan, strategies are extracted to describe specific aspects. They describe the objectives to target, detail the corresponding activities to undertake, and list the results to achieve.

The various words and concepts described above should be placed within a management framework. The five functions of management (see Figure 13.2) developed from Henri Fayol, can be summarised as follows (Doswell, 1997):

- *Plans* set clear directions and how to achieve them.
- *Organisation* tackles the mobilisation and deployment of resources and technology.
- *Direction* provides the leadership to maintain the necessary sense of purpose.
- *Coordination* keeps everybody and everything working together.
- *Monitoring* or control keeps performance on track with the plan.

These functions are described in more detail in Chapter 17.

Tourism Development Planning

The sector is managed in an ongoing and incremental way. One learns from experience and adds, year-to-year, to one's knowledge. One reviews plans against actual performance, making corrections and refinements on a continuing basis. And as part of this process one implements as one plans. A developed sector has an excellent information system, forecasts of growth, development strategies, lists of project opportunities and investment needs, and marketing and human resources plans. One also knows the expected and potential economic contribution of tourism, and shapes and controls the social and environmental impacts.

A GTA should monitor performance, identify trends and project the expansion and growth of tourism. It should maintain an up-to-date development strategy. It should also provide inputs to other government departments, on tourism's contributions and needs.

A plan usually includes the following main areas – marketing, product development including recommended physical plans and land use, human resources development, research and statistics including an information system, the regulatory framework, a public awareness programme, international and public relations, and an organisational development programme for the GTA itself. The plan may also include a system to monitor tourism's economic, social and environmental impacts.

Such plans are often used as a device to kick-start tourism development. However, planning should not be separated from a GTA's ongoing responsibilities and functions. It is an integral part of the total management process. This process is assisted by setting clear objectives and assigning responsibilities accordingly. With strategies and objectives agreed, as far as possible, by the sector as a whole.

Consensus Building

In Europe the system of government is essentially adversarial. One side opposes the other and majority voting wins the day. Only some issues, it is judged, warrant any effort to build an all-party consensus. However, if people have to live and work together – as is the case with local tourism – it is better to try and build a consensus.

People tend to feel more involved in political decisions when their own lives and behaviour happen to be directly affected. As a result, local issues are often treated in an emotional and self interested way. National issues, by contrast, appear remote and tend to be approached more dispassionately.

As a consequence, governments try to leave the local and regional levels to decide for themselves. They retain for the national level the issues which must be decided for everybody. This is the principle of subsidiarity espoused by the European Union. Figure 13.1, as noted, shows the division of responsibilities according to the various levels of government. Figure 13.3 recalls the responsibilities to be found in a GTA's organisation chart.

There is a view that a consensus must necessarily represent the correct course of action. This does not follow. It can also mean that everybody agrees to do the wrong thing. For example, in the town of Eymet in France, the tradespeople voted to allow parking in the thirteenth century central square. A better decision, at least in the peak months of the tourist season, would have

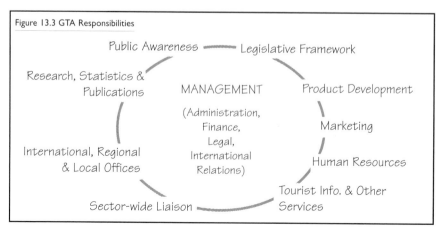

Figure 13.3 GTA Responsibilities

Public Awareness ——— Legislative Framework

Research, Statistics & Publications

MANAGEMENT

(Administration, Finance, Legal, International Relations)

Product Development

Marketing

International, Regional & Local Offices

Human Resources

Sector-wide Liaison

Tourist Info. & Other Services

been to pedestrianise the square, developing it as a focal point, to allow people to stroll, mingle, take refreshments, listen to music and generally enjoy an outstanding setting. Apart from enhancing Eymet as a tourist centre, this would create improved revenue earning opportunities for the shopkeepers and restaurateurs involved.

Public awareness, training programmes, and small enterprise advisory services, help people think through the options. Consensus building, as with all decision making, should be accompanied by the appropriate technical analyses and training.

Delphi is a technique used for getting agreement. It taps the experience and insight of people who know the issues well and can comment accordingly. It does this by soliciting their written response to questions. These comments are returned, processed, and the results are sent out for further comment. A consensus starts to emerge. The technique involves several successive rounds and normally maintains the anonymity of respondents. It can also use either conventional mail or E-mail. A facilitating group manage the exercise, reviewing and processing the results as they develop. Delphi is best used to predict outcomes based on the same hard data.

It is tricky to use Delphi to shape future strategy, since there are many different interpretations and viewpoints. However, a certain agreed stream of thinking can emerge. People move together in the same general direction. Delphi is also educational, it informs and guides. Positions can change, conflicts defuse, and opinions converge.

How does one go about this? The GTA convenes a meeting of people from across the sector. One agrees the terms of reference for a tourism strategy task group. A start is made. This group represents the sector and manages the Delphi process. It is free to co-opt anybody it wishes. It adopts a high profile approach with maximum transparency. Members are not anonymous and press releases keep the public informed. Meetings are open, individual presentations are heard, people are free to speak. The issues are aired, a strategy is shaped. Questionnaires are sent out and people respond. The Delphi process is set in motion.

Involvement, Participation and Change

The tourism sector is composed of diverse individuals and organisations brought together by common interests. The coordination of the public and private sectors lies at the heart of sound tourism sector management. The dangers of clashes between private and public sectors was discussed in Chapter 12 while Chapter 14 describes further aspects of their relationship. It also compares their different ways of seeing tourism.

References

Doswell, Roger. (1997). *Tourism – How Effective Management Makes the Difference*, Butterworth Heinemann.

World Bank. (1994). *Governance – The World Bank's Experience, p.vii.*

Frangialli. F. (1999). *Secretary General of WTO, Preliminary Remarks, WTO Commission for Africa, Thirty third meeting, Accra, Ghana, 4 May.*

chapter fourteen
Sales

T he chapter starts by describing forecasting and the development of sales targets. It goes on to explain distribution and sales and the importance of facilitation. It then brings together the previous references to tour operators, describing the approach which they adopt and how they put their programmes together. It goes on to describe the catalogue or brochure, and the increasing influence of the Internet and package travel regulations. The chapter then examines reservations systems and the role of retail travel agencies. It discusses the possibilities of checking the sales network and coverage provided. It then summarises the part played by airlines, and the selling of business and convention tourism. The chapter concludes by highlighting the importance of speedy sales decisions.

Forecasting

Forecasting is essential. One has to gauge likely future business and set realistic and attainable sales targets. However, forecasting can be wishful and naïve – "anybody's best guess" or the proverbial "picking figures out of the air". Or it can be systematic and methodical, based on a complete analysis of trends, market potential and change. The principles were already discussed in Chapter 8 on market research. Figure 14.1 sets out, as a matrix, the various approaches.

It is clear that in most destinations a market potential exists. Even a small share of world tourism is sizeable (one quarter of one per cent in the year 2000 represents over 1.5 million international arrivals). However, the feasibility of any sales targets depends on the existing products and the possibilities of regeneration, re-engineering and expansion. There can be no sales without products. And the nature of these sales are dictated by the types of products. In this sense, tourism is supply led.

If forecasts exceed current product capacity, they assume the addition of new product. If they are based on the possible regeneration of existing facilities, this also represents new product. Forecasts are therefore based on a product which does not exist. They are therefore a forecast of new additions or product improvements. This is the same as a forecast of new investment. A forecast of 5000 new rooms may therefore comprise a forecast of up to half a billion dollars in new investment.

Qualitative	Quantitative
EXPERT EVALUATION Knowledge and experience of the product/s and market/s. Familiarity with trends and developments. Complete data and analysis. The disaggregation of market segments. Full account taken of product limitations and any competitive advantages.	**MATHEMATICAL MODELS** Information technology application – computer-driven. Identifies key variables and relationships. Reveals major opportunities and bottlenecks. Dynamic model – simulates real-life interactions – calculates probable outcomes.
INTUITION – BEST GUESS Empiricism and cognition. Interpretation of trends and likely events. Seeing and knowing – entrepreneurial judgement. Can we do better than last year? Tends not to disaggregate the market – but looks at it as a whole. Delphi method takes a cross section of sector-wide expert opinion. Builds "best guess" consensus.	**EXTRAPOLATION** Projects forwards based on past performance. Results are extrapolated to form new forecasts. Tends to ignore improvement, development and change in general. The past may be full of deficiencies and lost opportunities. The future may hold major changes in the market.

Figure 14.1 Forecasting Matrix (based on a matrix idea in – Majaro S. 1993)

Forecasts of new investment, especially in tourism, are often wishful and naïve. They tend not to reflect the response of potential investors themselves. Capital projects depend on the investment climate and related conditions. They are influenced by market feasibility, availability of capital, evident opportunity, the tax regime, comparative risks, destination potential, and confidence in the government and the future. Sometimes investment does flood in, as it did in South East Asia in the 1980s and early 1990s. And capital tied up in hotels and resorts cannot leave easily.

World tourism forecasts (e.g. those prepared by WTO) are generally extrapolated; i.e. projected forwards based on historical trends and growth rates. At present nobody foresees any major changes likely to stop world tourism growth. Trends also indicate an increased share of this tourism by the south – the world's less developed regions. New investment would need to support such trends.

In situations of considerable uncertainty it is sensible to make three levels of forecast – a low, medium and high. Informed people can then be asked to weight the probability of attaining the various levels – or this approach can be incorporated into the Delphi method described in Chapter 13.

Selling Tourism

The term distribution applies generally to things like agricultural produce, fish and manufactured goods. Items which have to be moved from the port, farm, or factory to the shop, showroom or supermarket shelf. Effective distribution makes the item available and easy to buy.

Tourism, in contrast, is consumed where it is produced and is mostly bought where the tourists live. It is not the product itself which is distributed. One distributes the possibility of buying the product. In tourism therefore it is more appropriate to talk about a sales network. The tourism product arrives on the shelves of high street travel retailers as a catalogue or brochure. And, or, it arrives on the Internet.

The marketing mix focuses on product development, brand-image, pricing and the satisfaction of the customers needs. Promotion persuades customers that their needs have been well met. Sales enables the buying process.

As noted previously in Chapters 5 and 8, the skill of the tour operator is to pick and package the right holiday products and to promote and sell them effectively. And to do this under a brand-image signifying reliability and quality. It is difficult for newcomers to obtain a foothold either in contracting the product or securing the sales outlets.

Facilitation

Countries which want to develop tourism need ease of access. It has to be:

- easy to get there
- easy to get in once there

Chapter 6 on transport has a brief section on visas and facilitating entry. Entry to a country should not be overly difficult.

As also noted in Chapter 6, access by air needs well located and equipped airports, internationally accepted standards of safety and the capacity to receive various types of aircraft. It also needs civil aviation policies to encourage as many incoming flights as possible. National airlines, pursuing narrow protectionist policies, are notoriously good at blocking competition and restricting demand.

Access by other forms of transport – by sea, rivers, railway or road – also require open conditions. Minimal immigration requirements facilitate entry to a country, while ensuring adequate checks and controls. In many countries immigration doesn't work hand-in-hand with the tourism authorities, and inefficient and prolonged visa processing inhibits travel.

Where countries have suppressed the normal visa requirements, substituting the automatic issuance of a tourist visa on arrival, e.g. Indonesia, it has stimulated the rapid growth of international tourism.

The Product on the Travel Agent's Shelf

Mergers have tended to concentrate European tour operations into only a few hands. This can give rise to the dangers of oligopolistic pricing discussed in Chapter 10. Prices creep up to the highest levels. On the other hand, economies of scale can lead to reduced margins and commissions. This should mean sharper competition and lower prices.

In Chapter 5 on accommodation, the tour operator's role in contracting rooms and aircraft seats was compared to the multinational companies which process and market coffee. They have the expertise to buy a basic product internationally, and process, package, promote and sell it in the major markets.

In Chapter 8 on market research, the importance if monitoring the performance of tour operators was discussed. One should try to determine their role and monitor the volume of traffic they generate.

In contracting transportation and accommodation tour operators undertake risk. They develop their own marketing mix; their expertise is based on knowing the destination, contracting the right accommodation and transport, producing a marketable product, projecting the right image, and packaging and presenting it all attractively. Business decisions then revolve around the contractual flexibility to either expand or reduce the number of seats and beds. Success also depends on the stability of the conditions at the destination. However, tour operators depend ultimately on the effectiveness of their promotion and sales coverage. Once they have their thousands of packages ready, they have to sell them. It's a perishable product, it can't be stored.

A destination's risk is its willingness, through its tourism enterprises, to trust the tour operators' capabilities to project its image and promote and sell its products.

A tour operator normally sells packages based on a number of different destination areas within a country and various places, resorts and hotels within each of these. For example, if it has a large programme to Spain it may offer the Costa Brava, Costa Blanca, Costa del Sol, Majorca and Ibiza. Within each of these it may offer 10 to 15 different hotels, resorts and self catering apartments, 2 or 3 at the lead-in price, 8 to 10 in the medium price range, and 2 to 3 at higher prices. The Canary Islands, although Spanish, are distinctive and usually marketed separately.

Tour operators break the product up according to mainstream and special interest segments described in Chapter 3. Most tour operators sell holidays for leisure, recreation and holidays (serving the mainstream and special interest markets). Some specialise in providing trips for niche markets related to religion and pilgrimages, health treatment, and sports, conventions and incentive groups.

Each tour operator has developed its own marketing mix aimed at specific types and groups of customer, each the subject of a sales target. Large tour operators serve the mainstream markets, with principally summer sun holidays. They may also aim at other parts of the market, breaking their overall product range into some or all of the following types of holiday:

- Cities/short breaks
- Winter sun (short or medium haul)
- Summer sun (short or medium haul)
- Specialist holidays for over 55s
- Long haul – novel and cultural appeal
- Winter sports (short or medium haul)
- Lakes and mountains (short or medium haul)
- Cruise – principal cruise areas -mainly fly-cruise holidays
- Flights only

Of these, summer sun holidays account for the mainstream of the market. This is the domain of the major tour operators – the market leaders. Smaller tour operators base their programmes on special interest holidays, or on distinctive types of destinations – usually long haul. They all serve market segments they know well. Customers have similar needs and trust these operators to provide the type of specialised holidays they are looking for. There are companies which specialise in an area such as golf, diving, cultural and historical interest, mountaineering, winter sports, senior citizens' holidays, yachting, or ecotourism.

To pick one thing and do it really well is a sound strategy. The brand image and the whole of the marketing mix can be sharply focused. As noted in Chapter 11, if the product range is too diverse the marketing mix can become blurred.

If a tour operator sells flights only, visitors then make their own accommodation arrangements – in a hotel, resort or any other form of accommodation. Some of these travellers may fit the visiting friends and family category.

The Tour Operator's Catalogue or Brochure

The catalogue or brochure is the most important promotional and sales tool in leisure tourism. It lists the details, prices and conditions of the package holidays offered, and is produced with a long lead time. How many catalogues or brochures there are depends on the particular tour operator and the size and range of its programme:

- a catalogue may cover similar types of holidays in various parts of the world. For example, upmarket soft adventure holidays featuring, among other holidays, safaris in East Africa, or touring in Mongolia, or cruising in Eastern Indonesia.

- a catalogue for a region of the world covering a number of countries may include multiple destination holidays, main destinations and a choice of add-ons or secondary destinations. For example, a region like South East Asia.

- a catalogue may cover one country but several different destination areas. The example of Spain was given in the preceding section.

- a catalogue may also cover one destination but offer several different resorts and hotels. For example, Bali, the Seychelles or Barbados.

The catalogue or brochure portrays both the image of the tour operator itself as well as the images of the destinations included. It also reflects the tour operator's selling strategies and priorities, and how it wants to slant its sales to favour major product lines. Each tour operator decides how it wants to picture a destination's image. Each destination, in turn, tries to coordinate diverse approaches, to seek consistency and avoid contradictions.

The quality of the paper used, the illustrations, graphics, layout, the whole feel and look of the catalogue or brochure, combine to create an overall impression. It is a selling tool designed to provide all the necessary information and seize the imagination. It should make people want to travel.

Technology and Internet marketing should eventually make the catalogue obsolete. The web site replaces both the travel agent's manual and the tour operator's catalogue. Consumers can access all the necessary information from a screen, reach their decisions, and make their buys in a more convenient and timely way. Chapter 9 indicated the possibilities of "virtual reality" applications in allowing a consumer to see and experience a destination.

Figure 14.2 illustrates the pattern of tour operator sales.

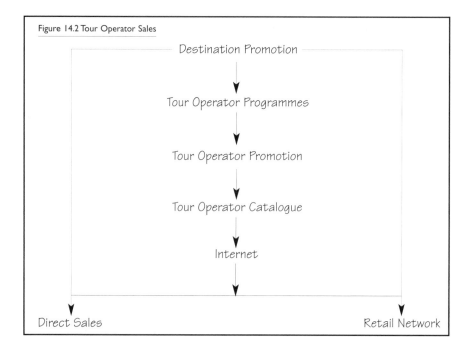

Figure 14.2 Tour Operator Sales

Destination Promotion

Tour Operator Programmes

Tour Operator Promotion

Tour Operator Catalogue

Internet

Direct Sales   Retail Network

Consumer Protection

In tourism many people buy something they have never seen, often far away, usually paid for in advance, to be consumed (in international tourism) in a foreign environment.

These circumstances require that people have certain kinds of consumer protection, and that the travel trade is regulated accordingly. Travel trade regulations, in both tourist generating and receiving countries, govern both outbound and inbound tourism – international and domestic.

A tour operator in Europe is required by law (the EC directed Package Travel, Package Holidays and Package Tours Regulations 1992) to include certain data in its catalogue or brochure: details of the the destination and transport, accomodation and its location and category, whether meals are included, the itinerary, visa requirements, health precautions, and the price and timetable for payment.

It should also describe the arrangements:

- if the holiday is cancelled because a certain minimum number of bookings has not been reached;
- if there are outward or homeward delays;
- for the security of moneys paid in advance;
- for the repatriation of holiday-makers in case of insolvency.

The above information is also provided in a written contract required on purchase of a package. The following additional questions are also covered.

- details of suitable health insurance.
- a local contact, normally a telephone number.

There are normally special conditions if the tour operator wishes to levy surcharges arising from unforeseen circumstances. Also included are provisions for the transfer of bookings, procedures when a part of the services are not provided, and liability for contract performance.

Including these details is not only a regulatory requirement but also makes good business sense. Regulations can be viewed as a tool in the management of tourism, and are further discussed in Chapter 19.

Reservations Systems

Philippe Bourguignon who took over the direction of Club Med in 1997 talked at that time about "the obsolescence and slowness of a reservation system incapable of acting as a useful sales tool" (Le Figaro, 1997).

The lack of an efficient state-of-the-art reservation system seriously handicaps sales effectiveness. Customers should be able to know immediately about availability. A good system does this; it also answers their questions and enables them to buy the product right away.

Systems are becoming more able to give options and alternatives, and answer the question – Where in the world can one go on these dates, for this experience, at this price?

A travel agent's on-line terminal can access one tour operator at a time. This means moving from system to system, having to repeat the same search and the same queries over and over again. Systems are also menu driven and slow to navigate. Home based teletext systems are even slower. A fully comprehensive and fast travel information and booking system remains to be developed.

However, as noted, the Internet will permit an increasing number of people to go on-line, plugging straight into central information and reservations systems – accessed both easily and internationally. In time this will revolutionise the retail selling function. Some web sites already invite bids for various offers, making selling more dynamic and competitive.

A travel agent's manual, produced by the destination, provides a ready reference for all key information. A destination web site can provide the same information in a faster and more complete and up-to-date form. It also gives the destination – the producer – a more direct presence in the market place itself. This tends to empower the destination from a marketing standpoint, and should change its relationships with the tour operators.

The Retail Travel Agency

The future of retail travel agencies has been questioned for years (Doswell, 1979). Tour operators, it was thought, would gradually increase their direct sales reducing the need for retailers. This would also save them a lot in commissions. Now – as noted – it is the Internet which is likely to bring major changes. However, tour operators have diversified into the retail field and retail networks are still important. Chain retail operations have expanded, absorbing many independent businesses.

Retail outlets provide the following:

- a personal contact able to provide face-to-face travel advice and counselling;

- an immediate and personal source of information and a place to pick up one's catalogues and brochures;

- a visible presence in prominent locations, acting as a promotional reminder of travel's appeal – adventure, escape, rest etc;

- a personal booking contact where reservations can be made and checked – where all questions can be asked and reassurances given;

- for tour operators a link to their customers. They can monitor their geographical coverage of all areas of potential sales. They can see where sales are made or not made and why, and where further support should be given and additional promotion undertaken. What sells, how much sells, to whom and where, are questions of major importance. A small proportion of retailers may sometimes account for the largest proportion of sales.

As already noted, the strength of a tour operator's sales network is one of its major competitive advantages.

As also noted, the Internet is able to do all of the above. It will eventually revolutionise travel retailing and change the role of the retail agent.

Checking the Retail Network

As the part played by the Internet develops, tourism and travel marketing will change. However, for the moment the current retail network and sales coverage remain important considerations.

Until now, the complexity of a large market makes it difficult to compile a complete list of the tour operators selling the destination. Also an extensive programme which includes many tour operators, with a very diverse marketing mix, can make it difficult to ascertain the precise retail network. Given a large and important market, the destination may choose to assume that the retail sales network is adequate. It is more important in smaller markets, with fewer tour operators involved, to try to check whether this is so.

Tour operators, not the destination, currently control the sales network. Retailers book holidays on behalf of the tour operator and only indirectly on behalf of the destination. It's the tour operators who pay their commission. And tour operators are reluctant to share information on their sales networks, even with a destination.

However, destinations should try to maintain a direct relationship with the retailers. One should provide them with newsletters, information updates, printed material and other promotional support. One should also invite them to participate regularly in familiarisation trips and trade shows.

It is currently regrettable to conclude that a destination cannot monitor the coverage provided by its sales networks. Yet to return to the example of coffee, cited in Chapter 5, producers do know the wholesaler or manufacturer to whom their coffee is sold. They do not necessarily know how and to whom the final retail product is sold nor, most would say, do they need to know. However, to distance themselves altogether from major considerations influencing the international marketing of their coffee, seems both shortsighted and misled. In tourism, it seems similarly shortsighted to sell one's product to a tour operator and leave it at that. The Internet should open up other possibilities.

Airlines

As noted in Chapter 6, the difference between scheduled and charter airline operations has become increasingly blurred. Tour operators now sell `flights only' travel, competing with scheduled services. Scheduled airlines promote holiday traffic as the major component on many routes. Holiday seats, although lower priced, act as a valuable filler to top up load factors on mainly business routes. Many scheduled airlines now operate subsidiary charter companies. Airlines are actively involved with tour operation, often as partners and associates, sharing the risks and rewards.

Selling Business and Convention Tourism

Business trips in Europe are recorded as 20 per cent of total travel (European Travel Monitor, 1997). It is a major market with particular needs. A number of specialised travel companies have sprung up to provide comprehensive services. These can cover the provision of in-house travel management schemes. Such a scheme can include travel policies, planning and approval procedures, health requirements and hotel and car rental bookings. By channelling buying power and controlling the travel budget, costs can be reduced.

Conventions are another specialised market, often called MICE (meetings, incentive groups, conventions and exhibitions). Destinations need attractive convention facilities and competitive attractions. A convention bureau is usually organised to spearhead a sales programme, to follow up leads and prepare bids for major international events.

The Speed of Sales Decisions

The rate at which a product is selling should be closely monitored. Promotion can be intensified and the sales coverage widened. Special sales incentives for retailers can be provided and discounts and rebates introduced. Adjustments in pricing may also improve performance. However, as noted in Chapter 8, rapid action needs up-to-date information. Tour operators may also need to adjust sales forecasts and anticipate `worst scenario' outcomes. They may not avoid some failures, but can still lessen the losses incurred.

Destinations are notoriously slow in keeping abreast of sales trends and often take three to four months to process tourism statistics. They also need up-to-date information. Without it they can put themselves completely in the hands of the tour operators. A destination itself should be aware of current trends. Things change. This has been noted elsewhere. One needs a speedy response.

References

Doswell, Roger. (1979). *Further Case Studies in Tourism*, Barrie and Jenkins

European Travel Monitor. (1996). *European Travel Behaviour*, IPK International, Munich.

Virage à 180° au Club Med. (1997). Le Figaro, 19 July.

Majaro, S. (1993). *The Essence of Marketing*, Prentice Hall.

chapter fifteen
Management Tools

T his chapter starts by further discussing the relationship between public
and private sectors. It then describes their distinctive ways of
seeing and the corresponding differences in focus. It then explains
the different types of approach to the management of the sector. It goes on
to list the tools and explain their relative uses. It also explains public awareness
programmes. The chapter concludes by emphasising the need for management
tools.

The Relationship Between the Public and Private Sectors

As already discussed, successful tourism requires a sense of partnership
between public and private sectors. People talk to each other, express
viewpoints, and try to hammer out differences. One aims at sector-wide
agreement and Chapter 13 discussed the possibilities of consensus building.
However, public and private sectors tend to view each other more or less
suspiciously.

- Private business is wary of government. It thinks of it as wasteful,
  interfering, and inefficient. Business usually wants a better deal and
  speaks out accordingly.

- Government thinks of business as narrow and self serving, unable to
  see the broader needs of the economy and society. It gets impatient
  that business never stops asking for things.

Each side lobbies the other, arguing viewpoints and trying to win support.
Businesses usually join together, lobbying through their professional and
trade associations. However, large and important corporations sometimes
lobby separately. So does the media. In turn, the government and political
parties lobby business.

All lobbying should stop short of bribery, the act of giving or promising
something to influence a person's judgement or conduct. Politicians should
be wary of accepting fees or expenses from particular sets of interests. An
involvement with a particular company or industry may clash with the proper
exercise of a politician's public duty. Politicians are given guidelines to follow

and links with business normally have to be reported and registered. Allegations of any transgression are investigated through an appropriate disciplinary committee or board.

The dividing line between right and wrong is sometimes ambiguous and remains a question of individual conscience. Political life is full of euphemisms for actions which are less than honest. The best safeguard is to maintain open government, keeping a good eye on both politicians and bureaucrats.

The division between private and public sectors tends to be reflected at local, national and international levels. The World Tourism Organisation (WTO) is, for the most part, public sector; The World Travel and Tourism Council (WTTC) is private sector.

The GTA has to listen, talk, inform and educate – it has to work towards the idea of sector-wide harmony and consensus. However, its starting point reflects different ways of seeing.

Different Ways of Seeing

As noted in Chapter 13, the tourism sector is diverse, covering a wide range of different activities and enterprises and involving many different aspects of society. It brings together businesses and government agencies which, through tourism, have common interests.

As also indicated in Chapter 13, a government tourism administration (GTA) coordinates all government agencies and private sector interests. It can be set up as a corporation or a statutory semi-independent board or organisation (a quasi autonomous non governmental organisation – QUANGO). Or it can take any other form which permits it to embrace both private and public sectors. This is a macro-management approach, through collaborative, regulatory, indicative and advisory actions, guided by agreed plans, policies and strategies.

Once one knows what to achieve, it is a question of how to best go about achieving it. Tourism is to develop in certain ways, take various forms and aim at certain targets. The tools are used to try and make this happen.

Both the public and private sector are concerned with marketing, financial, operational and human resources criteria. The public sector takes a macro-view since it deals with the whole sector, while each tourism enterprise tends to take only a micro-view of its own business These same macro and micro approaches were illustrated, as they related to positioning, in Chapter 11. The macro and micro levels interact – overall conditions influence each business and each business influences overall success.

Figure 15.1 shows the public and private sectors' different ways of seeing.

Areas of Concern	Private Sector	Public Sector
MARKETING	Looks at the specific range of marketing mixes (product, image, price, promotion and sales network) for a particular operation. This will accord with its established marketing strategy.	Has to see the whole spectrum of marketing mixes which the sector represents. Seeks ways to harmonise and adjust these with the overall development strategy, trying to provide additional promotional and sales support.
FINANCIAL	Has to achieve a minimum return on investment, meeting the needs of owners and shareholders. Is concerned with the level of capitalisation, structure of operating costs and resulting profits and cash flows.	Is concerned with the general prosperity of the sector and its contribution, through taxation, to government revenues. Must identify investment needs for product improvement, and identify and promote investment opportunities for sector-wide expansion
OPERATIONAL	Looks at its operational management to achieve specified quality standards, customer satisfaction, efficiency and targeted profits. Human resources management and training should be part of this.	Is concerned with the achievement of certain minimum standards of quality and service.
HUMAN RESOURCES	Sees training as linked to the improvement of operational efficiency, quality and customer satisfaction. However, many enterprises do not prioritise training, and only some have formal in-house training programmes.	Sees sector-wide training needs in the context of the labour market and overall employment trends. Tries to structure tourism careers, and to coordinate occupational standards and a national system of certification. Links training to the improvement of standards.

Figure 15.1 Different Ways of Seeing

Types of Approach

The management of the sector tries to get people:

- to develop tourism according to agreed policies (see the full list in Chapter 16);
- to observe particular codes and standards (further discussed in Chapter 18);

- to share responsibility for certain objectives and targets (see the consensus building in Chapter 13).

To do this it tends to adopt five types of approach; each of them is intended to get people to act in a certain way. Some are obligatory, people are required to do certain things. Some are voluntary, people are motivated to do things. Each approach, to be successful, requires people's maximum involvement and participation. They need to be a part of, and believe in, the directions chosen. "A feeling of ownership and commitment" is now a cliché, yet remains a key to successful management.

The approaches are:

- To require; this relates to regulations and legislation which set out minimum standards, and define what people can or cannot do. People's actions are required to conform.

- To encourage but also called "to lever"; although not obligatory people are encouraged to act in a particular manner. People may be encouraged, through a system of incentives, to improve their properties in certain ways or to develop new facilities in certain locations. They may also be encouraged to train staff, take certain marketing actions and observe certain operational standards.

- To enjoin; membership of trade or professional associations implies adherence to a certain organisational ethos. This includes certain aims, courses of action, codes of practice, and comprises an attempt by the sector to exercise control over itself.

- To provide; this covers the provision of infrastructure to create adequate conditions for the development of facilities and installations. It can also be part of "encouragement" or "leverage".

- To target; agreement on the achievement of certain objectives and results for the sector and its component segments.

People choose to invest where all the above conditions are satisfactorily met. These conditions indicate that certain minimum standards are observed, that some actions are prohibited and that certain other actions are encouraged. They also mean that adequate infrastructure is provided and maintained. And they also stimulate the achievement of targets, and the critical appraisal of performance.

Sometimes people may be required to do certain things, sometimes they may be merely encouraged. It is better for people to act by choice rather than by obligation.

Figure 15.2 illustrates the dynamics of management tools.

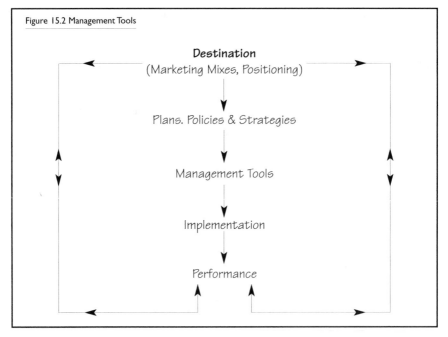

Figure 15.2 Management Tools

Destination
(Marketing Mixes, Positioning)

Plans. Policies & Strategies

Management Tools

Implementation

Performance

Using the Tools

In each area one can deploy a range of tools. For example:

- positioning, discussed in Chapter 11, provides an essential tool.

- effective institutional marketing, reflects positioning, and includes clear statements about the image, appeal and pricing of the destination, the target market segments and sales forecasts. It then indicates the intended promotional and sales programmes. It also includes visitor surveys, and market research to check on customer satisfaction and market behaviour (see Chapter 8).

- environmental planning and control in the development of new and existing facilities, including land use plans and zoning, are discussed more fully in Chapter 20. These denote which areas and zones may be used for which kinds of project. They may go further, indicating that only certain categories and sizes of facility can be constructed in certain locations and zones. They may also include the compulsory acquisition of sites or buildings for redevelopment purposes.

- the provision of certain types of educational and training facilities and programmes, with occupational skill standards, and a corresponding system of certification, form the basis for a national training system. This is fully discussed in Chapter 22. They should cover all needs everywhere; all skills, at all levels, for all occupations, for all types of tourism enterprise, for each area of the country. The outputs in certified staff provide an indication of the adequacy of training coverage. Visitor surveys and market feedback, mentioned above, permit an assessment of training effectiveness and the identification of any training weaknesses.

- additional physical planning regulations or codes can stipulate setbacks between buildings and from roads, shorelines, lakes and riversides, site coverage ratios, floor area ratios and height restrictions. They can also specify requirements for size, layout and external appearance, site access, car parking, and aspects of landscaping. They can also cover the availability and provision of infrastructure such as roads, water supply, drainage and waste disposal.

- planning regulations do not control how a building is constructed; this is the function of building regulations. Building regulations list the minimum specifications for construction work, and can include various aspects of safety, fire prevention and hygiene (these may also be covered by separate codes and regulations).

- the protection of buildings – which form part of a country's declared national heritage – is included. Any development involving such buildings is subject to scrutiny and control.

- the planning and control of infrastructure ensures an adequate provision of services (roads, ports and airports, railways, waterways, water, power, waste disposal and drainage), while preventing the denigration of the environment.

- carrying capacity indicates a limit in the number of visitors that can be satisfactorily received at a given time. It serves as an important guideline but can sometimes be increased. Facilities or attractions can be modified and, or, improved to permit more people to be accommodated.

- environmental legislation establishes various provisions, and impact assessments for new projects cover all questions affecting protection and conservation.

- regulations governing the display of outdoor advertising may be separate or incorporated in the environmental legislation listed above.

As noted, incentives aimed at encouraging the development of certain types of new and existing facilities may be introduced and promoted. These may be available selectively in only particular zones and locations, if projects meet the criteria stipulated. The following kinds of incentives, and combinations of these incentives, may be offered:

- tax holidays on profits, exemptions on customs duties, and reductions and exemptions from other government taxes and levies. Incentives (discussed in Chapter 16) may also include a generous allocation of work permits for the employment of key foreign personnel. Foreign companies may receive clearance for the repatriation of profits and dividends.

- the provision of land, either free, on attractive terms, or in exchange for nominal equity or rent, and, or, the provision of supporting infrastructure. Sometimes, for particularly desirable projects, governments may provide financial grants.

- the arrangement of loan finance at concessionary rates of interest, or the provision of government guarantees in support of lines of credit. These mechanisms are often used in the development of small tourism enterprise credit schemes.

- licensing controls aimed at establishing minimum operating standards for hotels, travel agencies and other tourism enterprises.

- the granting of any casino licenses sometimes requires the provision of infrastructure and, or, hotel facilities.

Other important management tools, which can be used, are as follows:

- regulations on travel enterprises which organise package holidays require certain minimum information to be included in brochures and catalogues. Basic consumer protection is needed, with guarantees on advanced payments and the repatriation of tourists in case of insolvency. Also full details on all other aspects of the package. These various regulations are discussed in Chapters 14 and 19.

- regulations governing hotels and other accommodation units, restaurants, discotheques, bars, night clubs and similar establishments, ground transportation (tourist buses, taxis), marine transportation and water sports. These regulations establish minimum standards and protect users. They are discussed in Chapter 18 and 19.

- apart from the enterprises and activities indicated above, many countries regulate tourist guides. Guides are usually required to pass a test or examination to satisfy specified minimum requirements.

- gambling casinos are usually regulated to protect users from unfairness, to ensure proper accounting and administrative procedures, and to exclude criminal elements.

- the classification and grading of facilities into categories may exist in addition to, or as a part of, licensing. The system may be administrated by the government on a mandatory basis. Alternatively a system may be run by the private sector through consumer and trade organisations, and various guide books and publications. These systems, noted in Chapter 5, are described in full in Chapter 21.

- visa controls should facilitate entry to the country (while still satisfying the requirements of the immigration authorities), encouraging an increase in the number of visitors. These were discussed in Chapters 6 and 14.

Government can employ any, or all, of these tools to achieve stated objectives. However, it should be consistent – not say one thing and do something else. It should agree with the sector what needs to be done and use the tools accordingly.

Quality and standards are further discussed in Chapter 18.

Public Awareness

All development brings change and impacts on the local community in a number of ways. These need not be negative. There should be little cause for concern providing that:

- tourism growth does not exceed a destination's carrying capacity;

- economic benefits are both up to expectations and well distributed;

- the environment is protected, conserved and enhanced;

- changes are compensated by greater prosperity and improved human welfare.

A public awareness programme explains tourism as a development option, the benefits it brings and the opportunities which it offers (Doswell, 1997). It also explains the significance of tourism, who the visitors are, why they come, what they are looking for, and how they perceive and judge the destination. This benefits not only tourism, but the local community itself. It helps to create a service-oriented environment, adding to the overall quality of life. Also part of the tourism product is experienced in the streets and reaches all walks of life. Everyday contacts with ordinary people influence a visitor's reactions to the place. The quality of the welcome and the way visitors are treated are important factors.

A public awareness programme:

- **informs people about tourism** – the economic benefits it brings, how well it is doing and is expected to do, its perspectives and future development, what it means and what will make it successful. It also tells people about the job and business opportunities in tourism and how to take advantage of them.

- **stimulates people's interest in tourism** – the background of visitors, their expectations and cultural differences, cross cultural contacts and their characteristics, and the challenge and cultural contribution of tourism.

- **involves people in tourism planning and development** – zoning and land use policy for tourism, future expansion and growth, what will be added where, what will be regenerated or re-engineered, the development of infrastructure, implications for urban development and city centres, and environmental considerations. In this, uses appropriate meetings and discussion groups.

- **alerts people about quality and standards** – lets them know about the visitors' motivations and needs. It explains the elements of good service. It stresses the importance of the welcome, courtesy and the concept of hospitality.

- **organises activities** such as skills competitions, award schemes, beautification programmes, tourism festivals and exhibitions, a tourism week, and programmes in schools

- **enables tourism to be assimilated** in a harmonious way, without social friction or disruption.

In pursuing these objectives, a programme makes extensive use of the media:

- **press** – articles on tourism and on the experiences of visitors, interviews, coverage of new developments, letters to the editor, tourism statistics and the performance of the sector. Press coverage should keep the sector in the public eye. Some advertising may be used.

- **television** – programmes can inform people on various aspects of tourism. News programmes should cover events. Panel discussions can feature various tourism issues.

- **radio** – similarly a variety of programmes can keep tourism to the forefront. Call-in programmes, panel discussions, news flashes, and interviews, can all make contributions. Selected radio advertising may also be used.

- **posters and printed material** – posters with public awareness themes can be distributed for display in public places. Brochures and leaflets can also be used to highlight particular aspects.

- **outdoor advertising** – bill boards can be used to feature an awareness of tourism – what one can get from it – and what one should give to it.

The sector, through its trade, professional associations, and the government tourism administration, should maintain close relations with the press. This should include holding press conferences as necessary, and issuing regular press releases.

A Sector-Wide Training Programme

Although Chapter 22 deals with human resources development, there is a distinctive training angle to public awareness. One can organise a tourism sensitivity course which can be offered to all personnel, from all sub-sectors, who have dealings with tourists. A course of this nature can contribute significantly to the sector's quality objectives.

The course can be designed to cover general knowledge about one's own country, and the cultural background of visitors. It can also include an introduction to the sector, and its components, including the tourism product, the various aspects of tourism demand, and quality and standards. And it can also teach basic hospitality skills, covering behavioural science, tourist related crime, cross cultural studies, and service techniques covering hospitality and visitor care.

The course can be offered part-time or full time, with a normal duration of 20-30 hours. The sector trains trainers who are then accredited to run the courses. On successful completion, participants will be awarded a certificate which authorises them to wear a badge or other emblem. This indicates that personnel have passed the course.

Developing the Destination

In analysing a tourism sector, one lists the tools already in place – indicating what they are intended to achieve. One assesses how well they are working and what they have achieved in practice. This overall approach shows what's happening now and indicates what's right and what's wrong. It identifies the gaps and brings us to the question – what are we going to do about it?

Regeneration, re-engineering and expansion are discussed in Chapters 16 and 17. Proposed steps have to be practical and feasible. The management tools exist – one must decide when and how to employ them.

Reference

Doswell, Roger. (1997). *Tourism – How Effective Management Makes the Difference*, Butterworth Heinemann.

chapter sixteen
Regeneration & Re-engineering

This chapter discusses the future development of the tourism sector, emphasising regeneration and re-engineering. It starts by defining these terms and referring to the concepts of cycles and positioning. It goes on to look at future development and the need to plan. The chapter then lists examples of improvement opportunities, and restates the possibilities of modifying markets and repositioning. It then explains tourism policy and the different degrees of development. The chapter identifies the specific development incentives more fully, and concludes with a section about the listing of regeneration and re-engineering projects.

Cycles and Positioning

Regeneration means to bring back to full life again – it is a term which can denote resurrection, resuscitation, redevelopment, revitalisation and renewal. Re-engineering is a term often taken to mean downsizing. However it is more than this. It means the best possible adjustment to the prevailing conditions and opportunities, a rational response to current and future circumstances. As such, it includes improvements of various kinds.

Expansion, discussed in the next chapter, has been related principally to new projects and sites. However, expansion can also take place through regeneration and re-engineering. The concepts are interrelated.

All tourist destinations in what they do and what they sell face the challenge, at some time, of renewal and revitalisation. How to stay alive and keep relevant are the recurring themes of management theory. A destination grows old and tired, products are no longer competitive, prices cease to offer good value, access becomes difficult, promotion seems jaded, and the sales coverage is inadequate. What went wrong? How did it happen?

Everything tends to reach maturity and then fall away. This book repeatedly examines how this can happen to all or part of a tourist destination. For example, Chapter 7 looked at the cyclical nature of things and the need to adjust to continually changing requirements and circumstances.

The management of the tourism sector has as its primary objective the development of a range of marketing mixes which is:

- fresh, up-to-date, complete and relevant to marketing needs and opportunities;

- conducive to the destination's conditions and characteristics;

- within the capacity of local entrepreneurs and operators – are they able to do it or not?

It means what to do with what, and whether this is possible or not – given the resources and constraints.

It may mean:

- The improvement of the current product to better satisfy the existing markets. This means improving or adjusting the marketing mix to make it a better fit with customer needs.

- A change in the mix of marketing mixes, through an expansion programme (discussed in Chapter 17). One diversifies through the addition of more facilities of certain categories.

Or it could mean:

- An attempt to change the existing product to appeal to alternative markets – usually the higher spending ones.

However, to switch to new, higher spending markets has many implications. Existing products need to be upgraded, prices adjusted upwards, staff trained to new standards, the image modified, the promotion redirected, and the sales approach and network changed. Any number of actions need to be undertaken. This means the re-positioning of the existing product. Something difficult to do.

Future Development

Tourism represents – if countries have the resources and attractions – a development option. A country and its private sector choose to develop the sector to generate a variety of social and economic benefits. Generally they don't choose only one type and form of tourism. The private sector responds to different marketing opportunities. Tourism development may include a spectrum of projects from ecotourism projects at local farms to five star urban and resort hotels. Any feasible project may attract investment. Countries support any tourism which is in keeping with their policy objectives. For this reason, the sector operates with a mix of marketing mixes. The analysis of this, in marketing the sector as a whole, was explained in Chapter 11 – Positioning.

The nature of a destination's tourism marketing mixes – particularly its accommodation – determines who comes to visit. For example, the category, quality, appeal and price of the hotels either attract or don't attract visitors. This mix of accommodation develops over time often in a fairly random, unplanned way with little in-depth analysis. However, the resulting composition of the sector is today's starting point. One looks at it and asks – How can one best improve the destination? How is it possible – if the options exist – to regenerate, re-engineer and expand it?

However, people tend to take the short rather than the long term view. Contemporary culture urges them to stay in the "now" – to concentrate on what lies immediately before them. Beyond the next few years seems too far away. "Who knows what will happen?" people say. They leave future options in favour of short term success. They don't focus on long term views but on immediate objectives. Politicians do the same. Businessmen also tend to look at the short term, concentrating on this year's results. However, planning for the long term is essential.

In the main, countries analyse a tourism sector which they have not (to a large extent) planned, and then plan (in an indicative, supportive and collaborative way) how to improve and develop it in the future.

Improvement Opportunities

There are always opportunities to improve the existing product. For example:

- On arrival at some airports the ground handling is slow and offhand. Customs and immigration are unwelcoming and aggressive. The wait for luggage is too long, signs are unclear, and there is nowhere to sit.

- In some destinations, information is limited and hard to get. One cannot find out where to go, what to see, what to do, or what to buy and where.

- Places often have obvious shortcomings. There is a poor choice of restaurants, nowhere to play tennis, few people speak English or another foreign language, and there are no international newspapers. And there seems no interest in asking tourists what they need or want.

- Some destinations have not pedestrianised key parts of the town, to make it more agreeable to walk, shop, eat out and generally enjoy the surroundings. Instead one competes with the traffic, hopping between cars, enveloped by fumes.

- The many small guest houses could be easily improved. Advisory services, technical assistance, training and access to credit, could help businesses achieve greater customer satisfaction and profitability.

Modifying Markets and Repositioning

One cannot change markets easily. However, WTO record several countries which wanted to reposition to attract higher spending tourists. For example, Cyprus, Malta and Sri Lanka. "The desired income will be generated by a fewer number of higher spending tourists rather than a larger number of lower spending tourists "(WTO, 1995).

However, the quality of the existing product, and the image of the destination, its promotion and all of its established price range and sales channels, tend to become fixed. They do not permit a straightforward readjustment to higher spending markets. It is usually easy to make some improvement to these existing marketing mixes but it is hard to re-position.

It is easier to re-position through expansion. Expansion is straightforward in a destination that still has good development sites. A place which is only partially developed with plenty of remaining space. However, it will still depend on many other variables, not least the access and proximity to appropriate markets. Also the plentiful availability of investment capital disposed to support expansion. Bali is a case in point. In the 1980s and 1990s one added a significant number of major new up-market hotels and resorts. As a result, higher spending tourists accounted for a much larger share of the total market.

Regeneration and re-engineering themselves can include:

- the improvement of some types of operation, as already noted, through all or some of the following: a better product with more skilful staff, a more appealing image, more advantageous pricing, and no change in markets but more effective promotion and sales.

- the re-positioning of a proportion of the product with a decided change in the marketing mix. This includes upgrading, staff re-training, re-pricing, and re-development of the image, promotion and sales.

- the addition of some new facilities, representing a diversification in marketing mixes and the introduction of new markets.

To re-engineer the product usually involves some shift in marketing and the positioning of the destination. The product and the marketing mix will be re-engineered not only to better attract existing markets but also to attract new markets. One may not re-position every marketing mix, i.e. the whole destination. Some mixes remain almost the same, some are modified, some are re-engineered completely.

As noted, one makes changes to:

- better attract all or some existing markets.
- attract some new markets.
- substitute all or some existing markets with new markets.

Figure 16.1 Development Options

• To better Satisfy Existing Markets

• To Attract and Satisfy Some New Markets

• To Substitute Existing Markets with New Markets

These are the three options (see Figure 16.1), or combinations of options. As already noted, new market segments can be attracted, displacing the old market segments. One notes that:

• new markets can only be attracted for a new or improved existing product. It cannot remain the same, it has to have improved standards, a revised image and price structure and a new promotion and sales programme.

• an existing market segment can only be discontinued by ceasing to satisfy its needs, particularly on price. The marketing mix is discontinued or killed off, and may be re-engineered to satisfy an alternative market.

Tourism Policy

Policy was defined in Chapter 13 as the agreed underlying values and the corresponding guidelines which development should follow. A "vision statement" expresses policy. Policy interrelates with the plan and strategies. A plan is a function of management and includes policy and strategy formulation. Strategies themselves summarise the specific objectives, activities and results. The tools, listed in Chapter 15, are then used to implement these plans, policies and strategies.

A full list of policy objectives for a destination is likely to include the following:

• a contribution to the country's economy, e.g. gross domestic product, foreign exchange earnings, employment, government revenue and regional development;

• a contribution to the country's overall development and the avoidance of negative socio-cultural impacts;

• the development of local tourism businesses;

• linkages between the tourism and other economic activities, e.g. market gardening, commercial fishing, and arts and handicrafts;

• foreign and domestic investment in various facilities and services, in accordance with the tourism development plan;

- conservation and enhancement of the country's heritage and, as appropriate, its culture and way of life;

- the development of contemporary culture, particularly through the visual and performing arts and the organisation of special events and festivals;

- conservation, protection and enhancement of the environment, through zoning, land use and other planning controls and regulations;

- the development of infrastructure not only for the support of tourism but also, wherever possible, for the benefit of the local population;

- a tourism sector with complementary attractions, facilities and services representing a well balanced mix of marketing mixes;

- the establishment and control of minimum standards for hotel and tourism attractions, facilities and services;

- the development of training centres and programmes, creating career and employment opportunities;

- an informed general public, aware of tourism, its growth and its contribution to the society at large;

- the selection of the marketing opportunities which can best reflect all of the above policy objectives;

- the cohesive management of the sector, ensuring the effective coordination of all public and private sector interests.

The Degree of Development

How big can a place get before a halt is called? It either spreads upwards (increases its density by pushing buildings higher) or it spreads outwards (increasing its area) or both. It can also become denser by filling in vacant land. At a certain point a place can only develop in this way from within. From the re-development of sites and buildings and from the improvement and re-positioning of existing businesses. From regeneration and re-engineering.

There is no correlation between a destination's age and its marketability. Established destinations such as London, Paris and Rome continue to go from strength to strength. By contrast, coastal resorts such as Margate and Ramsgate – in the UK – have become unfashionable and unused. Different market forces have produced different results.

Chapter 7 – Cycles – describes four stages of development – fully urbanised environments, partially urbanised environments, small resorts and resort towns, and building-free destinations. One can also categorise destinations according to the degree of development (see Figure 16.2):

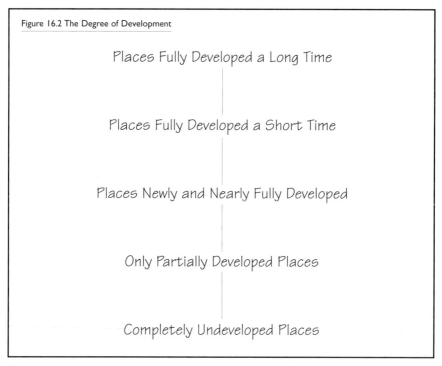

Figure 16.2 The Degree of Development

Places Fully Developed a Long Time

Places Fully Developed a Short Time

Places Newly and Nearly Fully Developed

Only Partially Developed Places

Completely Undeveloped Places

Places already fully developed a long time ago.

It may be that such a place cannot expand outwards; no further development is permitted beyond certain outer limits. Density and height restrictions are also controlled. Expansion through higher buildings is impossible. However, old hotels may be obsolete and run down and there may be some opportunities to gut existing buildings, redeveloping them from the inside while maintaining their exterior facades. There may also be opportunities to demolish some buildings and redevelop sites. There may be other opportunities to improve and upgrade existing facilities by adding bathrooms and central heating systems etc. Some such destinations may still be popular, maintaining and increasing their annual visitor numbers. Others may have suffered major market changes and a huge drop in visitors. In the first case one looks to reinforce the market position. In the second case one re-generates and re-positions the destination. This poses, for some places, a daunting task. For example, a seaside resort may have lost its appeal. It must now find a solution, possibly coupling its seaside location with heritage and cultural attractions.

Places fully developed but only a fairly short time ago.

This category includes many of the major Mediterranean resort developments of the last four decades. They were developed rapidly to maximise tourism's short term economic impact. As a consequence, planning regulations were absent or relaxed while infrastructure and environmental considerations were badly overlooked. Since then destinations have been re-engineered with improvements made to infrastructure, community services and the general environment. For example, Benidorm in Spain has been improved. While places appear fully developed there are usually opportunities for expansion. A destination can consolidate, gradually re-engineer itself, strengthen its marketing appeal, secure loyal repeat business, and continue to compete successfully.

Places newly and nearly fully developed.

The prognostic for such a destination depends on the soundness and control of its first development. Many new destinations have developed in a random higgledy-piggledy fashion. An abundance of small units sprang up, many from adaptations of existing buildings. They were then expanded with rooms tacked on here and there, defying any effective control. Kuta in Bali and Pattaya in Thailand serve as examples. These places always pose a re-engineering challenge, with urgent infrastructure and environmental requirements that have to be faced. Minimum standards should be enforced. Additional sites may offer the possibility of some new projects which can help re-structure the overall tourism product. These can enhance the destination's image and achieve some re-positioning.

Only partially developed places.

These are often destinations in their infancy, with plenty of opportunities for continuing expansion. Sound planning and control can stop haphazard development. Conflicts between small local investors and the large institutional investors from outside often occur. However, there is room for both in a well managed situation. Expansion should follow an agreed strategy. One decides carrying capacity and the limits to development. One knows what to create, in what time frame, for what markets and for what numbers of visitors. An investment promotional programme is put in place, projects are finalised, and planned development proceeds.

Completely underdeveloped places.

These are places with no development but important tourism potential. They are kept this way, conserved as places of natural beauty and, or, great environmental or cultural interest, to be visited and enjoyed but not developed. Planning concentrates on access and the reception and distribution of visitors. It provides for parking, reception, information, refreshment and toilet facilities.

In all of the above, one can see the need for planning and management. One has to be clear – with objectives defined, limits imposed, standards set, plans agreed and markets targeted.

Incentives

Incentives were mentioned in Chapter 15 – Management Tools. They can act as a spur to get facilities regenerated and re-engineered. They can also stimulate expansion. However, governments should be sure that incentives are really needed.

Incentives take different forms:

- various exemptions from taxes, customs tariffs or other government levies.

- accelerated depreciation allowances which also reduce tax obligations.

- the provision of loan finance at concessionary rates, or some form of government guarantee.

- cash grants towards the rehabilitation or improvement, or the development of a certain type, of facilities.

- the issue of work permits for a certain number of foreign technicians or professional staff.

- the grant of government owned land, free, or for a peppercorn rent, or for a nominal equity share.

- the provision of infrastructure to service a particular site or area, e.g. new roads, lighting, water and power supplies.

An incentive makes the conditions for an investment more attractive, it reduces risk and potentially increases returns. It gets (encourages or levers) people to do what one wants them to do. It makes the agreed strategy come true.

However, the process of handling applications for the appropriate approvals and licenses has to be quick, impartial and efficient. Bureaucrats should encourage and facilitate investment not obstruct it.

Listing the Projects

Once the existing sector is analysed (see checklists at Chapters 23 and 24) one can list the various types of project – the opportunities for regeneration and re-engineering (improvement and re-positioning):

As a part of the policy and long term plans one has clear ideas about the future. How to develop and position the destination. This is summarised in the tourism development strategy explained in Chapter 13. Implementation includes regeneration, re-engineering and expansion. Expansion can be quick (Chapter 17). Regeneration and re-engineering are normally a gradual process. Year by year one strengthens the product and its marketing. While the destination changes it also improves. It keeps ahead of the game. Dangers of obsolescence and decline are avoided.

One selects the appropriate management tools to achieve the objectives. The projects should be listed as follows:

Regeneration

One may develop new plans for particular urban zones or other areas. The authorities can have clear concepts for these, arrived at after wide consultation, discussion and reference to the development strategy. One may then earmark particular buildings and sites for redevelopment. For such individual projects one may only provide general guidelines. One can confer with owners or use compulsory purchase to pursue these aims. One sticks to the concepts but allows for wide entrepreneurial interpretation. The actual projects should result from detailed private sector feasibility and design studies. Some sites or buildings can be made subject to competitive tendering.

However, it is no good doing bits and pieces while losing sight of the whole tourism product. Chapter 4 discussed the development of a more complete product. Completeness is always the aim and regeneration is a part of this.

Re-engineering

As noted, re-engineering can take the form of improvement or re-positioning.

- Improvement projects. Improvement of existing businesses through the upgrading of facilities and equipment. Also additions or improvements to the service. A number of the management tools can help. For example, through small business, technical assistance and advisory services, workshops and in-service training, cooperative marketing schemes, incentive and grant schemes.

- Re-positioning projects. These involve changing all or part of a product's marketing mix. One redevelops the product, image and pricing and then re-aligns the promotion and sales. Doing this one abandons one's existing market to target new markets. This is the risk. Losing what one has while failing to achieve something new. Market research should support convincingly the feasibility of any change. The image, in particular, can become deeply attached to a product and its price and is difficult to change.

A marketing mix, as noted, may also be modified according to seasonal needs and opportunities.

Reference

World Tourism Organisation. (1994). *National and Regional Tourism Planning* – Methodologies and Case Studies, Routledge.

chapter seventeen
Expansion

This chapter starts by looking at the development of public sector planning in the context of management. It goes on to further explain the five management functions – planning, organising, directing, coordinating and monitoring – as they relate to tourism. The chapter then explains the importance of carrying capacity criteria, giving examples of various solutions. It then describes investment promotion and investment facilitation requirements. The chapter then restates the possibility of repositioning through expansion. It concludes with a list of key points related to expansion decisions.

Planning as a Part of Management

Governments have separated planning into two main types. First, "development plans" which are really in the realm of economics, prepared mainly by economists. They have a public sector focus and usually encompass prevailing economic conditions, the intended public sector expenditures, sectoral opportunities and needs, macro-economic projections of the economy, present and intended government policies, and the likely private sector response (Lewis, 1966). Such a development plan has to exist in some form for a government to function. Without it, there would be no government budgets or fiscal policies and plans.

Second, physical plans – also known as "development plans" – are aimed primarily at land use. They allocate land for particular uses and designate the corresponding zones. They also establish the planning regulations governing particular areas and sites. These plans lie in the realm of the urban planners, architects, engineers and environmentalists.

These two kinds of plans have been separated historically for the convenience of various specialists, disciplines and government departments. However, they represent different dimensions of the same thing and should be put together to form part of an integrated sectoral development plan – e.g. for the tourism sector. Tourism sector development plans are prepared but often in a separate and unrelated way.

As a result there are three types of plan – the economic plans, the land use plans and the sectoral plans. Despite the overlaps between different government departments and planning levels, they have to be reconciled together.

Regrettably, planning has tended to become a specialisation in itself – often divorced from management. Planning is considered as one thing and implementation as something different and quite apart. This is wrong. Planning is an integral part of management. A plan is prepared, then implemented and then monitored. In the light of performance one adjusts the plan as part of an ongoing management process. One doesn't only plan an economy, one has to manage it – not directly but indicatively. One doesn't only plan land-use, one also has to manage the environment and related development. One certainly doesn't just plan tourism – one manages the sector.

Sustainable means something which can continue. One needs to conserve and enhance the world for future generations. Not all new projects can have an indefinite life (see Chapter 7 – Cycles). Each succeeding generation evaluates what is there, what it wants to keep and pass on, and what it wants to replace or redevelop. Projects may not be sustainable in themselves. Many buildings are not created forever but for a given period of time. Once degenerated and obsolete they may be demolished and replaced. Or at the end of their life they may be regenerated or re-developed.

Chapter 16 noted that much of tourism's future lies not in new development but in making better use of what's already there. This includes many options, e.g. the re-planning of some urban areas, the re-development of key sites, the regeneration of existing buildings and businesses, and improved transport management and better landscaping.

The tourism sector should present its agreed development strategy to the government departments responsible, ensuring that their needs are included in overall plans.

Tourism Planning

As noted in Chapter 16 tourism plans deal with how to (i) improve tourism through the re-engineering or regeneration of existing facilities and services, and (ii) expand tourism through the development of new projects.

Meantime, government wants proposals to exploit the full potential of each sector. It wants sectors – including tourism – to fulfil their economic and social role, making the best possible contribution to overall development. It is therefore indispensable that each authority – at the national, regional and local levels – adopt a tourism development strategy.

The five functions of management, developed from Henri Fayol and applied to the tourism sector (Doswell, 1997), can be summarised as follows:

- Plans set clear directions and how to achieve them. A tourism development plan sets out how to regenerate, re-engineer and expand tourism. It sets out expansion – by how much, in what form and where. It therefore establishes the basis for particular tourism zones and land use planning. It also specifies the improvement opportunities offered by existing facilities and services. It also indicates the development of tourist attractions, and recreational and entertainment facilities. As a result it sets targets for visitor arrivals and earnings. It also indicates the targets for new investment, corresponding incentives and other tools, and the related promotional programme. It also includes the development of the legislative framework, the institutional marketing programme, a human resources development strategy, public awareness programmes, an improved information system, together with all the corresponding budgets. Finally, it examines the economic, environmental and socio-cultural aspects, and specifies steps to avoid undesirable impacts.

- Organisation tackles the mobilisation and deployment of resources and technology. It establishes the role of the government tourism administration (GTA) and its staffing. It agrees steps in the recruitment, selection and training of staff to improve institutional capacity. It ensures that all key staff are fully involved in the formulation of the agreed tourism development plans. It translates these plans into departmental annual working plans, to ensure that all activities are fully integrated in the GTA's ongoing functions and responsibilities. It designs the interlocking organisational mechanisms whereby other government agencies and the private sector can participate effectively in tourism management.

- Direction provides the leadership to maintain the necessary sense of purpose. It sets out the GTA's role in the implementation of agreed plans. This deals with how to spark the development of new projects and improvement programmes, and how to mobilise the private sector to tackle them. It includes the use of the various management tools to produce action, and translates plans into concrete activities designed to achieve targets.

- Coordination keeps everybody and everything working together. It follows through and ensures that the necessary consultation and participation takes place. It sets out how to link with the other government agencies involved in various aspects of tourism development, to ensure that they act in accordance with agreed plans. This means consultation with the employers and unions. It also means activating a whole system of committees, boards, councils etc, designed to capture the participation and involvement of all branches of the private sector.

- Monitoring or control keeps track of performance and compares it to the plan. This means an information system that monitors performance and results. It also means establishing trends, anticipating results and taking remedial action in time. It requires a comprehensive approach to intelligence gathering, that generates complete information on both supply and demand. For example, in the analysis of all tourism assets and the development of certifiable workforce skills. it also involves ongoing market research and models to monitor the economic, environmental and socio-cultural impacts.

These five functions can be reduced to three by simply saying – planning, implementing and monitoring.

As noted, where there are possibilities of expansion, one includes clear and feasible targets in terms of the number of new hotels and accommodation units, their size, category, style, and location and markets. This addresses the positioning and feasibility of these projects, along with the formulation of their marketing mixes. And it also includes the management tools to encourage and control such development. For example, it means investment promotion and possibly incentives, infrastructural development, and overall marketing support.

Generally plans can be written up in the following way (see Figure 17.1):

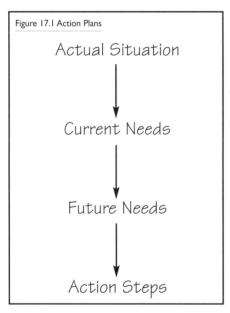

Figure 17.1 Action Plans

Actual Situation

Current Needs

Future Needs

Action Steps

• **Description of the actual situation.** What is happening? What exists? Current characteristics.

• **Current needs.** Weaknesses and deficiencies. Current needs – what precisely needs to be done now.

• **Future needs.** Future opportunities which are offered. What needs to be done.

• **Action steps.** The translation of needs into specific action steps, within a time frame.

As noted, Chapters 23 and 24 comprise a checklist for the analysis of the tourism sector and the development of a comprehensive plan.

Carrying Capacity

Carrying capacity (listed in Chapter 15) defines the optimum number of people that can visit somewhere, or use certain facilities at the same time, without:

• causing damage,
• or impairing other people's enjoyment.

Damage occurs through the sheer weight of people and, or, the lack of proper planning and control. People's enjoyment disappears through overcrowding, queues, delays, and unfriendliness. Steve Hide reports that the Inca Trail, near Machu Picchu in Peru, is at risk, "(It is) a four-day hiking route to the site that attracts 30,000 tourists a year. In the high season, campsites are overflowing and walkers queue to negotiate the steep stone steps carved by the Incas" (Daily Telegraph, 13, March, 1999).

A place can become so crowded that it ceases to be attractive, jeopardising its marketing mix.

To improve the carrying capacity, one can:

- Enlarge various areas and facilities so that more visitors can be received.

- Re-organise the layout, flow and circulation, to remove bottlenecks.

- Improve the crowd control methods – so that one can manage and move visitors more effectively, e.g. through the better use of signs and widening of passageways and doors.

- Coordinate better with tour operators so that visits can be staggered.

- Protect vulnerable materials or finishes from excessive wear and tear.

- Price differently to spread visitors better, according to hour of the day, days of the week, and times of the year.

If people arrive by car the same things apply. The circulation of vehicular traffic, the positioning of parking, access to the site, and the possible pedestrianisation of areas all need to be studied. For example, parking areas may be sunken or hidden, screened by trees and planting.

Whether one is dealing with a famous museum or monument, a popular cafetaria or restaurant, a large hotel, a football ground or conference centre, many of the same principles apply.

There are many quantitative techniques – e.g. linear programming and queuing theory – to study crowd management. Models can be created to test revised layout and design. Additionally, in qualitative terms, one can use market research and surveys to test the visitors' level of enjoyment.

The boldest step involves the radical expansion of carrying capacity. For example, the traditional housing and organisation of art and culture seldom match tourism's growth. Chapter 4 has already made reference to the new theatres, concert halls, opera houses, museums and libraries in major cities. The performing and visual arts exist, they need adequate places to be seen and enjoyed. It is here that one often finds that insufficient capacity exists. Generally one can:

- re-organise the existing premises. In a museum one can extend the opening days and hours, re-plan the layout, re-design some areas, rehang some paintings and make other changes to the display and organisation. In a theatre, one can increase performances and seating.

- expand the existing premises, by building extensions and adding more physical capacity. For example, the Royal Opera House in London or the Sainsbury Wing at the National Gallery also in London.

- add new facilities to enrich the places current cultural attractions. For example, the Guggenheim Museum in Bilbao.

- construct new buildings while leaving the existing premises to play a more limited role. One can switch a number of exhibits or performances to the new venue.

- adapt and convert other existing premises elsewhere, usually effecting a change of use. For example, the former power station which has become the new Tate Modern Gallery in London.

Florence has important renaissance art housed in the city's major museums. Principal among these is the Uffizi. However, the city's accommodation capacity appears to exceed the Uffizi's. Chapter 4 already discussed the importance of matching space. Enormous queues develop and many visitors find it impossible to visit the museum, a converted palace. It is not an ideal place either to display art or receive large numbers of people. There is a case to create new museum space, to display a selection of the key works.

Investment Promotion

Investment promotion requires a foundation of complete information. What does a potential investor, either domestic or foreign, need to know? Information should be available and accessible. It should include an investment pack describing the opportunities, tax regime, investment incentives and local conditions. Potential investors need information at two levels:

- first to capture their serious interest;

- second to provide them with all the information for the preparation of a thorough feasibility study (one can include a lot of this information or indicate where it can be obtained).

Information needs can be listed as follows:

- **on the country** – its background, history, geography, demography and its economic, social and political development. Where it stands and what it hopes for.

- **on tourism performance** – a comprehensive annual report on the sector, analysing the trends and developments.

- **on the tourism development strategy** – a summary of the agreed future development of the sector, and its needs and opportunities.

- **on the country's investment climate** – its tax regime, incentives and other conditions. Also the country's legal framework for tourism and the scope and purpose of legislation. It should indicate the licensing and registration requirements, and the minimum standards.

- **on the construction sector** – the structure of the sector, its capacity, type of local company, methods used, technology, and typical costs for various kinds of building.

- **on operational costs** – labour legislation and costs, costs of supplies, energy and other costs.

- **on the competition** – why the possibilities of investment are better than other countries or regions. A summary of the competitors and what they offer, and why an investor should choose the destination in question.

Most countries have an investment board or council charged with promoting and facilitating new investment for all sectors. A GTA should establish a close working relationship with it.

Promotion is intended to alert and attract investors. The first step is to identify potential investors – who and where they are and why they might be interested. The research needed to develop a good database and mailing list is ongoing. Data collection is incremental, one thing leads to another and one builds up the information. Leading banks and financial institutions, multilateral agencies and intergovernmental bodies may all help.

The promotional approaches listed in Chapter 12 also apply to investment. The extent of investment sought, particularly foreign investment determines the scope of a promotional programme and budget. Investment promotion is sometimes undertaken in too general a way, with insufficient reference to specific project opportunities. One should list these opportunities. One can also invite bids for particular types of project. An invitation is advertised and promoted and tender documents produced with all the necessary information.

A promotional programme can include the following:

- **Advertising.** Bids are invited on particular projects. Supplements for magazines and newspapers are produced, promoting the country and its investment opportunities. Other advertising may be undertaken – particularly when new resort areas present major new expansion opportunities. Advertisements can be reprinted to serve as promotional material.

- **Printed material.** Much of the normal tourism promotional material can be used. The investment framework and tax regime can be printed as a booklet – and a tourism investment folder can also be produced. All the relevant material is normally put together to form an investment pack.

- **Audio visual.** If justified, a tourism investment promotional video can be produced. A CD can also be developed, using the information on a web site.

- **Internet.** A web site specially designed for the destination should also serve for investment promotion.

- **Direct mail.** A mailing list should be compiled, kept updated and used for direct mail shots promoting investment.

- **Direct sales.** As a follow up to other promotional initiatives, sales trips should be undertaken and direct calls made on selected people. These should be undertaken by informed and knowledgeable people able to answer questions and provide information.

- **Financial journalists.** Journalists involved with investment may respond positively to an invitation. As with travel writing, the destination can benefit substantially from this kind of exposure.

- **Invitations to visit.** Investors who have expressed a serious interest are worth inviting. Depending on the case they may pay their own travel and accommodation expenses. However, the GTA together with any local investment board or council, will handle visits, interviews, discussions and other activities..

- **Overseas representation**. The country's embassies around the world should be kept briefed on activities, and be capable of playing an effective complementary role – establishing contacts and following up leads. Any GTA overseas promotional offices should be able to undertake a similar role.

Investment Workshops

One can invite potential investors to participate in investment workshops. These:

- present the tourism development strategy and the related investment needs and opportunities;

- present the whole picture of the country and its investment climate and conditions, investment code and tax regime;

- visit particular sites and areas offering opportunities for development.

However, although this sometimes works well it is not always the best approach. For example:

- the right persons do not take up the invitation.

- investors may resent being put together, talked to and approached as a group.
- it is difficult to follow up with people separately, to respond to their individual concerns, interests and requests.
- investors can collide with each other over the same opportunities.

Alternatively, one can contact potential investors with full details of investment conditions and opportunities, without such a workshop. They are targeted as individual entities, matched to specific projects or types of projects, invited and welcomed separately and dealt with as individuals with individualised sets of needs. This is a preferable approach.

Facilitating New Investment

The processing of new investment proposals should not stumble into bureaucratic difficulties.

- One needs a common understanding among government agencies, of the pre-conditions and requirements for investors to get their project approved. A range of different approvals is required from a variety of different agencies. These agencies should not make different interpretations or ask for different documentation.

- One should also establish a "one-stop shop" or a mechanism whereby all approvals can be considered together within a guaranteed period of time (the one-stop shop has proved a difficult concept to implement and has now become something of a cliché). In some countries, approval criteria seem to be applied haphazardly and subjectively and there may be a reluctance to say either "yes" or "no". An investor can also go from one agency to another, gradually accumulating approvals, only to be blocked by the last agency contacted.

- One should also harmonise and coordinate any inspections. A number of different agencies may have the right to inspect sites and facilities, e.g. the ministries of environment, commerce and tourism as well as the local authority.

Conflicting ideas and approaches can act as an obstacle to new investment. Agencies working together, applying commonly agreed criteria within the same time-frame, help to facilitate it.

Repositioning Through Expansion

The possibilities of re-positioning through expansion were mentioned in Chapter 16. In many newer destinations, it is an opportunity which should not be missed.

Expansion can double, triple, sometimes quadruple or more, the existing number of rooms. If management tools are deployed to ensure a minimum standard of new facility, this can change the destination's image and lead marketing mix. For example, this might happen where the initial development centres on a fishing village, with expansion outwards along the coast or in other peripheral areas. Bali's initial development, mentioned in Chapter 16, was centred on Kuta and Sanur, but expanded in the hitherto undeveloped area of Nusa Dua. This changed the structure and image of the sector and produced a new lead marketing mix. However, if expansion is unplanned and random, the result will be equally higgledy-piggledy – an ill defined product with a haphazard marketing mix. If instead it is carefully studied and conceived, it can succeed in positioning the destination much more advantageously.

Expansion Decisions

Expansion is based mainly on land use planning for the development of sites or the change of use of existing sites. The following sets out 27 related points:

- land use for tourism must be made a part of overall land use planning – for all sectors, for all parts of the country (tourism is often treated too sketchily).

- planners must not overlook tourism; the tourism sector itself – through the GTA – should ensure that tourism is properly included.

- comprehensive tourism development strategies must be agreed and included to act as the framework for the related tourism planning content (this is not always done – even in developed countries).

- at the national level guidelines should be established for land use planning at the regional and local levels. Regional authorities may also establish criteria for the local level.

- local and regional plans indicate the approved land use for the expansion and development of infrastructure and building.

- planning requirements are therefore indicated from the top (national level) but formulated from the bottom (regional and local levels).

- land use planning should involve the community at large, in the review, discussion, approval and appeal of proposals.

- a local authority can indicate a preferred type of project for a site but should leave the matter open for the developer's recommendations – based on an in-depth feasibility study.

- planning decisions should be consistent in using the agreed criteria. The more detailed and comprehensive the criteria, the easier it is to evaluate the planning application.

- planning applications and appeals need rapid and efficient processing.

- the regeneration of sites in already developed areas (inward expansion) can be preferable to building on new sites (outward expansion). This depends on the place and its stage of development.

- to abandon old areas to build in new areas can be a major mistake. For example, the inner city becomes a slum while new projects move to the outskirts and suburbs.

- in the same way, one should complete old tourism development zones before starting on new zones. This does not always follow, but different zones compete with one another for resources. It is often best to focus development in established zones with room for expansion. This concentrates infrastructure and resources and achieves economies of scale.

- such expansion also adds to the numbers of visitors in one area. This enlarges the market, generates activity, adds revenue, and further enhances the atmosphere.

- approved development in new areas must be on a scale to justify the cost of infrastructure e.g. roads, lighting, public areas, power, water, sewerage, drainage etc.

- such new areas are best phased, with investment plans and cash flows based on the forecast pace of development.

- the ratio of infrastructural costs to subsequent development in hotels and other facilities is often about 30:70 but can rise to 40:60.

- plans that open up sites and investment opportunities should be based on thorough marketing studies. If not investors will not respond and the GTA will lose credibility.

- market research is essential – all expansion decisions must be based on sound marketing data.

- one major project of recognised standing and quality can help to trigger other investments. It can serve as the destination's flagship and act as a springboard for further development.

- while most buildings are in private ownership, the local authority acts as the guardian of the overall environment

- small tourism enterprises can widen the ownership and participation of local people.

- as noted in Chapter 4, the completeness of a destination is important. "Make it complete" – is an appropriate slogan.

- one should try to differentiate destinations in the same country. They will still compete for market share but with complementary appeal.

- a clear vision of the eventual objectives of regeneration, re-engineering and expansion should exist. It should include the final mix of marketing mixes and show how the destination will position itself market by market (see Chapter 11).

- as noted in Chapter 11 the mix of marketing mixes should achieve a sense of balance. Some products should be more prominent, while one product should not clash with another. The different marketing mixes combine in suitable proportions to make up the destination as a whole.

- the objective is never quite achieved – the tourism product always remains unfinished and one is constantly adjusting and modifying things. One continues to regenerate and re-engineer, to improve and reposition. And – if the opportunities exist and it makes sense – to expand.

Chapter 20 discusses physical planning regulations.

References

Hide, Steve. (1999). *Inca City `in Danger'*, Daily Telegraph, 13, March, p. T2

Lewis, A. (1966). *Development Planning – The Essentials of Economic Policy*, Harper & Row.

chapter eighteen
Quality & Standards

T his chapter examines the concept of quality and how this interrelates with the development and use of standards. It explains quality and quality management, and describes the control cycle. It goes on to identify the International Standards Organisation and the ISO 9000 approach. It then examines the concept of management style, differing values and their influence on quality. It also looks at quality circles, the tangible and intangible product components, and the concept of empowerment. The chapter then goes on to discuss examples of various quality control and improvement ideas. It concludes by discussing quality improvement workshops and other training initiatives.

Quality and Quality Management

Quality itself is a relative term. It means:

- achieving the standards set for the whole of the marketing mix (product, image, price, promotion and sales) all of which are designed to meet or exceed customers' expectations.

- making sure that these standards are realistic given the operational circumstances. That they can be met satisfactorily not once, or now and then, but all the time.

- aiming therefore at invariability – that the customer always gets the same thing. This is difficult because of the spontaneous and intangible content of much of the tourism product and marketing mix.

One has quality management at the micro level – the concern of each owner or manager of a tourism enterprise. And one has quality management at the macro level – the concern of the government tourist administration (GTA), national and regional trade associations, and other sector-wide organisations.

Chapter 15 on management tools discusses the various approaches to sector-wide "macro level" standards and quality. It lists "require, encourage, enjoin, provide and target" as ways of achieving the desired results.

These amount to either:

- requiring minimum standards as they relate to various building and operational aspects,

- or helping enterprises to achieve improved standards and quality.

By mandatory means (reflecting the management tools in Chapter 15), one could:

- ensure that appropriate planning and building regulations, together with environmental protection, are in force (see Chapter 20 on physical planning).

- impose minimum standards that reflect and support the above planning, building and environmental regulations (see Chapter 19 on legislation), adding any additional requirements judged necessary.

- establish appropriate regulations to control the conduct of tourism enterprises (also see Chapter 19 on legislation).

- enforce classification and grading standards, where it is decided to adopt a mandatory rather than voluntary system (see Chapter 21).

In other ways (also listed under management tools in Chapter 15), one could:

- provide instructional materials and training programmes to help enterprises to tackle quality management effectively (see Chapter 22 on human resources).

- distribute fact sheets or newsletters, or any other published material, to the sector giving suggestions and hints on quality management and quality improvement.

- include quality management criteria in the curriculum and occupational skill standards curriculum and testing, developed in collaboration with the sector and adopted on a national basis (see Chapter 22).

- participate, if requested and supported by the sector itself, in the development of voluntary classification and grading which list establishments according to agreed quality criteria (classification is dealt with in Chapter 21).

- assist in any way possible in the assessment of facilities, services and attractions and all other aspects of the tourism product, for guide books or other private sector publications (see Chapter 21).

- incorporate quality management principles within the tourism public awareness programmes (also discussed in Chapter 15) aimed at influencing people whose work is related to tourism.

- provide feedback on all data collected and analysed through visitor surveys (see Chapter 8 on market research) to monitor the sector's quality record.

- organise an annual tourism quality management conference, and regular workshops, to review the sector's success in maintaining and improving standards and to discuss future needs and programmes.

• organise other quality management training activities as appropriate.

Quality management:

- tries to ensure that customers get the required standards;

- illustrates the standards through documentation (e.g. illustrated manuals and instructional booklets) or audio visual aids (posters, videos, cassettes);

- lists procedures about what has to be done – what, how, who, when and where;

- teaches the standards and procedures through training programmes;

- empowers personnel to use their discretion in unforeseen and unusual circumstances, and decide and take action to satisfy the customer;

- establishes some daily routines, continuously checking customer satisfaction;

- tries to record any variance from the standards;

- tries to prevent any such variance from occurring again;

- keeps the standards under review, changing or adjusting them as necessary.

The Control Cycle

The management functions – planning, organising, directing, coordinating and monitoring – were explained in Chapter 17. As a part of planning one sets standards. In implementing the plan one ensures that these standards are maintained. In monitoring performance one checks that this is the case.

This process, illustrated at Figure 18.1 can be called the control cycle. Planned results include standards and targets. Actual results – as opposed to planned – tell management what really happened. Management compares this actual performance against the plan and identifies variances. It takes action to eliminate these variances or it decides to modify the plan. One then starts the cycle again.

The International Standards Organisation

In 1987 the International Standards Organisation (ISO) adopted a British standard from the British Standards Institute – BS 5750 – which then became ISO 9000. It has now become a prominent and widely used international standard for quality management. ISO has continued to refine and develop the ISO 9000 approach, producing various versions. The approach has also become recognised as an important image and promotional tool. Its ISO 9000 affixation announces that an enterprise is serious about the quality it offers its customers. Increasingly people look for this and find it reassuring.

ISO 9000 does not in itself develop organisational behaviour or a particular management style. It offers a methodology and a system of tools, checks and procedures. Staff should conform with these. How one gets staff to do this is up to the enterprise. For example, it could result in a mechanistic and autocratic approach. Or it could also be used to encourage a more open and human style of management.

Like training itself, quality is part of everybody's responsibility. Total quality management (TQM) means using all the means available, adopting both the social (people) and technical (things) approaches.

Management Style

Building peoples' capacity is founded on a belief in human potential. Douglas McGregor (1906 – 1964) was a professor of industrial management at MIT – the Massachusetts Institute of Technology. He rejected (McGregor, 1960) the commonly held views that:

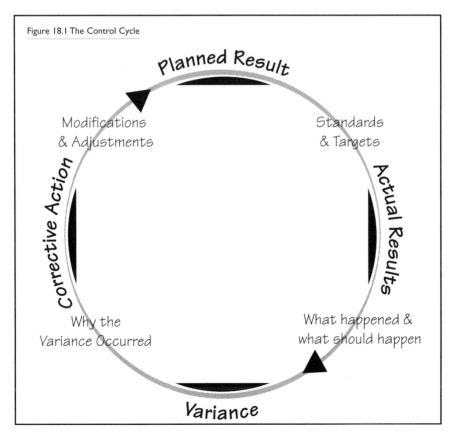

Figure 18.1 The Control Cycle

Planned Result

Modifications & Adjustments

Standards & Targets

Corrective Action

Actual Results

Why the Variance Occurred

What happened & what should happen

Variance

- people are basically lazy.
- they dislike work and try to avoid it.
- because people dislike work, they have to be controlled, told what to do, even threatened with punishment
- people don't have ambition. They don't want to take initiatives, and they avoid responsibility.
- the only way to motivate people is with reward and punishment – the "carrot and the stick".
- all that people want is security.

This pessimistic assessment of human nature leads to a very controlled, restrictive kind of management. McGregor called it Theory X. Nobody is trusted, nobody is developed, one is constantly checked or inspected. There is often an atmosphere of fear, anxiety and antagonism.

McGregor compared this view with that of Theory Y. This took an altogether more positive view of human potential:

- that giving physical and mental effort to work is just as natural as play or rest.
- that people exercise self control when they work on objectives to which they are committed. They don't have to be coerced or threatened.
- that one of the highest rewards for work is the feeling of job satisfaction and self fulfilment.
- that people learn not only to accept responsibility but to seek it.
- that creativity is widely, not narrowly, distributed among the population.
- that the intellectual potential of most human beings is only partially realised.

A Question of Values

The choice between McGregor's two contrasting theories is a matter of values. These vary from culture to culture. Cultural differences have already been mentioned in relation to markets (see Chapter 3).

If ones believes in Theory Y and takes a positive approach to one's staff, this leads to an open style of management. However, if one believes more in Theory X and adopts a more paternalistic, authoritative approach, this tends to be restricting. Power is concentrated at the top, communication is limited and there is little participation.

Various approaches have been adopted to maintain the participation of staff in quality control. Quality circles is one such approach. They bring together groups of volunteer employees to discuss quality problems, and propose solutions and ways to improve.

At the macro level this book has argued for the widest possible participation of the sector and community at large, in the development and management of tourism.

Quality Circles

The facilitator is the key resource person, within an enterprise, who makes a quality circle operational and effective. The facilitator explains the purpose, recruits volunteers, trains the group leaders, and helps the quality circle in its discussions.

A quality circle will normally have the following characteristics:

- ✓ participation is voluntary.
- ✓ groups normally number from about 5 to 12 persons.
- ✓ all members are encouraged to participate actively.
- ✓ results are attributed to the group – not to individuals.
- ✓ members are encouraged to be creative.
- ✓ the atmosphere is open and stimulating.
- ✓ proceedings are highly participative.
- ✓ management is wholly supportive.

The following are among the issues examined:

- ✓ improving quality.
- ✓ maintaining standards.
- ✓ building teamwork.
- ✓ reducing on-the-job mistakes.
- ✓ improving safety records.
- ✓ reducing waste.
- ✓ reducing costs.
- ✓ solving operational problems.
- ✓ increasing efficiency.
- ✓ improving morale.

Tangible and Intangible Items

One can set a clearly specified standard for tangible, measurable items. For example, a particular type of steak – that it should be so many centimetres thick and weigh so many grams. Checklists are useful to control standards which are easily evaluated or measurable such as the size of food portions or drinks, or the condition of a guest bedroom or bathroom. In inspecting and checking that things are correct, they enable the worker or supervisor to take a very thorough approach. A kitchen, for example, may display pictures or dishes on the wall with a reminder of the corresponding portion sizes. Cooks can check very quickly that presentation and portion sizes are correct.

However, the quality of the intangible aspects of service (discussed in Chapter 4) cannot be standardised. One cannot set a standard for a smile. One cannot say that it should be so many centimetres long, so many centimetres wide, and be held in place for at least ten seconds. It would be nonsense. Staff smile as a spontaneous response to a given situation, a question of approach and attitude. However, there are too many contacts – e.g. in a hotel – between staff and guests to permit their close monitoring. In tourism there are even more contacts between the host population in general and the visitors. Staff are largely responsible themselves for the quality of their contacts with visitors and the service which they give. Well trained and motivated staff will want to do their best. Staff should be empowered to give good service and to care for the customer.

Empowerment

Empowerment simply means to:

- give staff the responsibility to act without prior authorisation.
- indicate the kinds of situations in which such responsibility should be exercised.
- include this in job descriptions – e.g. "take all reasonable action to satisfy customers".
- train staff to interpret policy, make judgements and take appropriate action.
- be consistent in encouraging staff to take responsibility.
- establish a procedure for staff to report the actions they took.
- back-up and support staff when they decide to take action.

One should train staff to be empowered. First they should understand and subscribe to the values which contribute to excellence in the tourism product and marketing mix. Second, they should understand service elements and the importance of human warmth. One can help to develop their thinking and ideas by giving them examples of different situations. Skills alone are insufficient, staff also need to be interested and motivated. Empowerment can be included in the public awareness and training programmes described in Chapter 15.

Quality Control and Improvement

As noted, macro relates to the sector as a hole, micro to the management of particular companies or individual enterprises. At the micro level, management checks constantly whether the product meets market needs. One changes the standards to better meet these needs. Improvement is a part of product re-engineering. For example, in a hotel or resort:

- We should not serve tea directly in the cup, we should serve a pot of tea.

- The grilled beefsteak is too small – there are many complaints. We should increase the size from 150 grams to 230 grams.

- The glass for the water is very ugly. We should change to something more appropriate.

- We should start putting tooth picks on all the restaurant tables.

- We should keep the discotheque open for at least another hour. It closes too early.

- We should provide a hand towel in each bathroom as well as a bath towel.

- We should provide a colour television in all the rooms.

- Guests are waiting too long for luggage to be brought up to, or down from, their rooms. We should add two more bellmen (porters) to the staff.

- We should buy an Espresso coffee machine, and start offering Espresso coffee.

- The swimming pool is too small – we should enlarge it or build a bigger one.

These kinds of suggestions have cost, price, and revenue implications. Improving the product and incurring higher operating costs or increased capital investment, requires careful analysis by management. Does it make sense? Is it justifiable? Will it make the product more competitive? Will it produce more revenue? Is it important to the guests – will it produce, proportionately, greater satisfaction?

Some product improvement, however, may have no cost implications. There may be many ways of improving the service without incurring additional costs. This may be possible through better training of the staff, and more effective motivation.

For example:

- That the air stewardesses take note of the passenger's names. They can then, when giving them in-flight service, address them by name.

- That in a hotel, arriving guests are greeted and welcomed more warmly.
- That the head waiter goes round the restaurant tables, collecting customer requests for the pianist.
- That the hotel manager calls some of the arriving guests shortly after check-in. He welcomes them to the hotel and checks that they are happy and satisfied.
- That room attendants (e.g. housemaids) responsible for particular sections, introduce themselves to arriving guests and ask if they require anything.
- That the restaurant manager makes sure to check with customers at the end of the meal. He asks if everything has been satisfactory, and offers to make a table reservation for a return visit.
- That a travel agent takes time to describe very fully the client's holiday destination.

These are mostly a question of extra effort – not extra costs. Good service hinges on such attention to detail.

A the macro level, the trade and professional associations and the government tourism administration can generate ideas and suggestions for the sector as a whole, or for a sub-sector such as hotels or restaurants. They can produce publications on standards and recommended improvements and, or, organise related workshops and training activities.

Quality Management Workshops and Other Training Initiatives

Apart from the enforcement of agreed minimum standards, it is difficult to achieve sector-wide awareness of quality. The private sector tourism enterprises are numerous and diverse. Some companies may already operate with ISO 9000 or a similar quality management system. However, the many smaller enterprises may know little about quality and its importance in maximising customer satisfaction and profitability.

As noted, publications and instructional materials can provide guidelines and benchmarks aimed at improving operational standards. Regular quality workshops can review sectoral performance and provide the feedback gleaned from visitor surveys. They can focus on quality and help owners and managers to improve their operations. Such initiatives should be linked to the training schemes discussed in Chapters 15 and 22.

Various sector-wide standards are covered in the four chapters which follow. They all relate to quality, dealing with legislation, physical planning, classification and grading, and human resources development. They describe how these various tools (summarised in Chapter 15) can be used to manage tourism.

Reference

McGregor, D. (1960). *The Human Side of Enterprise*, McGraw-Hill

chapter nineteen
Legislation

This chapter describes the various components of a legislative framework governing the development and operation of tourism. These are the legislative tools described in Chapter 15 as part of the management tools. The chapter goes on to explain the differences between registration, licensing, classification and grading, and the concept of minimum standards. It describes the types of standards required in commercial accommodation establishments. It then includes a checklist for the development of various types of regulations. The chapter concludes with the right of appeal and the concept of an ombudsperson.

A Legislative Framework

The rule of law establishes a framework for the common good. It establishes what people cannot do and what they are required to do.

There are two types of legislation

- that which is specific to the tourism and related sectors;
- that which concerns all sectors of society including tourism.

Regulations governing tourism are generally designed to achieve:

- a register of each type of tourism business;
- the fulfilment other information needs;
- minimum standards of safety and security;
- minimum standards of hygiene and sanitation;
- minimum building and environmental standards;
- other consumer protection;
- minimum standards of facilities, furniture, fixtures and equipment;
- the prevention of bawdy or immoral behaviour;
- other acceptable and peaceful standards of operation, respecting the rights of neighbours;
- taxes from tourism to spend on tourism – particularly on marketing and training;

• taxes from tourism for the general good.

If a law exists it should be enforced. If it does not serve a justifiable purpose it should be repealed.

All Sectors of Society

As noted, the achievement of all social order requires rules. Every aspect of society is regulated by law. There is civil law, criminal law, banking law, and business law – there are laws for torts, contracts, consumer protection, property, monopolies, inheritance and insurance. There are taxes to be paid, and returns to be made. There are citizen's rights and laws to govern personal liberty, education, employment, freedom of expression, privacy, freedom of information, and housing and health.

The tourism sector monitors all law which, however indirectly, affects it. It may also lobby for exemptions or a better deal under the law. It argues its case accordingly and tries to justify its demands. It may also argue that new laws are necessary or that an existing law is unnecessary. It is up to the trade associations to lobby government on behalf of their members. They may do this either through the GTA or directly.

Where the GTA supports the position of the private sector it should take the lead role in making representations at the highest level of government. Whether it supports the private sector or not, it will be able to give detailed reasons and argue its position in full.

Registration, Licensing, Classification and Grading

A government tourism administration:

• wishes to maintain an up-to-date overview of the sector, with the details about each particular sub sector, e.g. hotels, guest houses, bed and breakfast operations, restaurants, travel agencies, and tour operators. It collects and holds some basic data about each establishment – e.g. its location, size, type, and category. This makes it possible to analyse the composition and characteristics of the sector. The data is normally incorporated within a total tourism assets inventory which forms a part of a complete and integrated information system (see Chapter 8 on market research). To do this requires annual registration and the supply of the data in question. This is usually made a statutory requirement.

• may wish, in addition to registration, to ensure that every establishment meets certain minimum standards. These include the planning regulations which cover areas such as parking, height, density and land use. Also the building regulations which cover, among other things, health and safety, fire prevention, energy conservation, ventilation, drainage, access and services for the disabled, and the various other planning and building regulations (see Chapter 20 on physical planning). Additional standards, not included in the planning and building regulations, may also be included. Some types of tourism enterprises – e.g. travel agencies and tour operators – may have to meet other requirements such as the provision of financial guarantees against performance. A license or permit ensures that all requirements are met.

• may wish to classify and grade hotels and tourism establishments according to their level of facilities and services, grading them accordingly. For example, hotels are normally awarded from one to five stars. A classification and grading scheme, among other things, provides guidance to the market and creates a system of industry-wide standards.

Where a GTA chooses to administrate a mandatory classification and grading scheme, it is often incorporated within a registration and licensing requirement. Chapter 21 discusses classification and grading in more detail, exploring the pros and cons of government schemes.

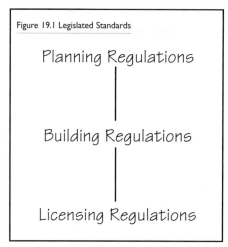

Figure 19.1 Legislated Standards

Planning Regulations

Building Regulations

Licensing Regulations

Standards are made part of either planning, building or licensing regulations (see Figure 19.1). The relative use of these three types of legislation differs from country to country. For example, where licensing regulations do not exist, the planning and building regulations (see Chapter 20) stand alone. Enforcement is then the responsibility of the local authority. If a licensing system is introduced, e.g. under the GTA, one works with the planning authorities, public health authority, and the fire department to ensure that their standards are met.

Before one decides on regulations one should ensure:

• that regulations are really needed – and that the sector cannot control and police itself.

• that the regulations serve the needs for which they have been written – no more and no less.

• that they are administrated efficiently by the appropriate agency – without bureaucratic waffling and obscurity. And without corruption.

Minimum Standards

As noted, these are the legislated minimum standards which every establishment must meet, regardless of their marketing mix, or any level of classification and grade.

These minimum standards can be of two types:

- the minimum requirements deemed necessary to satisfy safety, health, sanitation and hygiene requirements, use by disabled persons, fire prevention, freedom from nuisances, provision of parking etc.

- quality requirements aimed at protecting consumers and ensuring that they receive certain minimum standards of quality. For example, the size and minimum range of facilities, or access to daylight, are more to do with quality than any particular aspect of safety or health.

A licensing system for hotels and commercial accommodation, apart from any classification and grading system, may establish such minimum standards. These add to the standards already found in the planning and building regulations. If a mandatory government classification and grading scheme is in use, it will normally incorporate the minimum standards.

However, as noted, all minimum standards may be incorporated in the planning and building regulations (including public health and fire requirements). This avoids the dangers of duplication and overlaps.

In many places a hotel is defined as having at least 10 rooms. However, as noted in Chapter 5, the term hotel may cover all types of accommodation regardless of the number of rooms.

To set minimum standards one asks the question – What is essential in this type of establishment? Emphasis is on "essential" – items that are optional can be left to the discretion of the operator.

Minimum standards normally cover the surroundings and external appearance, internal cleanliness, maintenance including pest control, and the entrance, corridors and public areas. They also cover the guest notices to be displayed, e.g. safe custody for valuables, any operating permit or license, instructions on fire prevention and what to do in the case of fire.

In hotels, they may also cover:

- the guest bedroom – windows and natural light, artificial lighting and the door locking system.

- the minimum size of bedrooms, bathrooms and toilets. As an example, one might require a bedroom of 12 square metres (single occupancy) and 16 square metres (double occupancy), a bathroom of 4.5 square metres with toilet, 4 square metres without toilet, and 2 square metres for a separate toilet.

- the furniture, fittings, equipment for a bedroom, bathroom and toilet.

- guest supplies such as towels and soap, a glass, and in some countries, candles, candle holders and matches may be included. A first aid kit is required in case of accidents or emergencies.

- the minimum ratio of bathrooms to bedrooms, e.g. one bathroom for every five bedrooms and one toilet (either separate or incorporated in the bathroom) for every five bedrooms.

Standards may also be developed for restaurants and bars (either operating within a hotel or separately).

Food handlers shall be subject to an annual medical check up for contagious diseases. Other minimum standards required for a restaurant (and if applicable a bar) cover the dining room area of restaurants or bars, toilet facilities and kitchens. All kitchens should be clean and hygienic at all times, and have adequate arrangements for the washing of utensils, crockery, cutlery and glassware. The kitchen should be well ventilated, and equipped sufficiently to permit all cooking processes in the basic/entry level occupational skill standard for food preparation.

All parts of the kitchen premises should conform with health regulations regarding food storage, refuse, insect and vermin protection, and staff washing and toilet facilities.

Checklist for the Development of Tourism Regulations

An overall tourism law or proclamation acts as an umbrella to give the GTA power to regulate all of tourism's various sub sectors. It normally does this through the issue of a license or permit. For example:

- Travel agencies and tour operator regulations establish the conditions, standards and requirements for the conduct of this kind of business. They govern minimum standards and consumer protection (see Chapters 14 and 15), particularly in the event of default or bankruptcy.

- Local tourist transportation. These regulations are particularly concerned with safety and consumer protection.

- Hotel, restaurants and bars. These regulations also govern the standards, conduct of the business, safety, consumer protection and the control of undesirable elements.

- Tourist guides. These regulations govern standards, and appropriate conduct and behaviour.

- Tourism planning and design guidelines and standards. These regulations are the minimum physical standards, governing the design, size, site use and height of buildings.

- Diving and watersports regulations are concerned mainly with consumer protection and safety.
- Duty free retailing. These regulations govern the conditions for the conduct of businees, and safeguard society against abuse and malpractice.

Poorly drafted regulations tend to contain many inconsistencies, ambiguities and omissions. One should be sure that they:

✓ achieve precise objectives.
✓ do not repeat themselves.
✓ do not duplicate or contradict other existing legislation.
✓ are crystal clear – easy to understand – easy to interpret.
✓ cover everything necessary.
✓ have nothing unnecessary.

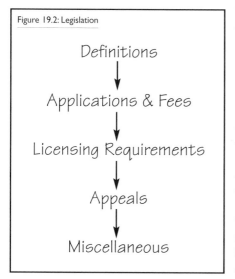

Figure 19.2: Legislation

Definitions
↓
Applications & Fees
↓
Licensing Requirements
↓
Appeals
↓
Miscellaneous

The following represents a checklist for the development of regulations, broken down according to a system of headings. These cover definitions, applications and fees, license or permit requirements, appeals, and miscellaneous (see Figure 19.2). Other articles or sections may be slotted in as necessary e.g. in the handicraft regulations the details of special award schemes, skills competitions, and certificates of authenticity; in the hotel, restaurant and bar regulations the inclusion of the rights and duties of hoteliers and restauranteurs; and in casino regulations the special powers of inspection.

Definitions of the various terms used in the regulations.

These are the precise definitions of all the terms employed. They ensure clarity and freedom from any ambiguity. As noted, to what and how the regulations apply must be clear.

Applications and fees

This section usually states:

- which persons and type of business must have a license or permit for the purpose of the regulations.

- any restrictions which apply – e.g. age and nationality of the applicant.

- when the application must be made. It also states where the application forms can be obtained.

- that any person operating the facility or service specified without a license or operating permit shall be guilty of an a offence and liable on conviction to a fine and, or, a period in prison.

- the length of time for which the license or permit is issued.

- that if, at the expiry of a license or permit, the holder does not wish to renew it, he or she will tell authorities within a period of 15 days before the expiry, giving the reasons.

- the conditions and procedures for renewing the license or permit or transferring it in the event of death of the holder, or sale of the business, or decision to stop doing business.

- any requirements for submitting documentary evidence with the application – e.g. report of a survey or independent inspection of vehicles or vessels, architectural drawings, cross sections and elevations, evidence of passing an examination, or copies of qualifications or certificates etc.

- the fees to be paid for the issue of the license or permit, and when they must be paid.

- on issue of the license or permit, how and where it must be displayed.

- any other requirements for signifying that a license or permit has been issued e.g. a badge and identification card for tourist guides, and the license or permit number on the hull of a pleasure craft.

License or permit requirements

This section usually states:

- any other licenses or permits which the applicant must already possess e.g. a business license or registration.

- that, where applicable, the enterprise must conform with local fire prevention regulations.

- that these same premises must conform with local health and sanitation regulations.

- that the premises must also conform with planning and building regulations.

- any minimum training and, or, qualifications which the applicant and, or, his staff must have.

- any financial guarantees which must provided and posted.

- any other requirements and conditions which the premises and, or, any items of equipment must satisfy.

- the insurance coverage which the applicant must have, and the evidence to this effect which must be provided.

- any requirement to post or display the prices or tariffs charged

- the standards of conduct which must be observed in the operation of the business.

- that the applicant or holder of a permit may make no false or misleading statements or claims with regard to the products or services provided.

- that any permit holder not maintaining or upholding any of these standards or requirements may have his or her license or permit revoked, or suspended until he or she has rectified the deficiencies.

- that in the event of any criminal or illegal conduct in the running of the business, the discretion exists to close down the premises with immediate effect.

- when something comprises an offence, the penalty which is payable, on conviction, indicating the amount of the fine and, or, the period of imprisonment.

- that license or permit holders shall inform the authorities of any changes to the information provided in the application, which may occur during the period of the validity of the license or permit.

- that the license or permit holder shall provide the authorities with an annual statistical report in the format indicated.

Appeals

This section usually states:

- to which authority an appeal may be made.

- the circumstances under which an appeal may be made to the high court.

Miscellaneous

This section usually states:

- which businesses do not fall under the provisions of the regulations and are exempt.

- when the regulations are not intended to infringe the rights of the local authorities to control certain other activities e.g. the control of local markets, stalls or pedlars.

- what regulations or notices are hereby amended or repealed.

- the effective date of the regulations.

The Right of Appeal

The right of appeal is fundamental. It extends the right to everyone to object and appeal to a higher authority. It also provides a safeguard against the possible errors committed by the bureaucracy. The constitution normally guarantees equality and fairness under the rule of law.

An Ombudsperson

The office of ombudsperson exists in many countries. It is intended as an effective safeguard against bureaucratic wrangling or administrative incompetence. It should often overcome the need for expensive and time consuming appeals. An ombudsperson checks the facts of a case and takes action accordingly.

chapter twenty
Physical Planning

This chapter covers the physical planning tools described in Chapter 15 as part of the management tools. It starts by examining the land use planning system and its objectives. It goes on to describe planning at the national, regional and local levels. It then explains the various aspects of carrying capacity and a project's environmental impact. The chapter then describes planning regulations and provides a checklist of the principal considerations. It explains listed buildings, controls on outdoor advertising and signs, and lists the items included in building regulations.

The Planning System

A planning system aims at the effective use of land, and ensures that the competing demands for land are met in the best interests of all. Sound land use planning applies a wide range of economic, social and environmental criteria. It:

- develops a land use plan, what goes where and in what shape and form;
- helps people to plan the use of their land within this framework of rules and regulations;
- encourages people, through possible incentives, to develop particular types of enterprise in certain areas;
- allows people the right to present and argue their particular points of view.

All governments should try to regulate physical planning to ensure that:

- the natural environment and the best elements of the current man-made environment are protected;
- the right things get built in the right places and that the wrong things do not get built;
- the man-made environment is continually enhanced, through better traffic management, landscaping and general urban planning;
- minimum planning and building standards are met – density, height, setbacks, safety, health and sanitation;

- people are able to enjoy an agreeable environment which adds to the quality of life;
- development and growth are `sustainable'.

This tries to enhance the quality of life, ensuring the minimum standards for people to live in agreeable surroundings under the best possible conditions. In Spain in the 1950s and 1960s the Mediterranean coast was allowed, for the sake of economic development alone, to develop haphazardly. The damage done is being rectified but far from completely.

Sound planning observes the following principles:

- the environment has to meet certain commonly agreed quality standards e.g. one may not want overcrowding, high rise buildings, an absence of sufficient car parking, and all the trees to be cut down. The standards reflect the community's values about how, and in what kind of environment, people would like to live.

- in tourism they also concern the sort of environment people would like to visit. To damage this environment can damage tourism.

- the environment should also provide certain standards of health and safety, e.g. pollution has to be prevented, satisfactory sanitation provided, flooding avoided, road safety assured, and access to light and views maintained.

- there has to be a zoning policy based on designated land use. Developments of certain types have to be channelled to certain areas, while rural land is kept development-free.

The planning system normally covers planning, environmental and building regulations, as well as fire and public health requirements. However, as noted in Chapter 13, the responsibilities – within government departments – often overlap. Tourism-related decisions should be coordinated in the most effective way possible.

Different Planning Levels

Planning covers a whole country and is normally broken down to cover three levels:

- **The national level.** At this level the government department responsible for physical planning serves a number of different functions. It provides the guidelines on strategies, standards and procedures, and also acts as the arbiter in the case of uncertainty or disputes. It also sets the guidelines for planning organisation and methods; the planning officers and committees, the scope of their activities and their independence and competence.

- **The regional level** normally follows the administrative division of the country into counties, provinces or states. The regional authority's planning department covers the broader strategy issues which are best decided for the area as a whole, e.g. economic development (including tourism, leisure and recreation), roads and other infrastructure, residential housing, transport policies, education and public health. In this, it liaises with the other government departments also operating at the regional level.

- **The local level** includes districts and municipalities, and tackles the full nitty-gritty of planning. It should come up with a land use and zoning strategy, together with planning standards and objectives. It should know what it is setting out to achieve, in accordance with the tourism development strategy described in earlier chapters. This strategy should be acted upon but this doesn't always happen. The development strategy often says one thing but the planning people move in a different direction. The planning authorities should participate in the formulation of strategy, the consensus building discussed in Chapter 13, and feel committed to its implementation.

As indicated in Chapter 13, and as illustrated in Figure 13.1, there should exist a dynamic interaction between the three levels – national, regional and local; a constant interchange of criteria and an inter-comparison of results.

Beyond the minimum framework of planning controls and regulations, people find their own design solutions. One expects both public and private sectors to implement strategy with conceptual vision and exciting creativity.

Environmental Impact

One assesses environmental impact before giving planning permission. However, the impact of any project should be monitored continuously. There are basically two impacts:

- the impact of the physical project itself, its infrastructure, buildings and facilities, how they were situated and planned, what equipment and installations they have, and how they will operate.

- the impact of the people who will visit, use or patronise the project; hence the carrying capacity (see Chapter 15 and 17).

All projects have these two impacts – clearly interrelated – the physical planning impact and the people impact. These impacts differ from project to project, e.g. a famous monument or museum may have a problem with the number of visitors – the people impact – while a restaurant in a resort area may have a worrying physical planning impact.

Planning Regulations

The building of tourism enterprise premises, or the reconstruction, change of use, renovation, extension or alteration of existing premises, should require planning permission. The process should always include the right to appeal.

Developers should be able to have informal discussions with planning officials, both before and after submitting an application. This can give them indications on any necessary additions or modifications.

The UK authorities issue planning guidelines to help people in the preparation of applications. This is a useful way of briefing applicants and putting them on the right path.

In many countries, one now finds that a separate environmental statement is required for review by a specialised environmental agency. This tends to create bureaucratic duplication and delay. Environmental characteristics are best included as part of the planning application. Planning officials are competent to judge environmental aspects, while consulting the specialised agency as necessary.

Land for tourism development is usually scarce. Its extravagant use decreases its tourism yield. One should avoid wasteful use (e.g. 20 rooms on a 5 hectare site). A planning authority may establish guidelines on minimum yields per hectare based on particular zones.

As a part of development plans, the planning authority designates zones for various kinds of development, including tourism. Within each zone, it establishes standards for setbacks, site ratios, floor area ratios and height restrictions.

- **Setbacks.** These are from neighbouring buildings, from access and surrounding roads and from shorelines at high water and riverbanks. For the latter they may range from 50 to 100 metres from the shoreline, down to 10 to 20 meters for riverbanks. In countryside and resort locations setbacks between buildings or from roads may be liberal, ranging from 30 to 50 meters. In urban areas they may go down to 2 to 5. Normally a planning authority determines setbacks according to local characteristics

- **Site ratios.** This is the ratio between the area covered by the proposed buildings and the total site area. In new destinations on beachfront locations it may be low ranging from 35 to 60 per cent. In urban areas it may range from 70 to 90 per cent. A low site ratio contributes to a spacious resort atmosphere.

- **Floor area ratios.** This is the ratio of the total floor area to the total site area. This may be low – say 40 or 50 percent in low density resort locations – but very high in city centres. A floor area ratio much higher than the site ratio, signifies a high rise building sitting in expansive grounds.

- **Height restrictions.** One can count an approximate 3 meters for each storey. In sensitive resort destinations height may be restricted to four storeys or less – just about under the treetops. In urban areas it depends on the particular location, but high rise building often become the norm.

The price of land tends to determine the density of building. High prices tend to mean high buildings.

Beaches should always be kept open to the public. When Tony Blair, the British Prime Minister, holidayed on the Tuscany coast in 1999, the local authority closed off a large expanse of beach. However, public access was re-established at Blair's request.

The planning application should include information based on the following checklist (also data for the environmental impact assessment [Doswell, 1997]):

Plans

- Submit a site plan, 1:100 scale drawings, cross sections and elevations.

Project concept

- Give a brief overall description of the project, and its business justification. This should indicate the revenues and the number of jobs which it is expected to generate. It should describe the project's nature, form, size, category, and range of activities. Also the number of people expected to use the facility, and the corresponding planned carrying capacity. Environmentalists and building specialists can advise on the protection and conservation aspects related to carrying capacity.

- Describe any changes to the area. Illustrate the visual impact and the effects on landscape and views. Show why the development has a favourable and acceptable overall impact.

- List the benefits and nuisances to the local community. Include details of the local labour force by department and occupation, together with its profile; gender, distribution by age, where they presently live and how they will journey to work. Also any staff housing needs. Describe the implications for health, education and other social services.

- Summarise the general effects of the development on the neighbouring buildings and population.

Location and site

- Show on the site plan the positioning of proposed buildings, access roads, parking areas, engineering installations, the form of the development and its landscaping, and the scale of the project and its relationship to adjoining sites.

- Give the precise details of the location of the project and its site (attach a map). Show the trees which exist. No tree may be cut down or removed unless agreed beforehand.

- Indicate the site coverage ratio, floor area ratio and the setbacks allowed from (i) neighbouring buildings (ii) surrounding roads (iii) the shoreline at high water (if applicable) or river bank (if applicable); and annotate the building elevations attached, showing the heights of buildings. In the case of a hotel or resort, indicate the ratio of rooms to each hectare of land or portion of a hectare.

Design/architectural solution

- Summarise this solution and highlight its key features. This should refer to the accompanying drawings, cross sections and elevations, explaining the functional interrelationships between areas and buildings, any site limitations, the way in which planning guidelines have been met, and the style and image of the proposed scheme. Also the merits of the architectural design of the building exteriors. Planning regulations can cover architectural style and particular finishes e.g. tiled roofs, for the development of facilities in particular areas.

- Architectural values reflect the product and image, and comprise an important part of the marketing mix. In this sense, a government department should not pre-empt private sector initiatives. However, one should guard against schemes which may damage the whole feel of the local area. One can also provide guidelines on the development of particular locations, with suggestions on scale, architectural character, and the use of particular building materials and external finishes.

Construction

- Provide details about the building materials, construction methods and timetable. Describe the organisation of work, materials and equipment during the construction phase. Also describe the site preparation, transportation of materials to the site, any blasting, excavation, and, or, earthmoving, and the disposal of construction spoil and waste. Also the control of dust, noise, drainage and runoffs during construction, and the measures taken to avoid water pollution.

Transport access

- Describe access roads and the volume of traffic generated. Indicate the implications, needs and solutions. Provide full details of the car parking (capacity and location).

Water supply

- Provide details about the demand for water, and access to water, during the construction stage. Also list any special operational needs – such as a swimming pool and indicate fire fighting provisions. Indicate the estimated monthly and annual water consumption.

- Detail the capacity of planned storage tanks together with any provision for water catchment.

Drainage

- Detail drainage needs, indicating if the site has any problematic aspects. Show the proposed stormwater drainage.

Sewage treatment and waste disposal

- Include full details of the treatment and disposal of sewage together with the full specifications of the proposed installations. Provide details of other waste disposal.

Electricity

- Indicate demand for electricity as the development proceeds. Show the eventual annual energy needs, together with the provision for any emergency supply. Indicate the use of alternate energy sources (solar) together with the resulting annual saving.

Telecommunications

- List the details of the proposed installations and needs. Describe the demand when the project is fully operational.

Pollution problems

- Describe the safeguards against all kinds of pollution; air and noise, water including the sea, and any rivers or lakes.

Coastline

- If on the sea, describe the project's interrelationship with overall coastline management. Indicate the provision of public access to beaches.

Flora and fauna

- Describe the effect on the site's vegetation and wildlife. Also indicate any dangers to the wildlife in the surrounding area.

Listed Buildings

One should list and protect buildings of special architectural and historical interest. In doing so one usually consults with any persons or organisations having special knowledge of such buildings.

As soon as a building is classified as "protected" and included on the list, owners are informed. They are not permitted to rebuild, demolish (wholly or partly), alter, extend, renovate or in any way change the appearance and substance of the building, without applying for permission. The application should include details of the proposed work.

In the event that an application is refused, the planning authority may suggest an alternative and acceptable manner to carry out the work.

Outdoor Advertising

Planning authorities should also control outdoor advertising and signs, their characteristics and positioning, e.g. posters, notices, boards, pole and canopy signs, directional signs, flag advertisements, traffic signs and place-names. Places of particular scenic beauty or historical importance are particularly vulnerable to obtrusive advertisements and signs. Where permission is rejected applicants have the right of appeal.

Some signs and advertisements may not need permission, e.g. "beware of the dog" signs, or the name of a surgery or company operating at the premises. The planning authority indicates the conditions under which these signs can be displayed.

Building Regulations

The planning system does not regulate how a building is constructed. This is done by the building regulations.

Building regulations are developed to ensure minimum standards of health, safety, energy conservation and, generally, the comfort and ease-of-use of disabled persons. From country to country they normally cover the same things although the way in which they are listed may differ. In the UK they are grouped under the following 13 headings:

1   Structure. Deals with aspects of loading and ground movement.

2   Fire safety. Covers the means of escape, the prevention of internal fire spread, external fire spread, and access and facilities for the fire service.

3   Site preparation and resistance to moisture. Deals with preparation of the site, absence of dangerous and offensive substances, and sub-soil drainage. Also resistance to weather and ground moisture.

4   Deals with toxic substances in particular relation to cavity insulation.

5   Covers resistance to the passage of sound and airborne sound through walls, floors and stairs. Also impact sound – floors and stairs.

6   Ventilation. Deals with condensation in roofs and the means of ventilation.

7   Hygiene. Regulates sanitary conveniences and washing facilities. Also bathrooms and hot water storage.

8   Drainage and waste disposal. Covers sanitary pipework and drainage, and cesspools and tanks. Also rainwater drainage and solid waste storage.

9   Deals with heat producing appliances.

10   Stairs, ramps and guards. Regulates stairs and ramps, and protection

from possible falls. Also vehicle barriers.

11   Covers conservation of fuel and power.

12   Access and facilities for disabled people. Covers access and use. Also audience or spectator seating.

13   Deals with glazing – materials and protection.

The local authority or municipality is usually responsible for the administration of such regulations. Application should be made for approval, attaching plans. These should include the technical specifications requested, e.g. relevant structural calculations. An inspection is normally carried out while other competent agencies, e.g. in charge of fire and water, are consulted. The authority must always be satisfied that regulations have been met. One should be able to appeal if an application is not approved.

Reference

Doswell, Roger. (1997). *Tourism – How Effective Management Makes the Difference*, Butterworth Heinemann.

chapter twenty-one
Classification and Grading

T his chapter starts by listing the purposes of classification and grading systems, and indicating the shortcomings of many government administrated systems. It goes on to examine the influences in a visitor's choice of accommodation and looks at who can operates a classification system. The chapter then explains the difference between classification and grading and goes on to discuss advisory services and training. It then describes the approach adopted by the Scottish Tourist Board, and the importance of effective inspection. The chapter concludes by describing the Michelin approach to private sector guides.

The Purposes of Classification and Grading Systems

The purposes of a system (see Figure 21.1) is to:

- set, maintain and improve quality standards, according to the concepts described in Chapter 18.

- define the various categories of establishment and the levels of facilities and services they should possess

- enable a GTA to analyse, structure and plan the future development of

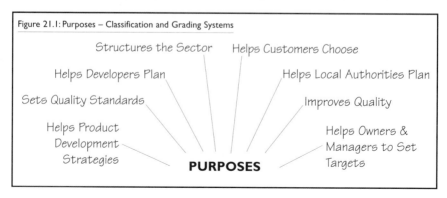

Figure 21.1: Purposes – Classification and Grading Systems

Structures the Sector   Helps Customers Choose

Helps Developers Plan   Helps Local Authorities Plan

Sets Quality Standards   Improves Quality

Helps Product Development Strategies   Helps Owners & Managers to Set Targets

PURPOSES

the sector according to these categories. The sector analyses the composition and developmental needs of the sector – according to levels, categories, location and prices of facilities. Chapter 11 on positioning and Chapters 16 and 17 on regeneration, re-engineering and expansion reflect this process.

- help a local authority to implement an agreed strategy and define a certain category of facility for a particular site. In the UK's National Planning Forum's report on "Planning for Tourism" cites a case where a local authority indicated that it wanted a four star hotel with conference facilities on a particular site (NPF, 1998).

- help a customer to choose an enterprise, based on the facilities, services and quality sought.

- help a developer to plan what facilities and services to incorporate in a particular project.

- help owners and managers to know the standards to target, in any attempt to upgrade and improve their operations.

These objectives are all necessary but a classification and grading system is not the only way to achieve them.

The Failure of Government-Driven Systems

Many government-driven classification systems can be criticised on the following counts:

- as noted, they tend to concentrate on entirely quantifiable aspects of the product, e.g. the range, size and furnishing of facilities, the type and availability of services, while ignoring any qualitative appraisal of these services. They therefore apply partial criteria which do not accurately reflect the needs or preferences of the customers.

- as a result, there exists a poor correlation between the classification awarded and the response of the market, e.g. the scheme says a hotel is of a particular category but it is clear that the customers don't agree.

- there is little help to upgrade standards through the counselling and training of owners and operators, or the training of staff.

- they do not mention the image factors which would influence a customer's perception of the establishment.

- they do not provide an accurate indication of the price/value relationship.

- they ignore the ease and convenience of purchase through an efficient reservations service, travel trade links and sales organisation.

- inspections are inconsistent and standards are loosely applied.

- the inspectors are sometimes insufficiently trained and motivated. They may also be poorly paid and open to bribery.

This means that systems do not serve either the interests of the market or the operators themselves. They are counter productive and, in most cases, governments would do well to drop them. Such systems can have the following negative effects:

- they can lead owners and operators into mistaken ideas about the acceptability of their establishments in the market place.

- this can induce operators to spend money on the wrong things.

- it may also lead them to price inappropriately, developing a marketing mix with little relevance to needs and realities.

- they also tend to encourage owners and operators to ignore the essential requirements of good service and in-house training.

The classification system itself is not only disregarded by the market, but also acts as an obstacle to the sector's improvement and development. It can also throw the pricing out of gear with the marketing mix. Establishments price according to their level of classification. For example a five star hotel charges the most, a one star the least. However, if the classification criteria do not reflect market needs the price is wrong – the consumer may see a different price/value relationship. If this is the case the system distorts the function of the market.

The assessment criteria in any classification and grading system must be the same ones a consumer would use. One identifies these through market research.

A government driven system as such is not advisable. However, a GTA coordinated system – with the extensive participation of the sector – can be successful. This is essentially a sector-driven system; the sector agrees its own standards and uses the system to control itself.

Helping the User Choose

Classification and grading systems are not widely effective as a marketing tool. They appear to be of most help in choosing the smaller establishments, e.g. guest houses and bed and breakfast operations. Users choose particular facilities based on a variety of influences:

- **Leisure visitors** often buy their accommodation through a tour operator (e.g. through an inclusive tour – by choosing a package they choose the hotel). The tour operator may also guide and influence them on the choice of other facilities and services. Alternatively, they may be similarly influenced by travel agencies and airlines, or the brand names of various hotel, restaurant or other companies or by particular advertising and promotion. They can also be influenced by personal recommendation or what they have heard, seen or read through the media. They may also trust particular guide books

- **Business tourists** are similarly influenced. They are also influenced by the company they work for, and those responsible for arranging and booking travel. They can also be expected to stay at particular hotels in particular places. Additionally, they can be influenced by the amount of their daily subsistence allowances and the corresponding prices which they can afford.

- **Other tourists** – e.g. travelling for MICE (meetings, incentive travel, conventions and exhibitions), health, religious or other reasons – will be similarly influenced. In particular, they be especially assisted through the associations or institutions involved in the organisation of the travel.

Equally, the bulk buyers of accommodation who work for tour operators or other travel organisers do not usually rely on the classification and grading system. They choose the product and rooms, based on their own criteria, and negotiate the prices and contractual arrangements accordingly. These buyers are usually highly experienced and specialised personnel who understand precisely the needs of their markets (see Chapter 5 on accommodation).

Tour operators develop a comprehensive set of criteria to evaluate an establishment, covering the location, accessibility, appearance, image, facilities, services, and operational standards. They are guided by their own range of marketing mixes at the destination, its products, image and prices.

Chain operations, e.g. hotels or restaurants, develop their own brand image in the market place. They have their own marketing mix well defined, usually together with a quality control programme. A classification and grading system offers them little advantage.

Who can Operate a Classification and, or, Grading System?

As noted, government-driven systems are not advisable. Alternative systems may be developed and operated in the following ways:

- the GTA, but set up as an independent statutory board (or as a quasi autonomous non governmental organisation – QUANGO), joining with the sector's representative organisations, consumer associations etc. The GTA coordinates a sector-driven system.

- trade associations, particularly hotel and restaurant associations, sometimes working in collaboration with the GTA. Such systems are based on product-oriented criteria and seldom reflect sufficiently the market needs and preferences.

- motoring and consumer associations, using their own staff, and gauging the needs and preferences of their members. To this extent these are market-driven systems.

- guide books using their own expert staff as researchers, reflecting their reader's tastes and preferences, and arriving at a qualitative assessment. They sometimes follow a clear set of criteria and a method for awarding grades. At other times they are written discursively, offering a wholly subjective assessment of an establishment. These publications aim to build up a following among their readers. People may find their tastes and needs well represented, developing trust and confidence in the recommendations made. These are also market-driven systems.

Free market mechanisms operate well for hotels, restaurants and similar commercial establishments. If one establishment doesn't do a good job people can go elsewhere. However, a historical or archaeological site – or similar tourist attraction – is unique. People have no choice. If they want to visit the place, they have to put up with things as they find them. For example, no information services, no refreshments, inadequate toilets and surly staff. If improvements are to be made, an external assessment of standards is important. It's the only way to signal deficiencies and trigger remedial measures. A GTA therefore can set up criteria for tourist attractions of this type and inspect them accordingly.

The Difference between Classification and Grading

The difference between registration and licensing was already explained in Chapter 19 on legislation. Registration means registering with the specified authority and supplying the information requested. Licensing enforces certain minimum standards of facilities and ensures that the regulations of other government agencies are complied with. For example, public health, commercial, building, and environmental codes and regulations.

The difference between classification and grading was also touched upon in Chapter 19. Classification tends to mean classifying establishments according to their range of facilities and services. This is quantitative and descriptive by nature and may not entail an assessment of quality. However, grading means an assessment of the quality of facilities and services provided.

The dictionary defines "classify" as arranging or ordering by class. "Classification" is the assignment of items to groups within a system of categories. The meaning is clear – one arranges a series of categories and classifies the items according to specific criteria.

It defines "grade" as a degree or step in a scale, as of rank, value, or quality and, or, a class of person or things of the same relative rank or quality.

One can classify according to any criteria but one grades according to quality. However, one could equally well classify according to grades. A classification system can cover quality as well as the size, range and type of facilities and services.

As noted, classification systems have tended to concentrate on the range of facilities and services. They have tended to ignore quality. The grading of quality, in some instances, has become added to classification as an additional and separate dimension. For example, in the system operated by the Scottish Tourist Board. However, quality – as noted in Chapters 4 and 5 – is inseparably linked to all aspects of the product. And as noted in Chapter 18, quality is the key factor in satisfying customers.

A review of international systems was conducted by the World Tourism Organisation (WTO, 1989). These systems were found to include some assessment of quality but this was limited to the facilities. There was almost no reference to the quality of services. Systems also relied on the use of descriptive adjectives as grades; for example, acceptable, good, very good/better, excellent, and the highest. There were no criteria listed, or methodology shown, as to how these grades were awarded. A system should be made as objective as possible with detailed criteria, a points system of grading, and thoroughly trained and experienced inspectors.

Registration and licensing normally go together. These are the two basic requirements which a government tourist administration (GTA) carries out on behalf of the sector (see Chapter 19).

Advisory Services and Training

Small hotels, guest houses, bed and breakfast operations and other small tourism enterprises, may not have a clear idea either of operational standards or their marketing targets. They need advice and training. A classification and grading system can help make their businesses more successful and profitable. It can indicate deficiencies, areas for improvement and training needs. This makes it a valuable tool in any overall improvement programme for the sector. Results tend to show up quickly, tourism improves and operators make more money.

The need to improve small units, which in most countries account for the biggest proportion of supply, is a key factor in tourism development. It makes a classification and grading system a valuable tool in assessing weaknesses and organising remedial measures.

These kinds of training initiatives were also discussed in Chapter 18. Training is also one of the key management tools listed in Chapter 15.

The Scottish Tourist Board

The Scottish Tourist Board (STB) serves as an example of a GTA coordinated sector-driven system. For serviced accommodation, it has taken a conventional approach to facilities, furniture, fittings and equipment but has added a comprehensive system of grading. This examines a total of 51 factors. These are graded on a scale (0-2, 3-5, 6-7, 8, and 9-10) with quite explicit criteria to guide inspectors. The award of stars, one to five, shows the overall quality of accommodation. Four and five star establishments are expected to provide a small number of key facilities in addition to meeting these quality standards.

The STB has developed its approach over a period of time. The system has grown with the sector itself, operators are familiar with it, and inspectors have worked with it. It has helped Scotland to do well, and one can note improvement and a growing awareness. One can also note a close correlation between customer satisfactions and the STB assessments. A good system is incremental, benefiting from additions and refinements.

However, developing a system from scratch one would choose to integrate classification (how much/many) with grading (how good) criteria. The quantitative and the qualitative. There is also an argument to group all aspects of service more closely together. Under the dining room, for example, one can include not only size, decoration, furniture, fittings, and equipment, but also menus, style of service, courtesy, cleanliness, comfort, freedom from nuisance, speed and rhythm.

Inspection

The final key to a classification and grading system is inspection. Whether a formal sector-wide system or a simple guide book, it requires responsible, impartial and objective inspection. In developed countries it is easier to recruit, train, pay and retain inspectors of sufficiently high calibre. These personnel become expert in hospitality operations, quick to see and assess quality standards. However, in developing countries it's more difficult. Inspection weaknesses, as much as shortcomings in evaluation criteria, bring systems into disrepute.

Private Sector Guides

There are many different private sector guide books which classify hotels and restaurants. The success of these publications indicate that they reflect the preferences and needs of their readers. People have tested the recommendations and come to trust them. Notable examples of such guides are Lonely Planet, Fodor, Baedeker and Michelin.

Michelin is world famous for its classification of hotels and restaurants. Hotels are classified as:

Luxury in the traditional style
Top class comfort
Very comfortable
Comfortable
Quite comfortable
Simple comfort

Categories also include "Other recommended accommodation at moderate prices", and give indications of "hotels with no restaurants" and "restaurants which also offer accommodation". Michelin therefore does not grade any establishment below "simple comfort" – its minimum standard.

Michelin also awards, famously, stars for good food. It tells consumers, "Certain establishments merit being brought to your particular attention for the quality of their cooking. We show some of the culinary specialities and the local wines we recommend you to try".

There are restaurant grades of one to three stars. The criteria are described by Michelin as follows:

✳✳✳ **exceptional cuisine, worth a special journey**. One always eats here extremely well, sometimes superbly. Fine wines, faultless service, elegant surroundings. One will pay accordingly.

✳✳ **excellent cooking, worth a detour**. Specialities and wines of first class quality. This will be reflected in the price.

✳ **a very good restaurant in its category**. The star indicates a good place to stop on your journey. But beware of comparing the star given to an expensive "de luxe" establishment to that of a simple restaurant where you can appreciate fine cuisine at a moderate price.

Michelin also indicates places which serve good food. These are judged to have less elaborate, moderately priced menus that offer good value for money. They serve carefully prepared meals, often of regional cooking.

Michelin has been publishing its guides since 1900, and has extended them to cover countries other than France. In France it sells about 600,000 copies annually, and estimates that five to ten times more people consult the guide.

Inspectors visit establishments anonymously, and Michelin does not publish the exact criteria used in an appraisal. However, its grades, comments and recommendations are trusted and followed.

Reference

World Tourism Organisation (1989). *Interregional Harmonisation of Hotel Classification Criteria on the basis of the Classification Standards adopted by the Regional Commissions.* WTO, Madrid.

chapter twenty-two
Human Resources

T he chapter starts by describing the place of human resources development and the approach and components of a strategy. It then describes the importance of working conditions. It goes on to deal with the forecasting of future workforce and training needs, and a framework of minimum standards. The chapter then examines the various types of training institution and programme, and the relative contribution which they make. It concludes by explaining a national council for tourism education and training, and its purpose and functions. The chapter reflects an up-to-date approach to human resources development (Doswell, 1997).

The Place of Human Resources Development

Any sector, if it is to be successful, should build up its human capital. One can do nothing without skilled and qualified people. Training is not something done only when times are good, it is an everyday part of operational life. It is a part of everybody's responsibility – an essential investment in the future.

A sensible strategy should encompass all types of training, at all times of life, at all stages of career development, for all occupations, for all levels of skill and knowledge, for all branches of the sector, wherever the needs arise. And it should create links between various levels and types of training, always opening up possibilities for further learning and advancement.

However, when one asks operational people they often reply, "If it's about training then talk to the training department." This is misleading. One cannot confine training to one department, it involves everybody and belongs everywhere. For this reason other chapters have already referred to human resources, in particular Chapter 15 which listed human resources development as a key management tool, and examined public awareness and a sector-wide training programme.

A Human Resources Development Strategy

A development strategy enables the sector to manage its human resources in a continuing way. At one level it monitors the sector's needs, on another it ensures that they are met. It should cover the following main areas:

- the national policy and system of vocational education and training and its relevance to the tourism sector. How well do they respond to tourism's needs?

- the existing tourism product and labour force – this will summarise characteristics such as numbers of staff, geographical distribution, age, gender, educational level, staff turnover, length of employment, seasonal employment, training background and experience, occupation, qualifications and levels of skill. It will also assess the level of technology, operational standards, and occupational skill standards. What is the exact profile of the existing labour force?

- the established working conditions and labour legislation. How well do the current regulations serve tourism?

- the future of tourism and the expected increase or decrease in the number of hotels and other tourism enterprises. The corresponding workforce and training needs, broken down by category of establishment and geographical distribution. What does the future hold?

- current training and education for tourism – both for pre-employment and post employment levels. The adequacy of present courses and programmes, location, capacity and output, and existing and future training gaps. How well does present training respond to the needs?

- the interrelation and harmonisation of the different programmes and institutions, into a national system of tourism education and training, rationalising the certification, accreditation and linkages, to meet training needs for all occupations at all levels of skill and knowledge. How coherent is the current system?

- the future development of all levels and types of education and training, located where it is needed and including the establishment of any new public and, or, private sector tourism training institutions. It may also propose measures to encourage the development of other new private sector training initiatives. How does one tackle future development?

- the organisation of a national council or committee on tourism education and training, and the possible formation of an association of hotel and tourism schools. How does one create the right representative mechanisms?

One should incorporate human resources into the national tourism information system:

- This includes labour force and training needs. Surveys monitor the characteristics of the current and future labour force, and identify the training needs of the existing staff and new entrants to the sector.

- A training standards, curriculum, materials and methods information system is also an advantage. It assures a constant inflow of information and includes links with training institutions in various parts of the world. It also includes participation in international organisations active in tourism education and training, and facilitates international recognition and accreditation.

The strategy should also take into consideration the following important criteria:

- Tourism needs qualified and experienced vocational teachers. It is difficult to attract the right people into teaching unless attractive career opportunities and rewards exist. Teachers also need links with the sector, and a chance to gain experience, add to their knowledge and augment their earnings.

- A human resources development strategy describes how each training need will be met. The strategy responds to identified needs and should cover all skill levels. It covers all pre-employment institutionally based training (university or equivalent, technical colleges of different categories and vocational secondary or high schools). It also covers work-based or in-service training at all levels, including various kinds of short, re-cycling and upgrading courses.

- The major training institutions can act as hubs in a sector-wide training network. They can monitor needs and establish an employment information system, undertake research, develop standards and curriculum, accredit other centres and programmes, help on in-service training, act as testing centres, develop trainers and teachers, advise on teaching methods and materials and field mobile training teams.

Working Conditions

In tourism, worldwide conditions of work have not always kept up with other sectors. The International Labour Organisation's (ILO) Hotel, Catering and Tourism Committee is of fairly recent origin and the first meeting was held at the ILO in Geneva in December, 1989. An agreement – an international convention – was reached on certain minimum working conditions in hotels, restaurants and similar establishments (lodging, restaurants and similar establishments providing food, beverages or both). ILO also adopts recommendations covering other aspects of the work place. Local labour laws and conditions should be reviewed against this background.

Future Workforce and Training Needs

Employment ratios, resulting from surveys, can be adjusted for trends and applied to the expected development of tourism. On this basis one can estimate future workforce requirements. These should be reconciled against labour market conditions and the sector's current recruitment and selection policies.

One should also survey the development of all training and education for tourism – both for pre-employment and post employment levels. As a result one can analyse the adequacy of existing courses and programmes, location, quality, capacity and output. All curriculum, training materials and standards should be re-assessed for their current relevance and effectiveness. This should include all in-service training and train-the-trainer courses.

Future workforce needs should be translated into future training needs. These can be compared to the capacity of the existing educational and training facilities and programmes. As a result, shortfalls or training gaps can be identified and rectified.

Minimum Standards

Minimum training standards deal with (i) the standards to which people are trained and (ii) the standards for training institutions and centres (Doswell, 1997).

Occupational skill standards

Occupational skill standards are the minimum standards of knowledge and skills for a particular job, at a particular level. They are the minimum acceptable – staff can do better but no worse. Once standards are agreed (normally at three levels – basic, intermediate and advanced), one develops the curriculum, tests and certification.

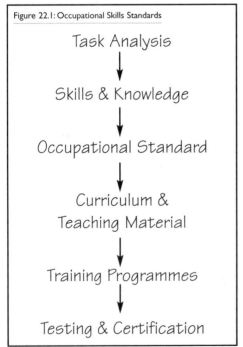

Figure 22.1: Occupational Skills Standards

Task Analysis

↓

Skills & Knowledge

↓

Occupational Standard

↓

Curriculum &
Teaching Material

↓

Training Programmes

↓

Testing & Certification

The starting point is task analysis. One identifies the tasks which make up the job – what a worker has to be able to do. One then breaks down the task into components, analysing what is done, when, where and how. Then how often and under what conditions. One can then decide the level of skills and back-up knowledge required. Finally one describes acceptable performance and the way it can be measured and verified.

These steps (see Figure 22.1) can be summarised as follows:

- The standard is based on the TASK ANALYSIS. It indicates the necessary skills and knowledge.
- Curriculum and teaching material keep to the standard.
- The test checks that trainees can achieve the standard.

Skill standards help career planning and counselling, performance appraisal interviewing, recruitment and selection, and training plans and targets. They also enable inter-company comparison and the monitoring of sector-wide training standards. National certification gives all workers the chance to achieve the same recognised standards of proficiency.

Standards agree the minimum skills and knowledge for every establishment of a certain category. However, each enterprise – in serving the needs of its own market – may have certain characteristics not shared with other enterprises. Standards therefore allow some room to meet these particularised needs.

Where classification and grading schemes (see Chapter 21) exist for hotels and other tourism enterprises, they can choose to include minimum training requirements. These can cover a minimum number of nationally certified staff.

Minimum requirements for training institutions

A set of criteria for the licensing of training institutions may or may not exist. In either case one can use the following checklist to review, or establish, the necessary minimum standards:

- A plan – usually for five years – for the courses offered, the needs they meet, student recruitment and links with the employers;
- The curriculum and the standards they represent., including their relationship to any nationally recognised occupational skill standards. Other relevant facts on accreditation and certification. Examples of teaching materials and methods.
- Details of instructors and teachers, their qualifications and experience, and teacher/student ratios;
- Details of students, the capacity of the programmes and the annual numbers of graduates;
- Physical planning: land area, floor area ratio, range of facilities, planning ratios, classrooms, offices, laboratories, library, student facilities, and other areas;
- The organisation chart and staffing plan;
- The employment of graduates and their expected impact on the sector;
- A financial plan showing sources of revenue (including any fees), costs and expected cash flows.

Training Institutions and Programmes

The vocational secondary schools can teach a number of basic skills. In doing so they can provide a stream of new entrants with basic level training. It is also more appropriate and less costly to teach many of these basic skills at the secondary rather than tertiary level.

As noted, tertiary level institutions can – apart from teaching and developing different courses and programmes – act as a hub. They can provide a range of research and back-up services. For example, they can:

- maintain libraries and centres of documentation;
- help develop national vocational skills standards and curriculum, and trade testing and certification;
- develop training material;
- help to train future vocational teachers.

A GTA can liaise with institutions to organise training for its own officials. It can also encourage, as appropriate, improvements in physical facilities, teaching materials and equipment, as well as the standards of their teaching.

If there is a shortage of training, a GTA may also wish to encourage the creation of new institutions. It may help by providing guidelines on the needed programmes, location, size and student capacity for any new facilities. Incentives may be offered to set up these facilities.

Universities exercise a degree of leadership in relation to socio-economic development. They educate not only the future technocrats, but also influence attitudes to development options. Some may not have recognised tourism as a an important field of study, research and technical assistance.

A wide range of university programmes should include tourism studies. For example, tourism should be taught in the social sciences, business studies, architectural, environmental and physical planning studies, and language and communications studies. One may also justify and include full time degree courses in tourism studies.

One should find out what the universities are currently doing in support of the tourism sector, and propose ways in which they can improve and expand this support. University activities should base themselves on the link between teaching, research and documentation and the concept of service to the community.

Post employment education and training includes in-service or in-house training programmes. In-service training should contribute significantly to the improvement of operational standards for the sector. The professional and trade associations should be encouraged to help organise this training, working closely with their members.

Larger enterprises should be encouraged to appoint specialised training personnel and develop in-house training departments and programmes.

Mobile training teams can be used to cover basic skills training in the more remote parts of the country. These teams can journey from area to area, organising basic level training courses.

The formulation of specialised clubs and societies among different hotel and tourism specialists, can greatly assist the objectives of human resources development.

Specialised training is needed for small hotel and tourism enterprises, including community development projects. Help can be given in the following areas:

- identifying opportunities for the improvement and, or, expansion of existing businesses and the creation of new ones;
- formulating projects and preparing feasibility studies;
- learning business management skills and knowledge;
- obtaining appropriate loan finance;
- talking to other small businesses and comparing ideas;
- getting further help.

There may be opportunities to create cooperatives, for example of small hotels. These would pool marketing efforts (particularly in promotion and sales), and maybe some training and purchasing.

Other educational and training courses and programmes include the development of vocational teachers. They also include the government tourism officials, essential to the effectiveness of the GTA.

Tourist guide skills are a major influence on the quality of the overall tourism product. While English has become the major international language, its importance and widespread use has not replaced the need for proficiency in other languages. For example, in Japanese or Arabic. Tourist guiding should also be included among the occupational skill standards and system of trade testing and certification.

Proficiency in foreign languages is essential to a successful tourism sector. One can introduce agreed standards for foreign language competence, as a part of the relevant occupational skill standards. They are then incorporated into a range of courses and programmes.

In Spain the provincial government of Navarre, through its Department of Industry, Commerce, Tourism and Labour, serves as an example of a sound training initiative, offering a range of courses in different centres. In 1999 these included marketing, sales and customer satisfaction, financial administration for rural tourism enterprises, merchandising wines, operating bars, tour guiding for taxi drivers, and managing tourism for a municipality.

A National Council for Tourism Education and Training

A national committee or council brings together representatives of all the public and private sector interests involved with tourism education and training. It should deal with all aspects of training. It monitors needs, programmes and centres, takes initiatives and provides advice.

It should:

- monitor labour market conditions, future workforce needs and all related trends;
- keep track of existing and future training needs for management, supervisory, and skilled staff.
- check on present programmes and their relevance, recommending changes as appropriate;
- recommend the development of any new centres or programmes – indicating their intended objectives and programmes;
- work with the university system, monitoring the extent and relevance of its involvement.
- encourage private sector training institutions;
- encourage tourism enterprises to develop in-service training programmes;
- establish career development guidelines for vocational educators and trainers, and encourage participation in the corresponding training programmes;
- encourage management and supervisory upgrading, and the training of trainers;
- coordinate the development and monitoring of occupational skill standards, testing and certification;
- enhance the image of the sector as an employer, and improve recruitment;
- encourage the teaching and learning of foreign languages for tourism;
- maintain links with education and training initiatives abroad and exchange information;
- give awards, and coordinate study tours and attachments abroad;
- undertake any other activities to develop tourism education and training and improve standards.

An association of the country's hotel and tourism schools can also play a useful and complementary role.

Reference

Doswell, Roger. (1997). *Tourism – How Effective Management Makes the Difference*, Butterworth Heinemann

chapter twenty-three
The Tourism Sector Checklist – part I

This chapter contains the first part of the tourism sector checklist, Chapter 24 the second part. The chapter starts by putting the checklist into the context of the management of the sector, including the recapitulation of the book's key points. It goes on to discuss the checklist approach and the advantages which it offers. It then indicates the checklist's structure, content and headings. It then presents the first four of these headings: description of the destination, tourism policies, positioning, and the mix of marketing mixes. The chapter concludes with the checklist's SWOT analysis of the sector's various marketing mixes.

Managing the Sector

The five functions of management – mentioned in Chapter 13 and explained more fully in Chapter 17 – are planning, organising, directing, coordinating and monitoring.

Monitoring both completes the process and starts it again. It checks the plan against performance and enables it to be reviewed and modified. One checks the pulse and general health of the sector, sees what's happening and what's not happening, what's right and what's wrong, and arrives at a diagnosis and prescription. One identifies the strengths, weaknesses, checks trends and opportunities, and anticipates the threats, problems and downturns. If possible one takes evasive or corrective action without waiting. One checks and corrects as a part of ongoing management. One looks ahead as well as backwards, and takes action before things go wrong.

There is no tourism sector anywhere, in developed or developing countries, which is perfect. It is essential to watch the sector closely. To know what needs to be done and to do it.

The purpose off the tourism sector checklist in these last two chapters is to recapitulate the book's content and show how it can be used in a practical way. However, the checklist can only contain a number of the key points.

When developing and using it, therefore, one should refer back to the relevant chapters. One can then fit the destination in question into the mould or framework, to evaluate its characteristics fully.

The Checklist Approach

Whether checklists are composed as a series of points or questions is not important. They make one ask the questions; for example – What exists? What doesn't exist? What's obsolescent? What's the strategy? What are the opportunities? What been done or hasn't been done? Do adequate tools exist? Are they being used effectively?

One is forced to provide a series of answers. The checklist helps. It looks at the situation in a complete and thorough way. It enables a thorough review. For example, it can help to:

- structure the sector sensibly, making it is straightforward for someone to work through it and analyse it logically.

- address all the points, so that one doesn't miss anything.

- recognise interrelating and interdependent questions.

- ensure that what should be counted is counted – how many, when, where?

- use the right criteria – through the way in which the checklist is phrased – to arrive at an answer.

- recognise the need, when one can't arrive at an answer, to undertake research or conduct surveys.

The tourism sector checklist draws together the various approaches described in the book. It can be used easily as a framework and further developed to suit any particular place.

The checklist enables the formulation of an agreed development strategy. This makes way for the use of the necessary management tools, discussed in Chapter 15. It also provides the basis for regeneration, re-engineering and expansion of the product/s and marketing mix/es – including improvement and re-positioning – discussed in Chapters 16 and 17.

The Structure of the Checklist

The checklist should enable a comprehensive overview of the current situation of the sector. What is happening now and the projects planned for the future. These are the planned projects certain of implementation with details of expected completion dates and budget appropriations.

Plans are often no more than wishful thinking. They are prepared but not implemented. To make implementation straightforward, they should list agreed action steps rather than recommendations. The checklist uses the following structure and headings. This denotes a sequence. However, in practice, one will cross relate different sections of the checklist in an open and dynamic way. There are a great number of factors, most of which interdepend and interact.

A. Description of the Destination.

B. Tourism Policies.

C. Positioning.

D. The Mix of Marketing Mixes (product/s, image/s, price/s, promotion, sales network).

E. The Development Strategy.

F. Human Resources Development.

G. The Management Tools.

H. Organisation and Management.

The checklist contains the key points. The user goes through it and provides the answers. The sector then evaluates and considers the answers and puts them to work.

A. Description of the Destination

This section should list the precise characteristics of the place as described in Chapter 1. Exactly where it is located, its population growth, natural characteristics, the built environment, the people and patterns of life, the economic situation, political systems and standards, historic and artistic characteristics, media, entertainment and recreation, international links, the pace of change and urbanisation, current trends and future plans. This provides a comprehensive overview of the destination.

The checklist then goes through the destination's broad marketing characteristics and opportunities – as a main destination only, as a secondary destination or in relation to secondary destinations, and as part of a multiple destination. It lists the destination as a stopping point, a same-day destination and as part of a destination area. This will require a broad indication as to markets and market segments for general interest leisure tourism, special interest tourism, visiting friends and family, business, MICE, health, religion and pilgrimages, and other purposes. It can start to indicate the characteristics of each market segment.

The destination can be described according to the six categories listed in Chapter 7:

- an established place, town or city with a mixed economy. Where tourism developed as an additional sector only but is now of substantial importance.

- an established place or seaside resort where tourism has developed over many years. A major economic sector historically, currently levelled off or in decline. Remains an important but problematic sector.

- a major resort complex created to serve only tourism, with visitors and facilities mainly segregated from the host population.

- a new or relatively new destination; has changed a small existing community into a large one dependent on tourism. Large and important tourism sector.

- a destination serving a particular type of special interest tourism, e.g. skiing.

- a small destination serving tourism alone, but providing only a single product to a narrow market segment.

- a micro destination; small villages or rural communities serving a small specialised market segment.

The above categories are included only as a guide; each destination tends to combine its own particular set of circumstances and characteristics. The checklist should enable a comprehensive description of the destination and describe the stage of development which tourism has reached. These stages were also summarised in Chapter 7; fully urbanised, partially urbanised, opportunities for redevelopment and improvement, major or limited opportunities for expansion, and building-free environments. In considering re-engineering in Chapter 16, these stages are expressed simply as:

- Places already fully developed a long time ago;
- Places fully developed but only a short time ago;
- Places newly and nearly fully developed;
- Only partially developed places;
- Completely underdeveloped places.

Here one can also include tourism statistics for the last five years, indicating trends (see Chapter 8 on market research). Any omissions in the available statistics should be noted.

B. Tourism Policies

The tourism policies underpin all sectoral management and development. Once stated they tend to be re-stated when used to guide subsequent decisions and actions. This leads to an inevitable degree of repetition. This is a good thing. It helps to reinforce policy, turning it into practical and living guidelines.

Tourism policies may not exist, assembled and published within one document.

However, they may exist in a looser, more fragmented form framed by various ministries and agencies as a part of their particular sectoral policies and plans. For example in fields such as education and training, infrastructual development and economic development. The tourism sector checklist should identify whatever policy statements exist, from whatever sources, listing them according to the system of headings below. If a comprehensive list does not exist it should hammer one out.

Where no policy seems to exist, the facts about tourism speak for themselves. They indicate the policy, or the absence of a policy, which is actually being followed. It may be a policy by default, an ambiguous mish-mash of customary practice, or a guiding light that is barely illuminated. Later sections in the checklist require an assessment of what is possible and what to do. A workable policy is needed, not one which isn't feasible and can never be applied. The checklist should also identify any gap between a stated policy (sometimes only a statement of wishful thinking) and the reality.

First the policy should be defined and listed, where appropriate with the existing facts. However, policies should be re-checked once the whole checklist has been worked through. The headings are as follows:

Contribution to the country's economy

List any relevant policy statement, plus the economic targets which have been set for the sector. Include any data on the current economic impact of tourism. Provide details of an economic model to measure tourism's contribution, or of plans to develop such a model. Make reference to the employment created, contribution to local GDP e.g. income generated and income multiplier, contribution to government revenues, and the relative impact on local economies.

Contribution to the country's overall development.

State the intention to develop tourism. Describe the general contribution of tourism, the views of the general public – and attitudes towards tourism. Provide details of any social manifestations against tourism or of any communities where the presence of tourists is resented. Refer to the effectiveness or otherwise of public awareness programmes. Give details of other steps – already taken or proposed.

Local tourism entrepreneurship and linkages with other sectors.

Identify the intention to develop the number of small, locally owned tourism enterprises. Identify the trend in number of new businesses (by type) coming on stream, and schemes for the promotion of new small and medium sized enterprises. Identify cross sectoral linkages, e.g. tourism's impact on small agricultural enterprises and retail shopping.

New tourism investment from external sources, both national and foreign.

Indicate the intention to promote and support new investment. List any existing incentives, and the current pace of investment. Describe the existing investment promotion programme. List projects terminated in recent years, projects currently being executed, and projects already planned for future execution.

Conservation of the country's national heritage, culture and way of life

Indicate the general intention to conserve these features. List the heritage sites, the measures to assure their protection, and whether and how they are being used as tourist attractions. List the various activities to link the culture and way of life with current tourism development. Indicate any evidence of local reaction against inbound tourism.

Development of contemporary culture

State the perceived link between tourism and the development of contemporary culture. List any festivals or other activities organised, in connection with tourism, to promote both the visual and performing arts. Indicate the evidence of tourism's support of local artists, including craft workers, bands, musical groups and dance groups.

Conservation and protection of the physical environment

Identify the intention to conserve and protect the environment. List any local protected areas or national parks, and the measures to link them with tourism. List the current regulations intended to control the environment, particularly in relation to tourism development. For example, land use planning, planning regulations and environmental legislation, environmental impact assessments and building regulations.

Infrastructure to serve the local population as well as proposed new tourism development

List the recently completed and planned infrastructural projects to facilitate tourism developments and expansion, indicating the benefits which these have brought to local residents. In any cases where infrastructure has been developed for the exclusive benefit of tourism, indicate the socio-economic justification for the corresponding public sector investment. Relate this to the provision of infrastructure as a management tool, in a later section of the checklist.

Matching capacities in facilities and services.

Indicate support for this policy. List any apparent deficiencies and shortfalls in various facilities and services, to support current tourism. Examine this in particular relation to the mix of marketing mixes, a later section of the checklist. Establish the basis for including it in the proposed SWOT analysis.

A selective marketing strategy, targeting those markets considered best.

Indicate support for this policy. Selective marketing strategies should be used later in the checklist, in relation to the destination's positioning and the development of its mix of marketing mixes.

Controls over the tourism product.

List the range of controls which currently regulate the product; e.g. the environmental controls, planning regulations, and building regulations mentioned above. Also others such as licensing and registration requirements, classification systems and standards, and skill standards. Relate these to the management tools section of the checklist in Chapter 24.

Adequate training facilities.

Review the policy statement about human resources, in establishing and influencing the human resources section of the checklist developed in Chapter 24.

Coordination of all public and private sector tourism interests.

Similarly review this policy statement in setting the criteria for the organisation and management checklist included in Chapter 24.

Public awareness.

Similarly review this policy statement in the light of the public awareness checklist included in Chapter 24.

C. Positioning

Under positioning the checklist follows the points covered in Chapter 11. Positioning describes how a destination is perceived and ranked in relation to other destinations. A destination is the aggregate of all of its various marketing mixes. One establishes the destination's overall market position, and then positions each component marketing mix in its corresponding market. This positioning overview helps to open the way for a SWOT (strengths, weaknesses, opportunities and threats) analysis. For example, to show where and how each marketing mix should be improved and possibly re-positioned.

Positioning therefore requires the identification of the marketing mixes in question. It then requires the completion of a positioning matrix firstly at the macro level – then at the micro level for each particular mix (see Figures 11.2 and 11.3). As indicated, each matrix observes the following system of headings:

- **Market segment/s.** The characteristics and the profile of each market segment served.

- **Product segment/s.** The product or products designed to satisfy the identified markets.

- **Access.** How you get there and the ease and characteristics of access.

- **Image/features.** The core image and predominant features. The brand-image. In the case of the micro product – the tertiary image – how this relates and how it adds particular "spin".

- **Price.** The price range, discount policies, and relationship to competitors

- **Competing products.** The major competitors. What they offer – product, image, price? Advantages/disadvantages through their promotion and sales.

- **Promotion.** Current approach. Main focus. Techniques used. Budget and results obtained.

- **Sales network.** Current sales patterns. Tour operators. Airlines. Retail agencies. Hotels. Group and individual travel

- **Position.** Current position according to the various markets. Main strengths and weaknesses.

The micro level adds one more item – the relationship to the total product. This shows how the particular facility, attraction or service fits in with the total product.

D. The Marketing Mix

Work on the marketing mix stems from the thinking already given to positioning (as above), and regeneration, re-engineering and expansion. The main purpose of checking it and its component mixes, is to assess:

- *how well they meet the needs of the current markets served.*
- *how they should be developed to serve any new markets.*
- *how they can improve and, if necessary, re-position.*

Also how well geared they might be to improve, through adjustment and diversification. For example, to introduce new market segments or concentrate more on one segment than another. Apart from quantification and objective assessment of the physical facilities and environment, the assessment of service and other quality is important. Recent visitor surveys, other market research data, up-to-date guide books and similar publications, can provide relevant feedback.

As noted above, each marketing mix should be analysed using SWOT. This analysis will follow the matrix shown as Figure 23.1. It takes the positioning matrix as the starting point – Figures 11.1 and 11.2 – and uses the SWOT analysis to indicate the proposed actions which will come to form part of the development strategy. These actions reflect the regeneration, re-engineering and expansion opportunities, including improvement and re-positioning.

The mix of marketing mixes, as discussed in Chapter 11, is also an important question. The particular structure of the sector, the location of each product, and the proportion of visitors for each marketing mix, indicate whether there is sufficient balance and harmony in the overall mix of marketing mixes. This then features as a factor in the SWOT analysis.

One is conscious that in a large destination (e.g. a country or region) the product and the range of marketing mixes are enormously diverse. Looking at the totality one forms a frighteningly complex picture. However, once one breaks it down into components – decentralising and placing responsibility into local hands – this picture is made manageable and becomes clear.

The contents of Chapter 8 on market research are particularly relevant, as is the section on forecasting in Chapter 14.

The SWOT Matrix

The SWOT criteria are as follows (example of the matrix at Figure 23.1):

✓ **Strengths.** The strengths indicate those characteristics which have made the marketing mix in question a success. One goes through the matrix and describes the strengths of the particular mix under analysis. For example, that the market segment is strong and that demand is growing. That the product is strong, of high quality, and competitive. That there is easy accessibility from major markets. That the image is strong, and that the destination is well known and perceived positively. That the prices are competitive, and the destination well established. That the promotion and sales network are also strong, stating the reasons why. It also describes the position of this marketing mix, and where it currently stands. In every case, reasons should be given, supporting data included, and conclusions well substantiated. A marketing mix may have many strengths or it may have few.

✗ **Weaknesses.** In the same way the analysis goes point by point, and identifies and explains all the weaknesses. The particular market may be weak and dropping away. The quality of the product may also be weak, e.g. business has dropped and the product has been poorly maintained. The ease of access may have worsened in recent years, or it may never have been good. The image may also be weak. The prices may be relatively high given the quality provided. As a result, the destination has become less competitive. Promotion and sales appear to be struggling. The positioning of this marketing mix may also be sliding, with many strong and improving competitors. As with strengths, a detailed analysis is required with the findings and conclusions fully justified.

? **Opportunities.** Here the analysis draws conclusions about the existing status of the marketing mix, and the opportunities for re-engineering – improvement and possible re-positioning – or, as appropriate, regeneration and expansion. Actions are likely to involve not only the product, but also the image, price, promotion and sales. In the first instance opportunities provide owners and managers with the chance to improve market relevance and acceptance, and profitability.

! **Threats.** These are any trends, events or possibilities which might threaten the development of tourism and, in particular, this particular product and marketing mix. For example, negative social attitudes, a declining market, changes in tastes and preferences, changes in air transportation, an imbalance in the mix of marketing mixes, or the emergence of new competition. One assesses the threats, relates them to the rest of the analysis, and proposes evasive and, or, contingent action.

Every part of the product may have its distinctive marketing mix. It requires a SWOT matrix for each one. As part of the quality workshops mentioned in Chapter 18, managers and owners can be asked to prepare an analysis for their particular enterprise, working together with the GTA. The GTA acts as a resource, providing the big picture of the total product and overall marketing mix, and explaining the key criteria. It thereby provides assistance and advice. To do all the marketing mixes is an extensive and complex job, although considerable information should already exist albeit dispersed over a variety of different places. Once brought together it can be built up, and kept up-to-date. In this way, it comes to form part of the information system (tourism assets). It provides a fix on the marketing mix at any time, and a means to establish and monitor the product development strategy and the implementation of regeneration, re-engineering – improvement and re-positioning – and expansion objectives. Because one works through it with (it is the only way) owners and managers, it also provides an excellent training and technical assistance tool.

This work on the positioning and development of the marketing mixes also establishes the marketing strategy.

The product, and corresponding marketing mix, can be broken down to fit the particular destination. Normally it includes the following:

Accommodation

Structure the sector by types of accommodation; the development of a series of product segments, describing their composition and characteristics. Chapter

Criteria	Strengths ✓	Weaknesses ✗	Opportunities ?	Threats !
Market segment/s. The characteristics and the profile of each market segment served.				
Product segment/s. The product or products designed to satisfy the identified markets.				
Relationship to the total product.				
Access. How you get there and the ease & nature of access.				
Image/features. The core image, brand-image and tertiary image.				
Price. The price range, discount policies, and relationship to competitors.				
Competing products. The major competitors. What they offer - product, image, price?				
Promotion. Current approach. Main focus. Techniques used. Budget and results obtained.				
Sales network. Current sales patterns. Tour operators. Airlines. Retail agencies. Hotels. Group and individual travel.				
Position potential. Regeneration, re-engineering & expansion (improvement & re-positioning possibilities).				

Figure 23.1 Matrix for Regeneration, Re-engineering and Expansion

11 gave, as an example, a possible destination in the Caribbean or South Pacific.

Follow the categories of an accommodation classification system, if one exists. If not, follow the estimated average achieved room rates. Show the distribution of units by each category (based either on the classification and grading system, or alternatively the price range), by number of rooms and number of beds, by geographical distribution. Also show the average size of units by category.

Also include an assessment of the quality of the accommodation categories listed and their apparent market acceptability (visit a sample of units and make on-the-spot assessments).

Restaurants and bars

List the food and beverage outlets which cater to visitors; this normally means all of them. They should be listed according to category (according to any classification system). In the absence of a formal system, they should be grouped by type and price range; e.g. restaurants, fast food outlets, cafés and cafeterias, bars.

The seating capacity should be shown, or just the capacity in the case of bars. The geographical distribution of units and seats by type. The average size of each type of unit should also be shown.

Tourist attractions

Show the tourist attractions by geographical distribution within the destination; archaeological and historical sites, religious buildings, museums and art galleries, national parks, sea gardens and aquariums, zoological and botanical gardens, fun fairs and leisure parks.

Culture and heritage

List all the events, festivals and other activities which link the local culture and heritage with tourism. These may be organised principally for the participation of local residents, but are available for the enjoyment of tourism.

This section does not include the cultural and historical and religious sites, museums, and major art galleries, which are included under tourist attractions. It covers rather the cultural and heritage "software"; the visual and particularly the performing arts, the music, dance, drama, the traditions, crafts, festivals and ceremonies which form part of a destination's culture and heritage. The activities which enliven and express the community and its values – which convey the character and flavour of a place.

Local ground transportation

List the services available through local ground transportation operators (inbound tour operators), including "meet and greet" services and transport from the ports of entry (transfers). Also list the excursions and tours offered, together with the guiding services provided. Include the organisation of local taxi services, and the availability of tours by foot, bicycle, horse and carriage, or on horseback or by other means

Also list – where these contribute significantly to the local tourism product – the local bus and train services.

Recreation and sports

List the facilities available for participative sports, and the events in terms of spectator sports. First what there is to do, second what there is to see.

The major participative sports tend to be tennis, squash, golf, fishing, cycling, scuba diving, swimming and snorkelling, yachting, horseriding, trekking, mountain climbing, canoeing, white water rafting, water sports (water skiing, para-sailing, wind surfing), winter sports and skiing, archery, clay pigeon shooting, aerobics and gymnastics.

The major spectator sports may be cricket, baseball, soccer, rugby, tennis, golf, yachting, rowing, boxing, athletics, show jumping and horse racing.

Entertainment

List the theatres, concert halls, cinemas, nightclubs and cabarets, discotheques, and karaoke bars. Also include any convention or conference facilities which are independent of the hotels.

Streets and shopping

List the major shopping areas, and describe the main characteristics. For example, the pedestrianisation of streets, attractiveness of the visual impressions, freshly painted houses, flowers, trees and landscaping, squares, piazzas and gathering places, outside cafés and bars, flags, awnings and sunshades, general cleanliness, outdoor music, and overall quality of the environment and ambience.

Describe the types and range of shops, fashion, books and compact discs, art, handicrafts and souvenirs, luxury goods, duty free shopping. Assess the range and prices of goods on offer

Information

List the tourist information services which exist – before arrival, en route and after arrival. Information from tour operators, travel agencies, diplomatic missions, tourist offices abroad, airlines, at destination airports, and in the destination itself. List the information offices which exist, and include an assessment of their functioning and effectiveness; layout, design, staffing, service, displays, and availability of printed material.

Travel services

List the travel agencies, rental car services, currency exchange services, credit card services – banks and cash machines, medical services, postal services, telecommunications services, hairdressing and beauty salons, religious services, and local transportation services.

Atmosphere and hospitality

This may not lend itself to the use of the same matrix, but a SWOT analysis is still possible. Make an assessment accordingly, covering the feel of the place, the local atmosphere, how welcoming and friendly people are, and whether it feels good to be there.

chapter twenty-three
The Tourism Sector Checklist – part 2

T his chapter completes the tourism sector checklist started in Chapter 23. It deals with the checklist's remaining four sections; the tourism development strategy, human resources, the management tools and organisation and management. Based on the checklist's first four sections (see Chapter 23 – the description of the destination, the tourism policies, positioning and the mix of marketing mixes), it starts with the tourism development strategy. It goes on to deal with human resources, specifying the steps to support the development strategy. It then lists the management tools that make the strategy's implementation possible. The final section deals with the organisational and management needs for the sector to reach its potential and achieve the stated objectives.

E. The Tourism Development Strategy

The development strategy reflects the other sections of the checklist already completed. In particular, the needs of the destination, its policies, positioning, and mix of marketing mixes.

It was suggested in Chapter 13 that this strategy document be used to build a sector-wide consensus. The chapter outlines an application of the DELPHI method, whereby the sector itself participates in the development of future plans and strategies.

The agreed strategy can be published as a short document covering the following main points:

Destination

The destination, its current stage of development, its past performance, and its prospects and opportunities;

Policies

The tourism policies and the sector's general objectives and requirements;

Positioning

Positioning of the sector, and the current mix of marketing mixes;

Marketing

The institutional marketing, reflecting the positioning, and including the destination's image and pricing, and the target market segments and sales forecasts. It also includes visitor surveys and market research.

Regeneration and re-engineering

The regeneration and re-engineering (improvement and any re-positioning) objectives, of the various marketing mixes;

Expansion

The expansion plans for the sector, indicating how this will add to or change particular marketing mixes, or introduce new marketing mixes. It indicates the types of project, number of projects, number of rooms etc. It will also explain whether this is expected to change overall positioning and, if so, how;

Spatial context

Expansion plans in their spatial context, indicating the zones, areas and sites designated for future projects;

Infrastructure

The infrastructural plans and improvements, including the transportation sub-sector;

Expected growth

The expected growth of tourism, the numbers and origins of visitors, their profile and characteristics, the expected receipts and the economic impact;

Promotion

The proposed promotional programme, covering advertising, printed material, direct mail, public relations, exhibitions, shows, familiarisation visits and other promotional activities;

Sales

The sales strategy, the strengthening of the sales network, and reservations and bookings systems;

Human resources

The current human resources situation, future workforce and training needs, and the corresponding improvement and development of the education and training system (as listed below);

Public awareness

The public awareness programmes planned and their objectives (as also listed below);

Management tools

The management tools not mentioned in the above (but emanating from the policy statements in Chapter 23). In particular the planning, building and licensing regulations, other legislation, classification and grading, and the investment incentives and promotion (as also listed below);

Information

The intended research programmes together with improvements to the current tourism information system;

Organisation and management

Any organisational or managerial improvements, indicating the involvement of the sector as a whole. In particular, the network of coordinating and working committees or groups, and the consultative committees or councils (as also listed below).

F. Human Resources

A strategy for the development of human resources reflects the content of Chapter 22. It also supports the objectives listed in the above tourism development strategy. The human resources part indicates how each training need will be met. It covers all pre-employment institutionally based training (university or equivalent, technical colleges of different categories and vocational secondary or high schools). It also covers work-based or in-service training at all levels, including various kinds of short, re-cycling and upgrading courses. It also includes public awareness programmes (explained in Chapter 17).

National vocational education and training policy

Indicate and explain the national policy and system of vocational education and training and indicate how tourism human resources development will relate to it.

Human resources Information system

Establish a labour force and training needs information system. It should monitor the profile and characteristics of the current and future labour force, and identify the training needs of both the existing staff and new entrants to the sector. It will incorporate the results of workforce surveys and will also assess the level of technology, operational standards, and occupational skill standards in use. It should also monitor the established working conditions and labour legislation. It can also include information on training standards, curriculum, materials and methods.

Expected workforce needs

Include the expected development of tourism and the expected increase or decrease in the number of hotels and other tourism enterprises. Indicate the corresponding workforce and training needs, broken down by category of establishment and geographical distribution.

Current education and training

Identify current training and education for tourism – both for pre-employment and post employment levels. Assess the adequacy of present courses and programmes, location, capacity and output, and identify existing and future training gaps.

Future development

Indicate the future development of all levels and types of education and training, located where it is needed and including the establishment of any new public and, or, private sector tourism training institutions. Include any measures to encourage the development of other new private sector training initiatives.

A national training system

Show how different programmes and institutions are integrated within a national system of tourism education and training, rationalising the certification, accreditation and linkages, to meet training needs for all occupations at all levels of skill and knowledge. Consider the following:

- vocational secondary schools
- tertiary level technical training institutions
- university level courses
- post employment training
- work based training schemes
- in-service training
- certification of existing skilled workers
- small and medium sized enterprises
- other post employment programmes
- specialised training
- tourist guide training
- host/hospitality training
- foreign language training
- government tourism officials

A national committee

Organise a national committee on tourism education and training, and an association of hotel and tourism schools. A national committee brings together representatives of all the public and private sector interests involved with tourism education and training. It can deal with training needs, in all parts of the country, at all levels of skill for all occupations. It can also monitor standards, testing and certification, and advise on all other aspects of training needs.

A support network and international links

Create a support network by setting up links with a range of training institutions – nationally and internationally. This assures a constant inflow of information on various methods, techniques, materials and approaches. It can also include the membership of international organisations, and can facilitate international recognition and accreditation.

Vocational teachers

Train vocational teachers. Include recycling and upgrading courses for existing teachers as well as full time courses for new entrants. Provide teachers with opportunities to gain experience and augment earnings. Attractive career advancement and rewards keep vocational teachers in teaching.

Hubs in a country-wide network

Designate certain training institutions to act as hubs in a country-wide network of programmes. Indicate their role in employment information systems, research, standards and curriculum, training material, and the accreditation of other centres and programmes. Also how they can act as testing centres, advise on teaching methods and materials, and field mobile training teams.

Public awareness

Inform people about the positive aspects of tourism. Ensure that people are consulted and involved in tourism development. Help them to take advantage of the opportunities offered by tourism. Explain the characteristics of visitors. Lack of knowledge of tourism can give rise to social, political and economic discontent, souring relationships between tourists and the host communities. Introduce training programmes for all personnel in direct contact with tourists; e.g. hotel, tourist accommodation, restaurant, bar and catering staff, shop assistants, taxi drivers, travel and airline staff, rental car and currency exchange services.

G. The Management Tools

The set of management tools which are normally necessary, are described in Chapter 15. Their use is indicated already in both the tourism policy and the tourism development strategy parts of this checklist. The section on human resources has also included a number. Here the tools listed are physical planning, incentives, and regulatory control.

Physical planning

Ensure that the following physical planning management tools are in place, and able to be used:

- Adequate current regulations covering effective environmental planning and control, land use plans, zoning, and the compulsory acquisition of sites or buildings.

- Regulations or codes which stipulate setbacks between buildings and from roads, shorelines, lakes and riversides, site coverage ratios, floor area ratios and height restrictions. Also size, layout and external appearance, site access, car parking, and aspects of landscaping.

- Building regulations – including safety, fire prevention and hygiene (these may also be covered by separate codes and regulations).

- Protection of buildings which represent the national heritage.

- Adequate infrastructure (roads, ports and airports, railways, waterways, water, power, waste disposal and drainage).

- The carrying capacity of key areas and installations studied and identified. Measures to keep to it, or increase it if there are feasible ways to accomplish this.

- Legislation to assess the environmental impact of new projects and establish controls over outdoor advertising.

Incentives

Review the case for incentives for regeneration, re-engineering and expansion. Consider the following provisions in existing or proposed incentives (some of these may not be feasible, and some may not be desirable).

- Extend tax holidays on profits, exemptions on customs duties, and reductions and exemptions from other government taxes and levies. Give work permits for key foreign personnel. Let foreign companies repatriate profits and dividends.

- Provide land, either free, on attractive terms, or in exchange for nominal equity or rent, and, or, the provision of supporting infrastructure. Provide financial grants.

- Arrange loan finance at concessionary rates of interest, or provide government guarantees in support of lines of credit (used mainly for small tourism enterprise credit schemes. Not normally desirable for large private sector projects).

Regulatory control

Regulatory control was dealt with in Chapter 19, and should be checked as follows:

- Review or establish regulations on travel enterprises which organise package holidays (tour operators). Require minimum information in brochures and catalogues, guarantees on advanced payments and measures for the repatriation of tourists (if necessary), and full details on all other aspects of the package.

- Establish regulations for hotels and other accommodation units, restaurants, discotheques, bars, night clubs and similar establishments, ground transportation (tourist buses, taxis), marine transportation and water sports, to establish minimum standards and protect users. Review the effectiveness of any classification and grading of facilities.

- Review whether there is a need to regulate tourist guides. Guides can pass a test or examination.

- Regulate any gambling casinos to protect users from unfairness Ensure proper accounting and administrative procedures. Establish controls to exclude criminal elements.

- Review facilitation and visa controls.

H. Organisation and Management

As noted, the term government tourism administration (GTA) describes all levels of government; local, regional, national and abroad. The term national – as in national tourism office (NTO) – tends to mean central government alone. Governments are tending to decentralise, placing more responsibility into local hands. GTA is therefore a more relevant term. Chapter 13 on governance includes the needs which the checklist should cover. The principal aim is to build a unified sector-wide approach.

Organisation and management concern a number of key issues:

- First how well the agreed strategy is disseminated and supported by the different ministries and government agencies, and by all branches of the tourism private sector.

- Second, the relative responsibilities of the three main levels of government – local, regional and national. Are their relative roles defined and understood? Do they work together effectively? Do they avoid overlaps and duplication?

- Third, whether different ministries and government agencies also work together effectively – locally, regionally and nationally.

- Fourth, whether the public and private sectors are able to work together – also locally, regionally and nationally.

- Fifth, whether there is an effective way to allocate relative responsibilities and establish objectives.

- Sixth, whether the five management functions (planning, organising, directing, coordinating and monitoring) are effectively observed.
- And finally how well everybody is able to combine, to make the concept of unified sectoral management workable.

One should review the following organisational provisions, examining how each body or committee is set up, at what level and with what functions.

Government tourism administration

Identify and check the following, recommending changes as appropriate:

- The main organisational modalities for the various government agencies and the corresponding effectiveness of their roles and responsibilities, e.g. the responsible ministry, any tourist board or other agency or agencies and their status – statutory, non statutory, QUANGO, offices abroad, development corporation, marketing board, training organisation etc. How well do they function? Are their deficiencies or gaps?
- The budgets and funding, and the relative contributions of public and private sectors. Are organisations cost effective?
- The mechanisms (e.g. committees or councils) set up to ensure close coordination between different government agencies and departments – at each level – local, regional and national.
- Management by objectives. The extent to which development strategies are translated into management objectives, across agencies, with results measured and validated.

International organisations and bodies

Assess the nature of the relationships and their usefulness.

Trade and professional associations

Identify the existence, constitutions and scope of the various trade and professional associations representing the various sub sectors. Assess their effectiveness and the comprehensiveness of the roles they play. Note, in particular, where appropriate associations do not exist and the nature of the gap which this creates.

Major corporate entities and the sector at large

Assess how direct contacts with the sector are established, and whether they are representative and effective.

Unions

Also review whether trade unions exist together with their scope. Assess the effectiveness and comprehensiveness of the role they play.

Consumer associations

Also review the various consumer associations which may exist, and assess whether they are able to play an effective role.

Public and private sector collaboration.

Identify and check the following:

- participation in the formulation of the proposed development strategies and objectives – and how it is achieved;
- the setting of objectives and assignment of responsibilities and how this is coordinated across the sector;
- consensus building and how this is achieved;
- the coordinating bodies which exist – councils, committees, working groups etc;
- covering all levels – local, regional and national;
- the composition of these various bodies and committees, and the extent of sector-wide representation;
- the overall extent and effectiveness of the collaboration achieved.

The media

Assess the nature and comprehensiveness of the relationships with the media, how they function and their effectiveness.

appendices
further reading
index

Further Reading

Baud Bovy, Manuel and Lawson, Fred. (1998). *Tourism and Recreation Handbook for Planning and Design*, Butterworth Heinemann

Bickerton, M. Simpson-Holley, K. (1998). *Cyberstrategy: Business Strategy for Extranets, Intranets and the Internet*, Butterworth Heinemann

Bray, R. Raitz, V. (2000). *Flight to the Sun – The Story of the Holiday Revolution*, Continuum

Brindley, T. Rydin, Y. and Stoker. G. (1996). *Remaking Planning*, Routledge

Brunt, Paul. (1999). *Market Research in Travel and Tourism*, Butterworth Heinemann

Buttle, Francis. (1986). *Hotel and Foodservice Marketing*, Continuum

Cooper, C. Fletcher, J. Gilbert, D. and Wanhill, S. (1993). *Tourism; Principles and Practice*, Pitman

Reily Collins, V. (2000). *Becoming a Tour Guide – Principles of Guiding and Site Interpretation*, Continuum

Davidson, Rob. (1996). *Business Travel*, Longman

Davis, Bernard., Lockwood, Andrew and Stone, Sally. (1998). *Food and Beverage Management*, Butterworth Heinemann

Dickinson, R.H. Vladimir, A.N. (1996). *Selling the Sea – An Inside Look at the Cruise Industry*, Wiley

Doswell, Roger. (1997). *Tourism – How Effective Management Makes the Difference*, Butterworth Heinemann

Downes, John and Paton, Tricia. (1993). *Travel Agency Law*, Pitman

Fennell, David. A. (1999). *Ecotourism*, Routledge

Foley, M. Lennon, J. & Maxwell, G. (1997). *Hospitality, Tourism and Leisure Management*, Continuum

Frechtling, Douglas C. (1996). *Practical Tourism Forecasting*, Butterworth Heinemann

Hanlon, Pat. (1999). *Global Airlines – Competition in a Transnational Industry*, Butterworth Heinemann

Harrison, David. Ed. (1992). *Tourism and the Less Developed Countries*, Bellhaven/Wiley

Holloway, J.C. (1998). *The Business of Tourism,* 5th ed. Longman

Holloway, J.C. (1995). *Marketing for Tourism*, 3rd ed. Longman

Ingold, A. McMahon, U. & Yeoman, I. (2000). *Yield Management*, 2nd ed. Continuum.

Inskeep, Edward. (1991). *Tourism Planning – An Integrated and Sustainable Development Approach,* Van Nostrand Reinhold

Institute of Commercial Management, (1999). *World Travel Atlas – The Atlas of the Travel Industry,* Columbus Press

Lashley, Conrad. (1997). *Empowering Service Excellence*, Continuum

Law, Christopher. M. (1994). *Urban Tourism – Attracting Visitors to Large Cities*, Cassell

Lawson, Fred. (1995). *Hotels and Resorts – Planning, Design and Refurbishment*, Butterworth Heinemann

Leask, A. Yeoman, I. (1999). *Heritage Visitor Attractions*, Continuum

Lickorish, Leonard. Jenkins, C.L. (1995). *An Introduction to Tourism,* Butterworth Heinemann

Lockwood, A. Baker, M. & Ghillyer, A. (1996). *Quality Management in Hospitality*, Continuum

Lundberg, D.E. Stavenga, M.H. & Krishnamoorthy, M. (1995). *Tourism Economics*, Wiley

Mawson, Steve, (2000). *The Fundamentals of Hospitality Marketing*, Continuum

McIntosh, R.W. Goeldner, C.R. and Brent Richie, J.R. (1994). *Tourism – Principles, Practices, Philosophies*, 7th ed. Wiley.

Medlik, S. (1999). *The Business of Hotels,* Butterworth Heinemann

Michael Hall, C. Page, Stephen. J. (1999). *The Geography of Tourism and Recreation*, Routledge

Middleton, Victor. with Clarke Jackie R. (2000). *Marketing in Travel and Tourism*, Butterworth Heinemann

O'Connor, Peter. (1999). *Using Computers in Hospitality*, Continuum

Owen, Gareth. (1995). *Accounting for Hospitality, Tourism and Leisure*, 2nd ed. Longman

Orams, Mark. (1998). *Marine Tourism,* Routledge

Page, S. (1999). *Transport and Tourism*, Longman

Pearce, Douglas. (1995). *Tourism Today*, 2nd ed. Longman

Quest, M. ed. (1990). *Horwath Book of Tourism*, Macmillan

Ryan, Chris. (1996). *The Tourist Experience*, Continuum

Tribe, John. (1995). *The Economics of Leisure and Tourism,* Butterworth Heinemann

Swarbrooke, John. (1999). *Consumer Behaviour in Tourism,* Butterworth Heinemann

Syratt, Gwenda. (1995). *Manual of Travel Agency Practice*, Butterworth Heinemann

Tuxworth Twist, Wendy and MacMillan, Sebastian. (1996). *Environmental Management for Hotels*, Butterworth Heinemann

Williams, Stephen. (1998). *Tourism Geography,* Routledge

World Bank. (1994). *Governance – The World Bank's Experience,* The World Bank

World Tourism Organisation. (1998). *Guide for Local Authorities on Developing Sustainable Tourism,* WTO, Madrid

World Tourism Organisation. (1996). *Towards New Forms of Public-Private Sector Partnership – The Changing Role, Structure and Activities of National Tourism Administrations A Special Report,* WTO, Madrid

World Tourism Organisation. (1994). *National and Regional Tourism Planning – Methodologies and Case Studies,* Routledge

Yale, Pat. (1995). *The Business of Tour Operations*, Longman

Yale, Pat. (1991). *From Tourist Attractions to Heritage Tourism,* ELM Publications

Index

D

E

T

U

V

W

Y

Z